Hyde Park Orator
Illustrated

2

Hyde Park Orator
Illustrated

Bonar Thompson

Union of Egoists
Columbus / Baltimore 2021

Hyde Park Orator *Illustrated*
Transcription, Editing, Index, Bibliographies, Map and "Outside the Gates"

Thanks to Cyril Pearce, author of *Communities of Resistance: Patterns of Dissent in Britain, 1914-1919* (London: Francis Boutle, 2020), and thanks to the Ashley family collection, for permission to publish the photograph on page 215.

This new work incorporates elements in the public domain in the United States, including *Hyde Park Orator* by Bonar Thompson.

Proof reading: Teresa Bergen and Richenda Walford.
Cover illustration: SYLAQ.
Cover design: Kevin I. Slaughter.

Columbus: Union of Egoists, 2021
Stand Alone 1175

Thompson, Bonar
Hyde Park Orator *Illustrated*
(English)
Hardcover ISBN 978-1-944651-19-0
Paperback ISBN 978-1-944651-18-3
1. Biography
2. Theater
Bonar Thompson (1888–1963); Trevor Blake (b. 1966)

Now buying (in multiple copies): *The Black Hat, Bonar Thompson's Monthly, Hyde Park Orator*, books, letters, manuscripts, signatures, photographs, recordings, films, ephemera, memorials, all and any material related to Bonar Thompson.

Trevor Blake
P. O. Box 3
Columbus, IN 47202
United States

127 House: At every turn in its thought society will find us waiting.

Hyde Park Orator Illustrated

Addendum

Illustrations

10

CHAPTER I

"Quick, Thy Tablets, Memory!"

THE date of my birth was the 16th of December, 1888. The event was not eagerly anticipated, nor was my first appearance hailed with shouts of joy. My parents were of low degree, the poorest of the Ulster peasantry; my father disowned and my mother was unable to support me. Had not an elderly relative, an aunt, undertaken to preserve me, I might easily have been laid aside and forgotten. My mother, however, struck a bargain with Aunt Eliza Thompson, who took me over and agreed to store me until called for.

At the time of my birth my aunt was about fifty years of age. She had worked, since she was a girl, as housekeeper to her brother, the schoolmaster, until his retirement a few years before I came on the scene. Her services being no

longer required as a housekeeper, she took a small, damp,
two-roomed cottage, a little way from her brother's house.

My mother, after depositing me in my Aunt Eliza's keeping, disappeared to England, unable to bear the disgrace of
having given me birth.

My aunt existed upon the profits derived from the sale
of eggs laid by a few faithful hens which she kept in a tiny
garden at the back of the cottage. A goat was also maintained
for the sake of the milk it sometimes gave. This animal was
kept tethered to a stake in the middle of the garden during
the daytime, where it fed upon roots, scrubs, old boots, nails,
and other odds and ends. When I grew old enough, I would
often tantalize the creature by getting hold of its beard and
allowing it to rush after me until it reached the end of its
tether. The goat's failure to learn by experience that it would
be nearly thrown off its feet by the terrific jerk was a constant
puzzle to me. My aunt could give no explanation, except
that it was, she said, the nature of the beast. She rated
me for badgering the old thing, and after a time I became
ashamed and sorry.

Of my experiences until about the age of six I can remember very little, and that of no special interest to any one.
(Students of child-psychology, please accept this, the only
intimation.)

At the age of seven I was sent to the National School. The
name of the school was Ladyhill. It stood by itself, a small,
whitewashed building with accommodation for sixty scholars,
a little way back from the narrow road which led to Antrim,
two miles farther on. My aunt's cottage was three miles away,
in the direction of Ballymena, so that I had a six-mile walk
to and from the school. The master was a young man named
Duncan, who wore a different suit of clothes every week, or

perhaps he had a half a dozen or so, which made me think of him as a man from another sphere. The scholars were boys and girls from the farms, most of whom came from long distances, Ladyhill being the only school for miles and miles. The master taught us the three "R's," and used his cane with considerable frequency. The pupils were a dull lot who displayed no interest in education. I felt myself immensely superior, as I was quick to learn; but certain subjects were obnoxious to me. I had no head for arithmetic and did not shine at geography. I had a gift for reading aloud, answering questions on history, and explaining the meanings of words.

I could not bear to be spoken to roughly, and I refused to suffer the indignity of being caned. On many occasions I defied the master, amid scenes of great excitement, out of which I derived intense emotional satisfaction. It seems that I was born with a strong sense of the dramatic. These school episodes gave me scope for the exercise of this inborn craving for drama. The other children were delighted with the performances, in which I played an heroic part, defying the tyrant to his face.

For long periods during the summer I was away from school, working in the fields. My aunt loaned me out to the neighboring farmers. She was glad of the sixpence a day I could earn as a day-laborer, a valuable addition to her meager income from the chickens and goat. Work on the farms was hard, back-breaking labor. By the time I was ten I was employed on such tasks as gathering potatoes, topping turnips, hoeing, dunging the byres, milking, lifting flax, driving cattle, digging turf, learning to thresh corn and drive a plow. We rose early, and had our meals in the fields. The work was not unpleasant, but there was too much of it. There was very little time for rest or recreation; but I learned a great deal that was useful: how to milk a cow, sow corn, plant potatoes, plow a straight furrow, smoke a pipe, swear, and drink whisky. By the time I was fourteen, I had learned all the best oaths, knew all the best girls, and had made contact with some of the best brands of whisky in the County Antrim.

The Ulster Sabbath was a holy terror. There was chapel in the morning, Sunday school in the afternoon, chapel again in the evening; and prayers offered up by lay preachers along the roadside in between. At home with my aunt, there were prayers, Bible-readings and psalm-singing. From morn till bedtime there was no surcease from the heavy monotony of droning religiosity. As the dreary hours crawled miserably along, there was nothing to fill the mind but thoughts of the tomb, the destination of the damned, the fiery pit, the undying worm.

Although I was made to believe in God, in a miserable uneasy fashion, the observance of the irksome rites of Presbyterianism evoked no genuine spiritual response on my part. What my aunt told me about Calvin's grim God was not calculated to inspire confidence. In spite of the persistent efforts of my elders to interest me in this God of wrath and fire, who, although mighty to save, was even more swift to strike, I could not take kindly to Him. Sometimes I broke out into fearful blasphemies, which sent my aunt into a state of terror lest I should be struck dead by an outraged Deity. I would become hysterical with rage, and awful curses would escape my childish lips. I always felt silly after these outbursts, but never repentant. My aunt did not punish me. She would leave that, she said, to God.

These explosions of pent-up emotion were the inevitable reactions of a sensitive temperament to the repressive influence of a Puritan environment, which manifested itself in the maintenance of an abnormal solemnity, an acute consciousness of personal and collective unworthiness, a laboring and straining after an abnormal holiness, and a deadly gloom over all.

The lunatic asylum near Antrim did a roaring trade in the victims of Calvin and Knox. Yet, in spite of everything, cheerfulness would keep breaking through, especially among the younger ones.

Aunt Eliza was a woman of devastating piety. A Presbyterian by, and from, birth, she was sustained her whole life long by an unquestioning faith in the goodness and mercy of Jehovah. She had had little education and had no interest in intellectual matters. Of what things were like outside the small area in which she had always lived she knew nothing and evinced no curiosity. Her ignorance of this world was balanced by an incredible certitude about the next. Every spare moment was given over to the study of celestial geography, topography, climate, and general flora and fauna.

"There will be no winter there," she often told me, speaking of heaven. "No cold, no rain. It will be perpetual summer there. And there will be no steep hills to climb, and no wasps, or rats, or spiders, or beetles; no stinging-nettles, no toadstools. There will be no chilblains or lumbago, no illness at all and no death. We shall have eternal life. That is the place which Christ has prepared for us, if we love Him and serve Him and worship and obey Him. But for the wicked, who turn away from Him, who are proud and stiff-necked and puffed up with their own conceit, there will be hunger and thirst, and every sort of ache and pain. There will be boils and blisters and insect-stings, and madness and sorrow, and weeping and wailing and gnashing of teeth."

Her descriptions of hell were even more detailed and authoritative than her graphic accounts of the Home of the Blest. She read the Bible continually and interpreted everything in it in the most literal way. Apart from the Bible, she read no other books, except the *Pilgrim's Progress* and *Grace Abounding,* and occasionally a stray copy of the *Quiver* or *Good Words.* The reading of novels or newspapers she looked upon as sinful and immoral. She would not allow the *Christian Herald* or the *Sunday Companion* into the house, because those journals contained serial stories. Even though the serials in both papers were often written by the Rev. Silas K. Hocking, she would have nothing to do with them. "A clergyman who writes stories is worse than an infidel," she declared sternly. "Such devil's work will never enter my house."

Her mind dwelt upon the somber side of religion a great deal. She could not disguise her satisfaction at the thought that the majority of God's creatures were predestined to everlasting perdition. She lived ever in the great Taskmaster's eye, but she had no fear or doubt of her own salvation. "For me and my house," she often said, "we will serve the Lord. I am glad that I, at any rate, have made my calling and election sure."

My aunt never married—she was too holy. "I am a bride of Christ," she once said, when I asked her why she had not taken a husband. "Then it is wrong to marry?" I inquired. "No, it is not wrong for the great majority. Paul tells us it is better to marry than to burn; but the chosen ones of Christ have no need to contaminate themselves by indulging in fleshly lusts. They are told to keep themselves pure and undefiled." I was troubled about this and wondered what Paul meant by saying that it was better to marry than to burn. "What does it mean, 'to burn?'" I asked my aunt, but she put me off with an ambiguous answer. I concluded that those who did not marry would burn; but where? And how? The whole thing was a mystery.

This pious woman taught me the *Shorter Catechism,* sent me to chapel and Sunday school, read the Bible to me on all possible occasions, and never failed to remind me that I was heading straight for hell.

To me she appeared stiff, staid, small-minded, and fussy. She seemed to be an imaginary invalid, in constant fear of illness, dosing herself, at all hours of the day and night, with pills, herbal mixtures, and genuine and quack remedies for a variety of non-existent maladies which she believed would, unless nipped in the bud, shoot her into the spirit-land prematurely, no reckoning made. No elephant ever possessed a tougher constitution. A cough and a corn were the only deviations from bodily fitness she was ever called upon to endure.

My aunt was not endowed with physical beauty. Her features were of the Carrie Nation type, common in New England to this day. In figure she was short, round, and dumpy, with large feet which were encased in elastic-sided boots. Two black dresses, a cape, and three bonnets, two white and one black with little trembling things standing up on top, two flannel petticoats and a nightcap, constituted the bulk of her wardrobe for the forty years during which I saw her. I was told that she had the same articles of attire when she was a girl of twenty. For trinkets, gewgaws, ornaments, and the pomps and vanities of this wicked world she cared nothing.

The black bonnet and cape were reserved for special occasions—chapel, a funeral, a visit to a neighbor, or a trip to Antrim or Ballymena. The white bonnets were for daily wear; the nightcap was worn during sleep.

My aunt sang a great deal. Her voice was out of tune and harsh, but she recked naught of that. She would stamp about indoors and out, her voice echoing to the reverberate hills, singing psalms, hymns, and spiritual songs. "God allows us to sing forth His praise," she observed once. "But surely not in a voice like that?" I said to myself. For music other than that of a religious and devotional kind she had no time at all, and spoke in hard terms of those who misused the gift of song by employing it for secular purposes. The music produced by my aunt, though not heavenly, was certainly unearthly.

The dampness of the cottage had no ill effects on my aunt's health, but it played havoc with mine. Every winter I was laid low with bronchitis and suffered acutely, drawing my breath in pain and coughing and wheezing continually. My aunt did what she could for me. Her main idea was mustard plasters, which she applied to my chest with unfaltering assiduity. As soon as I showed the first signs of an attack coming on, she would order me to bed and commence preparations for the campaign. Sometimes it was a linseed poultice, but she had a special passion, not shared by me, for the mustard plaster. Just as I was settled comfortably in bed and beginning to feel that the attack would pass off if I could remain warm until the next day, my aunt would throw the blanket off my chest, open my shirt, wait just long enough for me to catch pneumonia, and then dash a scorching plaster on my chest with great energy and abandon.

Taking advantage of my helpless position, she would scold me vehemently for not taking proper care of my health. "Out in all weathers and skulking the country at all hours of the day and night." This was a favorite phrase of hers. "You have been skulking the country again. No wonder you're ill." My bronchitis was directly due to living and sleeping in a damp room, but my aunt had no idea of this at all. Nor had I, until later.

Her own constitution was proof against the dampness of the house, but, although her health was good, she was never known to admit it. "Only middling," was her answer to all inquiries. "I've been ailing a great deal lately, you know."

She had a sister in America with whom she corresponded on the health question. The sister was a Christian Scientist, a fanatical believer in the efficacy of Faith Healing; a doctrine which my aunt toyed with, but could not accept at first in its entirety, though she often advised me to put my faith in God if I wished to be free from chest complaints. God might not cure me at once, she admitted, but He would, if my faith were strong enough, cure me in His own good time. Though I prayed a great deal when the attacks came on, there was no immediate result. I probably prayed in too half-hearted a manner, and while my words flew up, my thoughts, like Hamlet's uncle's, remained below. I continued to endure great pain. There were times when I thought I was going to suffocate. I must have been a pathetic and rather ridiculous object, coughing, wheezing, expectorating, and fighting for breath.

Letters from the sister in America contained lengthy accounts of the progress of her ill health. She suffered from a bad leg. Doctors, physicians, and surgeons having failed to effect a cure, the sister, as a last resort, had taken it—the leg—to the Lord in prayer. After a violent bout of intensive praying on her part, the affected limb appeared to show signs of improvement. She subsequently joined the Faith Healers and became convinced that every disease could be cured by faith alone. The doctors were dismissed and their physic thrown to the dogs. Later on, her leg still uncured, she linked up with Pastor Russell's crowd, the International Bible Students' Association. "Millions now living," declared Pastor Russell, "will never die." Sister Matilda believed herself to be one of those chosen to remain on earth until "caught up" into Paradise by a celestial attendant. She settled down, at the age of sixty, to the prospect of living for a couple of hundred years, maybe longer. Though her leg got worse, she remained firm in the faith. A year later she died.

From that moment my aunt turned her mind to the study of Pastor Russell's *magnum opus*: *The Divine Plan of the Ages*. She continued to pore over the sacred volumes until the day of her death. Her sister's death, which would seem to throw doubt on the validity of her beliefs, had a contrary effect upon my aunt. Perhaps she blamed the sister for not having sufficient faith. At any rate, Aunt Eliza convinced herself that she would succeed where others, her sister included, had failed. As the years went by she never seemed to grow any older. Although she always looked an elderly person, she did not become frail or feeble. While others, young and old, were cut down by the scythe of Time, my aunt lived on and on and on. Her death took place in 1931. It came as a shock to her relatives and friends: they had ceased to expect it, and considered that she had let them down. She was ninety-three years old at the time of her passing.

M Y schooldays were, on the whole, unprofitable. During the winter months, when I was supposed to be busy at my lessons, I "mitched," as we say in Ulster, that is, I absented myself without leave. The days stolen from school were spent in roaming about the country, climbing hills and investigating birds' nests, catching trout with my hands in the burns, watching birds in flight, or bees and butterflies as they moved about among the wild flowers. I was once chased by a bull as I was crossing Carnearney mountain. Instead of jumping a hedge and being caught from behind on the horns of the infuriated animal, I dropped into a ditch. Although the ditch was only about three feet deep, the bull could not get to me; I waited until he had gone off and then crept out, covered with wet clay and filth. Another time I was chased by a mad horse. I was used to horses and had never known an unfriendly one. When the animal sprang at me, I was taken by surprise. He did not pursue me far, but I was thoroughly frightened. It seemed uncanny. I have never seen a horse of that kind since, and I have no desire to do so.

Mr. Duncan, the schoolmaster, regarded me as a clever but lazy and unmanageable boy. Had I applied myself, he said to my aunt, I should have been his most brilliant pupil. But I would not apply myself.

Now and again I burst out in a queer way. Once, as I was walking home from Sunday school on a beautiful afternoon, I felt myself seized by some uncontrollable surge of emotion. Throwing my cap over a hedge and ruffling my hair, I removed my jacket, cast it upon the dusty roadway at a part which had been recently fouled by horse-dung, and jumping it, I broke into a torrent of foul and blasphemous language. My companions ran away in horror.

I had dreams of becoming a great figure in the world when I grew up. I wanted to become a great preacher or a great soldier. It was always some one great that I wanted to be; never any one mediocre or subordinate.

At the age of nine I fell madly in love. She was a golden-haired schoolmate called Peggy Adair. I dreamed about her and thought about her all day long. I could not eat or sleep. I dared not speak to her; she seemed too beautiful and good to have time for a lout like me. I sometimes hung around the lane near the house where she lived, a mile and a half from my aunt's cottage, hoping to catch a glimpse of her. I picked a bunch of wild flowers once, and offered them to her as she was leaving the school. She accepted them with a friendly smile and thanked me. I was ready to die with happiness. I often hoped she would ask me to walk home with her from school, but she did not do so. I had nothing to say to her when we met, so that we always parted without any progress being made. One day she was placed next to me in the class, and I had the undreamed-of privilege of letting her copy the answer to a sum from my slate. (By some miracle I had worked out the correct answer.) An exquisite thrill ran through me as she leaned her face close to mine, her golden curls touching my face. We walked home together that afternoon; but I could not speak—I was the victim of a dumb passion.

I mooned about after her for several weeks, worshiping mostly from a distance. Her people were fairly prosperous farmers. I was nobody—worse than that, I was one whose parents had neglected to bind themselves in holy wedlock. People pitied me; I bore the stigma of illegitimacy. My father passed me every day as I walked past him through the fields, without acknowledging me as his son. He repudiated me, though every one knew he was my father. My aunt brought me up to look upon him as an unprincipled scoundrel. I had no cause to honor him.

My love was hopeless. I continued to adore little Goldilocks in a mute, dreamy fashion for a long time, but I could not speak. What would have happened had I been able to tell my love, and had it been reciprocated, I cannot imagine; though I believe it would have been a lovely romance. I had no knowledge of the physical side of sex. What I had heard from lewd companions had filled me with incredulity and disgust. I could not believe that human beings came into the world in the way I had heard so brutally described. It was too horrible, and in my love for little Peggy such thoughts had no place at all.

Whether Miss Adair, who was a year younger than I was, had any inkling of the physiology of sex or not, I cannot say, though in the light of what I have learned since, especially from a reading of some of our modern novelists, I would not be too certain. On my part, however, the passion was as chaste as ice, as pure as snow. There were no psycho-analysts in those days to probe and pry into the far recesses of our inner consciousness. For that, at least, one should be thankful, for it is a terrible thing for any man or woman to fall into the hands of the living Freud.

My infatuation, which had been so wonderful and beautiful while it lasted, gradually faded away. In less than a year I could look upon the lady without a tremor. Thus ended my first, but not last, love affair.

In the evenings at milking-time I often sat among the farm-hands and listened to stories of the banshee, of fairies, ghosts, apparitions, and wraiths. Sometimes I would get round the turf fire at my Uncle Bonar's house and listen to him telling stories of great deeds done in the olden time, long, long ago. From him I learned a great deal of Irish history. John Bonar Thompson, or "The Master," as he was called, was a great historian, a great theologian, and a great politician. He was also a great scholar, moralist, teacher, and lawgiver. What he did not know was hardly worth consideration.

For many years he had taught school at Ladyhill. I did not commence school until after his retirement. He had no time for the new teacher, Mr. Duncan, whom he stigmatized as an effeminate nincompoop. "He has fine clothes on his back, but rags in his head," Uncle Bonar once said to me. "Children who are sent to him for instruction, they will grow up as stupid as their teacher." When I once mentioned to my uncle that his successor at Ladyhill was in the habit of eating sandwiches at his desk during the play-hour, his contempt was supreme. "Just what I would expect from the pampered mollycoddle," he said with disgust. "I would have died of hunger before doing such a thing. A glass of water was all I had between breakfast and late dinner. The man who needs sandwiches during school-hours is a miserable weakling."

Uncle Bonar was the oracle of the countryside. He was looked upon as an authority on law, philosophy, history, ethics, foreign affairs, and the correct interpretation of obscure points in theology and moral philosophy.

Relatives and neighbors would gather in his kitchen at times, to hear him reading a leading article from the *Belfast Weekly Telegraph,* or *The Witness,* amid a respectful hush, or holding forth on the progress of the South African War, which was then raging. Sometimes, by special request, he would recite "King Robert of Sicily," or "Lord Ullin's Daughter," in a strong, solemn, parsonic voice.

It was said that in his youth he had been engaged to a girl who eventually threw him over in favor of a richer man. She had the bad taste to invite the young schoolmaster to the wedding. He turned up rather drunk, ate heartily, swore loudly while eating, and insulted the guests; drank the bride's health, poured whisky over the bridegroom, smashed his jaw;

tore off the bride's dress, and, after cursing all women as faithless wantons, rushed madly into the road and was found later asleep in a ditch. From that day he swore he would never marry. He also swore he would sign the pledge, but better counsel prevailed.

This remarkable character was a tall, stout man, with a white beard and a pompous manner. He wore a black swallow-tailed coat, dark gray trousers, and gray top hat. Although he subscribed to the current religious beliefs, he was never seen at chapel. His opinion of the minister was a poor one. "A weak, daft creature," he said of him. "As ignorant of theology as a goat. He ought never to have been ordained. He preaches like a dummy." And no one ever contradicted "The Master." He was feared for his erudition and his sharp tongue.

His later years were darkened by the shadow of a great scandal. For a long time he had been involved in a law case arising out of a suit brought against him by his sister-in-law, Rachel Thompson. She lived in a small tumble-down cottage on my uncle's farm, where she had brought up her three children in very poor circumstances and in face of great difficulties. Every one believed that her husband, who was supposed to be living in Australia, had deserted her twenty years ago. One day a man from Australia turned up at Rachel's cottage to ask how she was getting on. He had known her husband in Australia and had worked with him on a sheep farm.

"Your late husband used to talk a lot about you," he told Rachel. "My late husband?" exclaimed Rachel in surprise. "When did he die?" The stranger informed her that her husband had been dead for some years. He had prospered with the sheep farm, and, having taken up with a woman, who lived with him as his mistress, had tried to forget all about his wife and children at home. Just before his death, however, he had been stricken with a twinge of remorse and had written to Uncle Bonar, begging him to look after the wife and family and enclosing a check for a large sum of money, something over a thousand pounds. "The Master" had written saying that he had made the money over to Rachel and would see that she and the children were well cared for, and more to the same effect.

This came as a stunning blow to poor Rachel. She could not believe it at first; when proof was forthcoming, she nearly went off her head with indignation against my uncle. He had not only swindled her out of what was lawfully due to her, but he had treated her most callously for years. He had even tried to evict her from the cottage and slandered her shamefully in many ways.

Many of the neighbors had been puzzled by my uncle's conduct. Rachel was a broad-spoken, pipe-smoking pagan, who swore a great deal and was no fine lady. She did not go to chapel and took no interest in such things. Among the respectable and the "unco guid" she was looked upon as a heathen. But she was a good-natured, generous, hard-working woman, who had battled strenuously for her children against heavy odds and was well liked by all who really knew her.

The story of my uncle's treachery got about and tongues began to wag. Rachel was advised to take action against him. She did so, and the case came on at the court at Ballymena. The proceedings dragged on for months. Documents had to be sent from Australia. Witnesses came from across the seas. Things began to look black against "The Master"; he was looked at askance in many quarters. At length the case ended. My uncle lost and was ordered to make reparation to the woman he had so shamefully swindled. He was disgraced, but the strait-laced, chapel-going, respectable ones would not believe in his guilt.

Rachel, they said, was a low, wicked, designing woman. She did not worship God in their way. She swore like a bargee, smoked a clay pipe, kept open house for the roughest and wildest of the country boys and girls, and refused to moralize over the awful wickedness of her fellow-creatures. Any girl who got in trouble over a boy was certain of sanctuary at Rachel's cottage. "Rachel's" was notorious, and I was continually warned by my aunt to avoid her house for fear of contamination. And although Rachel had been cruelly robbed by a silver-haired hypocrite, my aunt refused to believe it, insisting that my uncle could do no wrong.

On the memorable day upon which "The Master's" case came to an end, I saw him as he drove past our cottage in his gig. He looked old and pale and stricken. He was not seen about for many weeks after this. His day was done and he slowly sank in general esteem. As the enormity of his crime began to dawn upon people, he became an object of scorn and retired from public view. Even the God-fearing supporters ceased to call upon him. The facts could no longer be denied. A well-respected and scholarly man who had used his knowledge of the world and his position as a leader of rural society to cheat a poor woman who could not read or write, and persecute her into the bargain, was a humbug and a villain. Even my aunt's faith in him began to waver towards the end.

I learned a great deal from listening to his conversations and pronouncements on life and letters, morals, and religion. He remained a bachelor, though his mind dwelt a great deal upon women. I remember him, shortly before his death, walking about the rooms of his house entirely naked, half-drunk, and, in the presence of all, behaving in an indecent manner. His language at such times was unfit for female ears, though they always listened eagerly to all he said. He died in pain, refusing—unlike Cromwell—the ministrations of a field preacher who implored him to seek grace and pardon from his Maker before it was too late. "Go and ____ yourself!" shouted my uncle. A few minutes later he died, with an oath on his lips.

My aunt's ban on my visits to Rachel was lifted after a while, and I spent some happy times at her cottage. There was always plenty of fun; fiddles, jew's-harps, melodeons, and mouth-organs playing, bawdy stories being told, and laughter ringing through the house. My aunt did not know all that went on at such times, and I did not think it advisable to inform her—she would certainly have withdrawn my permit had I done so.

CHAPTER II

Figures of Earth

THERE are two villages about a mile from my aunt's cottage. They are almost deserted now, but thirty years ago they were scenes of thriving life. These villages, Upper and Lower Scolbow, stood a quarter of a mile from each other on the road towards Ballymena, which was seven miles away. Each village contained half a dozen houses, occupied by farmers and their families. I often went to one or the other on errands for my aunt. There were no shops, not even a public-house—the nearest public-house was three miles away, though there was a Mrs. O'Neil who kept an illicit still in a house not far away from Lower Scolbow—just houses and barns and byres.

In one of the houses lived a hard-working farmer by the name of Gawn, whose wife was a madwoman. Mrs. Gawn went off her head periodically and had to be taken to the lunatic asylum. The unhappy woman was quite sane and sober for long periods; a cheerful, industrious wife and mother to their four children. When the attacks came on she turned into a dangerous fiend, who raved, bit, and drew knives or other weapons upon her own children or any one whom she imagined had injured her in some way.

Aunt Eliza used to call at the house sometimes for a chat. I was allowed to accompany her on these calls, generally to carry a bag, or a parcel, or something of the kind. We dropped in one morning while the husband was at work in the fields and the children away at school. Mrs. Gawn made us welcome, gave me a "piece"—the Ulster term for a piece of bread and jam—and entered into conversation with my aunt, who, like most people, was fond of gossip and scandal. The two women were soon deep in the disembowelment of some one's reputation. I sat on a small stool eating my bread and jam and plotting some scheme by which I could rob the orchard at the back of Gawn's house before leaving, while the two gossips collogued together at the tea-table.

After an hour had gone by, during which my aunt went through the time-honored formula of pretending that she had only a moment to stay at least a dozen times, Mrs. Gawn went to the front door and locked it, putting the key on a high ledge well out of reach of my aunt, who was a short woman. A queer look passed over my aunt's face, but I went on eating bread and jam without paying much attention to what it might mean.

"You must stay a while longer, Miss Thompson," said Mrs. Gawn in a firm voice. "We'll go up to bed for an hour or two."

"Oh no, Mrs. Gawn," said my aunt, trying to speak in a normal way. "I must really be going; I have to feed the hens, you know."

"The hens can wait," announced Mrs. Gawn in a decided tone. "They won't die. Come on, we must get to bed."

My aunt was thoroughly terrified. She rushed towards the door, with Mrs. Gawn after her. For ten minutes or more the two women struggled about the room, Mrs. Gawn grim and awful-looking in her frenzy; my aunt deadly pale, disheveled, and perspiring terribly.

I cannot recall my own feelings, but I could not have been very happy. I believe I sat stock-still gazing at the two women struggling madly on the floor, for I remember their expressions quite vividly.

Mr. Gawn, coming suddenly in from the field, heard cries

and broke down the door. He took the madwoman to the asylum the same afternoon, conveying her there in a cart, in which she lay trussed like a fowl. A few months later she was back at the farmhouse, as sane as ever. She had no memory of the incident with my aunt. But the attacks became more frequent as she grew older, and eventually she died in the asylum.

Why she wanted my aunt to go to bed with her was never known.

There was quite a large percentage of insane persons in the district, most of them being the victims of religious mania. "Conversions" were common occurrences. Some man or woman would suddenly "get religion" in this sensational form. They would give up their bad habits, start pulling long faces and making every one uncomfortable, develop hysteria, and end in the "bughouse."

A great deal of misery was caused by the activities of the evangelicals and revivalists who came snooping round the farmhouses asking after the state of our souls. It was not enough that we had to live from the cradle to coffin under the dark shadow of Puritanism, but we were forced to suffer these half-crazy fanatics into the bargain. I am not a materialist, but sudden conversions under the influence of these old types of revivalist soul-savers have never impressed me as other than harmful. I think religion should be based on thought, not on crude and violent emotion, or hysterical fears and half-understood sex promptings. Many of the people who were "born again" during a revivalist wave ought not to have been born the first time. They were the village freaks, or the worthless scamps and trollops who lacked intellect, self-control, and strength of character. Every now and then one of these poor creatures would be carted away to the lunatic asylum.

Some of the persons who got converted were quite worthy, though extremely trying, types. They would suddenly, after what they imagined had been lives of sin, undergo a superficial transformation, abandon all frivolity, separate themselves from their former companions, and set up as unofficial ministers of the Gospel. They became "witnesses" to the "saving power of Christ unto salvation." A certain number would backslide after a time and return to their former way of life. But those who stood firm were a great nuisance. I was frequently intercepted while working in the fields, or playing with my companions, by some ardent missionary, who would wrestle with me for the possession of my youthful soul; without, however, any success. I lacked the religious temperament. It soon became recognized that I was hopeless material for their evangelizing efforts, and I was left to go my own way to the everlasting bonfire. They recoiled before a weapon I have always been able to handle with success against those who tried to convert me to anything—the weapon of ridicule. This seems to show a lack of genuine sincerity on the part of the proselytizers. They do not fear abuse, even threats of violence, not even death, but they wilt under ridicule. This applies especially, I discovered many years later, to socialists, communists, atheists, and other persons who want to convert people to their way of thinking. They cannot stand up to the man who laughs at them, and when ridicule is applied they curl up and wither away.

A familiar figure in the district at that time was the poet Samuel Owens. A doddering octogenarian, gap-toothed and bald, he shuffled around reciting to himself or any one who would listen the gems of verse which gushed from his fertile fancy in a perpetual stream. To the irreverent he was a handy butt, and sods of earth frequently struck him as he passed up and down the lanes. He was a man of varied activities and versatile gifts, a self-appointed politician and moral adviser, an amateur theologian, an historical expert and social reformer without portfolio. He was filled with an omnivorous curiosity about human nature in all its manifestations.

Once, when a prudish and super-respectable lady, who was visiting my aunt in connection with some mission work in which she was interested, was introduced to the old poet, who had called to read his latest effusion, he commenced to put her through a searching examination about her married life—when and where she had first met her husband, what he said to her during their courting-days, what it felt like to be a bride, and so on.

"And do you sleep in separate beds, may I inquire?" asked the queer old man.

The lady could stand no more. "How dare you ask such questions?" she demanded, turning red with annoyance and disgust.

"But these things are of the utmost importance," declared the poet. "How am I to find out if I don't ask? Now tell me: do you still desire your husband in a physical way as much as you did at first? Or have the fires of passion begun to die down?"

"Go away, you filthy old scoundrel!" cried the indignant woman. "You ought to be locked up in prison. I shall report this to the Chief Constable of Antrim."

At this point my aunt, who was almost fainting with horror—or appeared to be—ordered the truth-seeker out of the house, at the same time ordering me off to bed. As it was about six o'clock in the evening, with the sun shining, I did not relish the idea, but dared not refuse. I went upstairs, but instead of going to bed I stood at the top of the stairs listening to the two women discussing the affair for about an hour. I was surprised and indignant to find that my aunt knew far more about the mysteries of sex than I had ever suspected. And the ultra-respectable lady's indignation gave way to laughter after the poet had gone. I heard the two women giggling for quite a long time, and I heard my aunt telling things about Samuel Owens that I could not believe she even knew about. It was very puzzling. She sank a little in my estimation after that evening.

Shortly after this I obtained my aunt's permission to visit Antrim and hear the Church of Ireland clergyman, Mr. West, deliver a lecture entitled "The Success of Failure."

I always went on foot to Antrim and back, a distance of eight miles. I must have been a quaint youngster to walk such a distance for the sake of a lecture by a clergyman. Mr. West gave an excellent address, in which he sketched the careers of a number of celebrated men who had failed at first, but by means of thrift, enterprise, sobriety, piety, and ruthless determination, had risen on stepping-stones, as it were, of their dead failures to triumph and a sure success. A vote of thanks was tendered at the close of the lecture. The mover was Samuel Owens. He had risen before any one could stop him and continued long after every one felt willing to shoot him. He introduced a good quantity of new matter, pointed his own moral, and adorned his own tale by the introduction of a poem specially composed for the occasion. The verses were written in praise of Mr. West, and the rustic laureate began as follows:

"Wherever we may wander o'er earth's farthest
  clime—
To the north, to the south, to the east or the west—
There is none to compare in talents sublime
To the well-known preacher, the Reverend West.

Let us read, mark and learn and inwardly digest
The truths he has just now so ably expressed.
When our turn comes to depart to the Home of the
  Blest,
Let it be in the company of the Reverend West."

The rest of the noble panegyric was unfortunately lost, both
to the audience and to posterity, as at this point the noise
became so great that the poet's voice could no longer be
heard.

Samuel Owens, though inglorious, was not mute, and I
regret not having taken down more of his verses as they fell
from his inspired lips. Unfortunately he did not publish.

I have a final memory of his standing upon a stone at
the foot of Carnearney mountain during the Queen's Jubilee
celebrations, chanting an ode specially written by him for the
occasion, while the village youths pelted him with manure,
clods of earth, pieces of turf and other missiles.

MY aunt was always scolding me about something and
warning me against dangers and perils, especially the
dangers and perils attendant upon self-indulgence and the
pleasures of the flesh. She warned me against the dangers
of female society, against eating too much, smoking, tea-
drinking, late hours, bad company, and idleness. She allowed
me to visit Antrim every six months, on condition that I
did not loiter on the way and brought back the currants,

gooseberries, and apples she instructed me to buy without eating any of them on the way home.

The half-yearly market-fair at Antrim was a great thrill. There were coconut-shies and peep-shows, which I never saw because I had no money to spend. My aunt gave me a halfpenny, and sometimes as much as a penny, to spend on riotous living, but these sums did not go far. I lingered, despite my aunt's instructions, to watch the free performances in the High Street. There were ballad-singers, bagpipers, players on the penny whistle, pill-sellers, and fortune-tellers.

I once saw a sword-swallower at work in the High Street. He was stripped to the waist. He cursed his audience roughly. "Before I begin my performance, which I have given in every country in the world and before every crowned head in Europe, America, and Africa, including the Czar of Russia and the Sultan of Turkey, I want to see a sum of money equal to three silver shillings lying on that space of ground in front of me. I doubt if you possess that much money among the whole crowd of ye. You look more like a pack of starved, mangy curs than civilized and Christian men. I have had gold and silver poured out on the ground before me in other countries, where the people are civilized and able to appreciate my performances properly.

"If I was not a sentimental fool, I would not be giving my famous exhibition of sword-swallowing to the likes of you, a miserable collection of starved-looking curs. I should be giving my performances before a select audience of Christian men—aye, the highest in the land. It makes me sick to have to demean myself by performing to a lot of curs and swine like you. Are ye men or are ye dogs?" he demanded furiously. "If ye are men and not dirty savages and mangy curs or ignorant heathen, prove yourselves. Throw your money in. Come on, hurry. I have to appear before important people. Do you think I can afford to stand here shivering for the sake of three paltry, dirty, lousy shillings?"

The money was thrown in at last. As soon as the full amount had been furnished, the great artiste's tone altered completely. "Thank ye, thank ye!" he said gratefully. "God bless ye every one. May ye never want!" He gave a wonderful show, swallowing watches, swords, and a bayonet with hearty appetite. There was no doubt that he did these things. I heard years after that he injured himself internally while swallowing a sword and died as a result.

It amazed me to hear the things he said being taken so calmly by the crowd, big, strong, tough-looking fellows. Many laughed as he scourged them with his tongue and seemed to admire him for insulting them. I found in later years that crowds like to be castigated by speakers in this fashion. Each member of the crowd thinks that he is the exception; the speaker's remarks do not apply to him; it is the others who are being indicated. A speaker can never go wrong, therefore, in cursing his hearers roundly. He is really cursing a crowd of exceptions, each one of whom is delighted to hear the others denounced so trenchantly.

THE Presbyterian minister Mr. Moffit was a regular visitor to my aunt's cottage. He came every month, from his chapel three miles away, a long walk across the mountain and hills which stretch over towards Kells and Connor. Mr. Moffit had been the preacher at Eskalain Chapel for over thirty years. He worked hard and was accounted a good man, but he lacked intellectual depth, scholarship, and force of mind. He was a bad preacher who hesitated over his sentences in a painful way, "er"-ing and "er"-ing before every word. It is human for speakers and preachers to "er" occasionally, but with Mr. Moffit it amounted to a nuisance. I used to imitate his mannerisms, to the great scandal of Aunt Eliza, who warned me that all mockers should have their part in the lake which burneth forever. But though the manner of his preaching left much to be desired, the matter was according to standard. Threats of hell were more common in his sermons than hopes of Paradise. For the wicked there was a place reserved, a house of eternal pain, a furnace seven times heated, a pit of flames, an inferno of agony without end. Congregations loved this sort of thing, and Mr. Moffit could be relied upon to deliver the goods.

He was a kindly man, active in good works and well liked by all, especially the children. "Get your face washed, the minister's coming," the parents would say, as Mr. Moffit was observed coming over the fields. He carried sweets and biscuits for the youngsters and always had a kind word for every one. It was easy and natural for young people to laugh at him, good man though he was, for he was eccentric. About sixty years of age, slight and sandy-bearded with a shining bald head, he talked to himself and gesticulated as he skipped across the hills and fields to visit his parishioners. I often watched him vaulting the dikes and wire-fences, stopping every now and then to peer into a hedge or examine a wild flower. As soon as any one accosted him he became quite normal and ceased his fidgeting at once.

Every year a *soirée* was held at Eskalain Chapel, with Mr. Moffit at the head of affairs. At these gatherings, which were attended by young and old (including those who never went to a place of worship at any other time) and by some of the roughest and noisiest of the young farm-laborers and their lady-loves, it was the custom for tea and cake to be handed round, after which a concert would be given. The visitors were herded in tightly packed rows in the pews, where the boiling tea and thick slabs of cake were consumed in much discomfort. A great deal of hot tea was always spilled upon the trousers and skirts of the guests, who swore heartily at each other, or clicked their tongues, as the fervent liquid soaked through their clothing.

It was usual, after the multitude had eaten to bursting and drunken to saturation point, for the more active and undisciplined youths to dip pieces of cake in the tea and fling the sodden mass at the head of some unsuspecting elder, or other pompous person, amid howls of merriment. Mr. Moffit reproved the larrikins sternly from time to time, but without avail. Things became so bad at one of these socials that action had to be taken by the officials of the chapel to circumvent the activities of the high-spirited merrymakers. Mr. Moffit had rated them vigorously, standing on a form near the pulpit. "It is a sin and a scandal," he had said, his bald head shining in the lamplight, "that good bread, for which many of our brothers in East Africa would be only too grateful, should be thrown about in this disgraceful way. It is a sound proverb which says, 'Waste not, want not.' It is shameful that such things should be done in the House of God. Satan finds some mischief still, it seems—" Splosh! A lump of tea-soaked cake had landed full upon the indignant cleric's sparkling dome. His polemic concluded abruptly as, with pieces of wet cake sliding slowly down the sides of his face, he made sadly for the vestry. I felt very sorry for poor Mr. Moffit, though I had been throwing cake myself a few moments before.

A subtle device was introduced the following year. The building was crammed as usual, the potential cake-slingers being well in evidence and in militant mood. A groan of disappointment sounded through the hall when—instead of the liberal supplies of cake being served out according to custom—a small bun, studded with a few odd currants, was handed to each person, the bun neatly enclosed in a plain paper bag.

As many of those present had gone without food for at least half a day in order to do justice to the anticipated feast, a wave of anger swept over the congregation. "We want another bun!" "More buns here!" "Do you want us to die of starvation?" and similar cries resounded through the building. The chapel officials took no notice whatever of these displays of disaffection. Mr. Moffit, his face beaming with happiness and *bonhomié*, moved along the aisles nodding and waving his hand in greeting to his flock.

Mr. Moffit continued in the ministry at Eskalain until he was over seventy years of age. Although many grumbled at his bad style as a preacher and laughed at his eccentric habits, everyone was sorry when he became too old for his job. The congregation was never large, and Mr. Moffit's stipend was not more than about thirty shillings a week, upon which he had brought up a large family. A present of money was—I heard—made to him upon his retirement. It was no more than he deserved, for he was a good man.

His successor, a young intellectual from Belfast, did not last a month. He got on the wrong side of the congregation the first time he appeared in the pulpit. It soon became apparent from the tone of his remarks, which were all about loving our enemies, forgiving those that trespass (a dangerous point to make, with a congregation of farmers) against us, and showing toleration even to skeptics and Roman Catholics! Toleration towards skeptics meant nothing—few knew what a skeptic was; but toleration towards the "Papishes," the hated hellhounds of Rome, the spawn of the Scarlet Woman! It was a mercy he was not pulled out of the pulpit and ducked in a pond. He tried to put things right the following Sunday by plastering Martin Luther and the heroes of the Reformation with panegyrical superlatives, but it would not do. The congregation had him "taped." He was a mealy-mouthed half-and-halfer, a temporizer, an insipid muff whose Protestantism was so lukewarm as to render him suspect by every one. The root of the matter was not in him. He finished himself completely on the third Sunday by advising his hearers to read Dante! This was the end. Half of them walked out and the remainder stopped to let the wretched young man know just what they thought about him. He never preached there again. A man from Derry, a Mr. MacMeekin, was appointed in his stead and proved satisfactory in every way. His first sermon was based upon the text, "The wicked shall be cast into hell."

My aunt, who did not go to chapel, being excused duty on grounds of failing health, was as disgusted as any one with the young preacher's reference to Dante. "Dante, indeed!" she exclaimed. "The devil is busy when such names can be mentioned in God's house!" Neither my aunt, nor any one else, as far as I could gather, including myself, would have known any different if we had been told that Dante was a leader of the French Revolution.

IN one of the houses at Upper Scolbow there lived at that time an old woman named Margaret Livingstone, a widow. Her son Andrew lived with her and did all the work on the farm, which belonged to Margaret. Andrew was a man of great physical strength, known everywhere by his enormous red beard, and popular because of his good humor and easy-going disposition. He worked like a slave and was completely under the thumb of his mother. Although Andrew was over forty, "Big Margaret," as she was called, treated him like a child. She was a raw-boned, red-faced, loud-voiced, domineering woman of about seventy years of age. Her husband had been dead for about forty years, and she lived on in the house with Andrew, the only issue of her union with the late Mr. Livingstone.

"Big Margaret" wore a red hat with a large blue feather sticking up from the center; a white blouse and a short red skirt, white stockings and elastic-sided boots. We used to laugh as she stalked about among the chickens and geese, throwing them their bran and Indian corn from a large earthen basin, or carrying cans of milk from the byre to throw in the churn, whistling and singing like a man as she went about these tasks. Andrew was bullied and insulted by her all day long, but he took it without saying a word. "Let her say what she likes," he once told my aunt. "Hard words break no bones, and when she dies the farm will be mine." And though he was often twitted about his submissiveness, he only laughed, continuing to bear "Big Margaret's" insults with a patient shrug.

A time came, however, when Andrew, who had fallen a victim to love for the first time in his life, made up his mind to marry the girl who had stirred his giant's heart. "Big Margaret" would not hear of it, of course. But Andrew, for the first time in his life, defied her. He slipped off to Eskalain one Saturday afternoon, and came back home with his newly married bride sitting beside him in the buggy.

"What do you mean by bringing that hussy here?" called "Big Margaret" from the doorway. "Get off to where you came from, you brazen little bitch."

"This is my mother," said Andrew, after assisting the

young woman from her seat in the buggy. "Mother, this is Alice—my wife."

"Your wife, is she?" said "Big Margaret." "Well, you can go and lead your married life somewhere else, for you won't cross this threshold again."

The bride was frightened out of her life, and Andrew pushed her back into the buggy and drove away to Antrim, where they spent their honeymoon at the house of a friend of the bride.

"Big Margaret" would not relent. She sold the farm, shut herself up in the house, refused to speak to any of her neighbors, who were on Andrew's side, and died a year later. When her will was read it was found that she had left every penny, something like two thousand pounds, to a niece in England. And so poor Andrew got none. He had been working as a hired man since his mother turned him out, but he did not dream that she would cut him out of her will without a penny. The farm, he thought, would come back to him after her death.

The unexpected blow cut him to pieces. He worked on for a while here and there, as a day-laborer, while Alice went back to her people. But he aged quickly, his splendid red beard turning quite gray. Every one pitied him, but before many years had passed he sank and died—a worn-out old man. His child grew up a cripple. Alice married again. Her second husband, who was a man twice her age, died of heart failure, leaving what little money there was to be divided between Alice and a brother of his who was a hopeless drunkard. Alice invested her share of the money in setting up a sweetshop at Kells, but the shop failed and she went into service. As the years passed she found the burden of life too heavy to carry and she went out of her mind. The crippled daughter was taken care of by a neighbor of "Big Margaret's" and grew up to be a very intelligent woman. Alice lived on in the insane asylum; as far as I know she is still alive; of her past life she remembers nothing. Her daughter, who is a writer of children's stories and at present living in Belfast, goes to visit her from time to time. Alice, who is now a very old woman, quiet, mild, and harmless, does not recognize her.

THERE were two men well known to me in those days who ruined themselves rather gloriously. One was a man called Orr, who lived with a sister on a small farm near Carnearney. He drove his horse-and-trap to Antrim market every Thursday, with the ostensible purpose of doing business there. His business was to get blind drunk. He drove me in once or twice and insisted on filling me with whisky and port wine. My aunt put a stop to it; but I liked Orr. He was a kindly soul; I learned a great deal from him about life and the ways of men. Orr had been about the world a lot in his time and had a racy way of describing places and people; and he was no Puritan. Church and chapel people looked down upon him as a waster, and Mr. West came all the way from Antrim once, to pray over him. Orr took it in good part and offered the reverend gentleman several glasses of whisky, which Mr. West accepted under mild protest. "Oh, really, Mr. Orr, I should not be doing this. I have come here today to try and induce you to give it up. Well, good health."

Orr continued his drinking until he drank himself out of his farm and into the poorhouse. The sister also went into the poorhouse. She was old and nearly blind; in a few years she died. Orr had passed some time before. They lie side by side in paupers' graves.

The other was a young man by the name of Coulter.

When his parents died he became the sole owner of two large farms. Most of the work was left to the hired men, and Coulter exercised no supervision over them whatever. The men became slack, the crops were neglected and the cattle were not properly fed. Several valuable beasts died. The cattle were left to stray in the fields and trample out the crops. Much damage was done in this way. When things got bad, Coulter sold one of the farms. The hired men began to leave, as wages were not always forthcoming. Everything fell into neglect. Coulter's trouble—if trouble it can be called—was laziness. He lay in bed till two and three in the afternoon. If any one came to the house on business, they found the place deserted. There was no sign of life, no fire on the hearth, no sound within the house. Everything was in a state of disorder, and dust lay thick over the chairs and tables. After a time people stopped going near the place.

Coulter would turn out in the evenings and join some of the younger men in games of wrestling and running. He was full of fun and a good teller of stories. A handsome, vigorous, well-built man, with a cheerful and likeable personality, he was popular with women and liked their society. But he avoided marriage—it was too much trouble. As things got worse, he stayed indoors more and more and became a recluse. Long after the furniture had been sold he remained on in the big farmhouse, sleeping on the floor all day and most of the night. He had no visitors, and never went out. One day he was found dead in bed. The inquest disclosed nothing organically wrong—he had just ceased living. It had become too much trouble to breathe; so he gave it up.

I cannot remember a time when I was not fond of reading, although there was little cultural life among the people of County Antrim. The only books I ever saw in circulation there were the Bible (a book which I have come to appreciate and understand a little, but which was read and interpreted to me in the worst possible way); that over-rated classic *The Pilgrim's Progress*; a horrible concoction called *Foxe's Book of Martyrs*; and one or two old novels like *The Basket of Flowers, Christie's Old Organ,* and *A Peep Behind the Scenes.* Old numbers of the *Sphere,* the *Illustrated London News,* and an illustrated paper called *Black and White* were also to be found in some of the more intellectual households. My aunt disapproved of reading. She disapproved of theater-going, although she had never been to a theater, nor had any one else I ever met in those parts. But we heard tales of the awful wickedness and wantonness that went on in the playhouses of Belfast. My aunt also disapproved of dancing (but not singing), dressing in fine clothes, having photographs taken, reading newspapers on the Sabbath, stopping out after dark, stopping in bed after six in the morning, making love, or using endearing terms towards those of the opposite sex. Marriage was permissible, but falling in love was indelicate and improper. Strong drink was taboo, as was smoking or chewing tobacco; swearing and using words like "damn" were sins against the Holy Ghost.

She distrusted anything that gave pleasure to the flesh. I was forced to drink cocoa, and deny myself tea, because she knew that I liked tea and loathed cocoa. Brown bread was given to me because I preferred white, oatmeal porridge because I had a taste for cornflower. My egg was always boiled because I liked it fried. I was kept hard at work because my aunt suspected—and rightly—that I was lazy.

There was a young man called Billy O'Neil who dropped in to ask me to play with him sometimes. He was six or seven years my senior, a wild character, indolent and clever.

My aunt did not approve of him; but as I grew older she
could not stop me associating with him, though she warned
me against him. Billy lived with his father, a man of similar
ways and tastes to his own. The father knew Latin and
played the fiddle—he certainly played, and had taught Billy
to play it, rather well. He was humorous, kindly, and lazy.
Billy lived at home without doing any work, and his father
did no work either. How they lived was a mystery; but they
did, and seemed quite happy. The mother had died and there
were no brothers or sisters; father and son lived in a small
house at the foot of Carnearney mountain.

Billy was my hero. He was strong and good-looking and
devil-may-care; he had no reverence for his elders and no
respect for his betters; he was a swearer, a blasphemer, and
a mocker and scoffer. It was a tremendous honor to have
him as a companion. I was treated by him as an equal. He
allowed me to read some of his books, which I was obliged
to peruse in secret, going away into the fields where I had
hiding-places of my own. One of the greatest literary thrills
I ever enjoyed was when Billy lent me a small green-covered

story-book called *The Marvel,* containing a tale of "Jack, Sam and Pete." The famous boys' story-book cost, at that time, one halfpenny per issue. The well-known green cover will, I hope, be familiar to all who read these pages; as should be the *Union Jack* and *Pluck*. To buy copies of these halfpenny "bloods" was beyond my power; I was never given more than twopence a year to spend during the whole of my boyhood until I left Ireland at the age of fourteen. Billy also lent me a copy of *Chips,* a well-known comic paper. Years later I was able to complete the reading of a serial story entitled *The Human Bat,* by S. Clarke-Hook (not to be confused with H. Clarke Hook, also a writer of boys' thrillers), an eerie installment of which I read, with palpitating excitement, in the solitary issue lent me by Billy O'Neil.

My aunt got to know about my surreptitious reading of forbidden books. She burned Billy's copy of *Dead-wood Dick,* which he had given me to take care of. "Never let me catch you... " etc. The burning of Billy's book by my aunt proved to be a turning-point in my life. For the first time I rose in revolt against her silly tyranny. I turned wild, set fire to a neighbor's haystack, filled my aunt's milkchurn with stones, began making faces while she tried to read the Bible to me, refused to attend school, and struck work. My aunt became alarmed. She realized at last that I was growing up and that her authority over me was gone. She changed her tactics, became indulgent, almost humble. She talked to me as to an equal. "I shall not always be here to guide you," she said, with tears coming into her eyes (this was before she had become a convert to Pastor Russell's religious doctrines). I felt sorry when she talked in this way, and promised to reform, abandoned my mischievous practices, attended school regularly, worked hard, and became a veritable prig. Yet I could not forget that she had burned Billy's book.

Shortly after this episode Billy "found salvation." He took to singing hymns and saying his prayers and going about as if butter would melt in his mouth. His assumption of holiness was grotesque. It did not suit his personality. Fortunately the fit of piety did not last long. He dropped hymn-singing in favor of bawdy songs, spared the knees of his trousers any unnecessary wear and tear, and became his natural self again.

Billy was an emotionalist and a romantic. Some time after his recovery from the Salvation craze he was seized with an idea that there was going to be a Roman Catholic rising in Ulster, or an attempt on the part of the "Papishes" to put Northern Ireland under Popish authority. Home Rule, some one had said, was Rome Rule. The "Papishes" were plotting to bring the northern province under the heel of the accursed thing—the Vatican. Billy became obsessed with the idea of preparedness. "Every man will be needed," he told me solemnly, "in the struggle that is coming. Every Orangeman must arm in readiness for the attack when it comes." He bought a fowling-piece from a friend and took up shooting practice. One Saturday afternoon he took me to an old cave at the back of a hill. "We can hide here when the enemy comes ravaging and pillaging," he told me. It was not much of a cave. There was hardly room for us to crawl inside, and, once in, it was a problem how to get out again. But Billy found it sufficient.

I did not share his military enthusiasm or his strange ideas of patriotism, though I had been taught, of course, like every one else, to curse the Pope, cheer at the mention of "King Billy" (William of Orange), and look upon Catholics as vipers, traitors, idol-worshipers, and scoundrels of the deepest dye. I often joined in the old Orange songs like "Sleeter, slatter," and "Up comes a man with a shovel in his hand," and I took it for granted that the Pope was a monster and all Catholics damned to eternal perdition. But I did not think seriously about the question until many years later. Nor did any one else that I knew think very deeply about it; it was enough that there was an enemy to be cursed and, if only the opportunity should arise, to be fought and, of course, beaten to a frazzle.

Billy tired of waiting for the day which never came, and his enthusiasm petered out after a week or two. He sold the fowling-piece, stopped visiting the cave, and took up his father's fiddle again, upon which he would play very sweetly. Getting tired of reading and dreaming after a while, he placed a few things in a Gladstone bag one day and went north to seek his fortune in Belfast. I felt very lonely without him. He wrote once to say that he had got a job as a milkman in the city and was doing well. He was seriously thinking, he said, of turning Catholic—what he had been taught about them had been a pack of lies. It was not impossible, he stated, that he might one day become a priest. This interested me very much, and I too began to feel that all the things I had been told to believe about the Catholics might not be true after all. I said as much to my aunt, but she looked so horror-stricken that I had not the heart to pursue the subject.

I never saw Billy O'Neil again.

NORTHERN Ireland is a place of great natural beauty. The glens of Antrim are famous in song and story. On a clear day one can stand on the top of the Carnearney mountain and see Lough Neigh four miles away; or the Cave Hill, just outside Belfast, a distance of eighteen miles. Lough Neigh is full of historical and poetical associations.

I often saw Lord Masserene boating on Lough Neigh when I was a child. His lordship was a celebrated figure among the Antrim people. He was said to have been fond of having a "wee drap" among the laboring men in the public-houses, and that he cursed and swore like a lord. My aunt had the honor of being knocked down by him as he was driving furiously along the road near Carnearney. He apologized most elaborately and offered to drive her home. His offer was declined, but she always spoke with justifiable pride of having been run over by a peer of the realm.

I also used to see old Earl O'Neil, the lord of the famous Shanes Castle, walking into the town along the Antrim road. He had a nervous habit of lifting his head quickly up and down as he walked; as he held his head on one side, the movement looked all the more odd. I formed the impression that he was not "all there," but my elders assured me that he was.

TOWARDS the end of my thirteenth year a message came from my mother. She had lived in England since my birth, so that I had no memory of her. My aunt did not speak well of her, but neither did she speak harshly. Having brought me up so far, she did not like my leaving her; but my mother was anxious that I should join her in Manchester, and wrote to my aunt to that effect. The choice was left to me—I could go or stay.

I was tremendously excited at the prospect of seeing something of the great world. My aunt had never allowed me even to visit Belfast, for she regarded cities as cesspools of vice and sin. She did not want me to leave her, especially as I was able to earn a little money. But I had no enthusiasm for the life of a farm-laborer, having had a pretty tough experience as a hired boy. I jibbed at the prospect of toiling in the fields from dawn to dusk at a wage of three pounds a year, with bed and board—all board and no bed—little leisure or recreation, and no money to spend, no decent clothes, no scope for intellectual advancement, no cultural life. It was not good enough. I would go to Manchester.

The poor old lady wept as she bade me good-by. "But I shall be seeing you again before long," I told her. "No, no," she said; "I shall soon be gone. I'm not long for this world." She was none too pleased when I told her that she would live another twenty years. As it turned out, she lived for nearly thirty years more, and later she, too, came to Manchester and settled down with my mother until her death in 1931. I forgot her petty tyrannies and the many punishments she had laid upon me as we said good-by that day, and for a moment I saw things from her point of view. But I took my leave—and the boat for England.

I have often regretted the step. Ulster people are shrewd, hardy, good-humored folk; hospitable and kindly. In spite of Puritanism their sense of fun is high, robust, and keen; and they have "character," a thing lacking, for instance, in a Londoner. There is an abundance of the raw stuff of human nature in them. They live intensely and their lives are full of drama. The longer I live among people who are alien to me in blood and breeding, the more I appreciate the fine qualities of the Ulster people. I had grown up among the traditions of a proud and ancient race. Love and loyalty to kindred and country is a passion no Irishman can eradicate from his heart. It is strengthened by long absence. With me it grows deeper and more poignant, more intense and steadfast, as the years go by. I think of the old days at Carnearney; of the girls who laughed and joked, and the men who were boys when I was a boy, and who are gone, dust these many years.

CHAPTER III

City Lights and Satellites

FROM London Road Station to Oliver Street, Openshaw, Manchester, is a walk of about a mile and a half. Thirty years ago, a stranger, a country-bred boy visiting a big city for the first time, I walked from that station to my mother's house. There was no one to meet me at the station, and I had to ask my way. I walked up Ashton Old Road. It was a gray, dusty thoroughfare, with row upon row of dingy streets on every side, clanking trams loaded with men in overalls going to the Armstrong-Whitworth works, or the Gorton "Tank," women in clogs and shawls tramping their way to the mills, and with dust and waste paper whirling about in the wind.

But I did not see it like this. To me it was strange and new and thrilling. Among the things that impressed me most were the enormous posters. One which I remember particularly represented a tall, striking, and dominantly magnetic-looking man with a heavy black waxed mustache, who stood in an attitude of authority and command, looking the whole world in the face. At the top of this magnificent poster were the words "Dr. Bodie," and beneath, in large type, the challenging statement: "I lead: follow who can."

Other posters showed certain individuals in various positions of acute distress, dire peril, awful suspense, stark amazement, profound grief, and other rending emotions. Upon these posters were printed such exciting titles as *The Silver King, At War With Women* and *While London Sleeps*. Naturally these were the advertisements of the dramatic pieces to be seen at the Manchester theaters. I was filled with a desperate desire to see the plays as soon as possible. In a bookshop I saw displayed some of the novels I had heard about from Billy O'Neil—*Dead Man's Rock, The Woman in White, The Phantom Ship,* and many others. I wanted to buy them all and start reading right away. Alas, I had not the means to purchase many story-books, and was not to have for many years. I had never possessed as much as half a crown in my life. Perhaps I shall soon get a job, I thought, then I shall have some of the things which fortunate people enjoy as a matter of course.

My mother was waiting for me at the door of her small house in Oliver Street. She looked at me with intense curiosity and interest. Nearly fourteen years had gone by since she had last seen me, a small lump of life, like, I suppose, any other baby of a few days old. I regarded her with a like interest. She was a good-looking woman of thirty-eight, with an honest and kindly expression. Her face was lined with worry and sorrow, but she looked no more than her age. I was introduced to my stepfather, whose name was William Williams. My mother called him William, and so did I. He was a man of the artisan type, neat, rather handsome, and quiet in his manner. His wage was thirty shillings a week, and as my mother sold a few things, in the way of children's socks, shirts, shoes, overalls, and similar articles from a display in the window of their house, they were not extremely poor by my standards.

William was a plumber in the employ of the Manchester Corporation. He was a good man at his trade and drank heavily, as many good workmen did at that time. My mother and he lived quite happily together. They quarreled a good deal, which is often a sign that people love each other strongly.

My mother had a violent temper, which she has handed on, together with several other interesting but unprofitable characteristics, to me. Patient and placid for long periods, she would, I found, burst forth on occasion into a fit of apparently unrestrained fury. In the course of these demoniacal displays pots, plates, pans, knives, and other utensils would whiz through the air with great velocity. This was her way of releasing long-pent-up feelings, and I soon became used to the outbursts.

I noticed that after one of these bouts of violent temper she would, all passion spent, become more than ordinarily charming to my stepfather, and I became disgusted with the billing and cooing which followed a quarrel. I learned later that it was an old working-class custom, and accepted it as such.

William had his own way of showing displeasure. If anything upset him he took revenge on my mother by refusing to eat. At first this had been effective, but as time went on and their love became dulled by what Shelley called "the contagion of the world's slow stain," it became less so. He would come in from work looking stern and forbidding. No word was spoken on these occasions. The atmosphere was cold and dead. My mother would withdraw William's dinner from the oven and set it before him. He would appear to be ignorant of any such thing as a dinner and pretend to be reading the *Evening Chronicle* with extreme diligence. After a period of silence my mother would say, "Your dinner's getting cold," in a flat, indifferent voice. "I want no dinner, thank you," was the invariable reply, and it was uttered by William in a short, decided tone, without detaching his eyes from the newspaper. Instead of leaving the room to spend the next few hours weeping and sulking, as had been the rule earlier, she would take the dinner away from him and say cheerfully, "If you're not hungry, I'll eat it myself." And she did. She sometimes offered the rejected meal to me, but I could not very well accept it without offending William, so I was obliged to let it pass from me.

William had been told all about me before my arrival and made me welcome for my mother's sake. I liked him, and in later years got to like him more. He was not an educated man, but he had good natural intelligence and talked well on many subjects when he felt in the humor. I quarreled with him now and then, but he bore no malice and neither did I. He thought I might enter the plumbing trade as an apprentice, but my mother urged the need for me to be earning something right away. So in less than a week I was answering advertisements for errand-boys, office-boys, van-boys, and other juvenile laborers.

I soon found work in Stockport Road. The wage was

five shillings a week. Three people worked at the shop: Mr. Upchurch, the boss, who sat in a little office making up the accounts and answering letters; Mr. David Soddington, a bad-tempered, middle-aged man with a bald head, who cut cardboard on a guillotine and gave orders to Miss Burr, a tall masculine woman who stood by herself all day, in a large room, and pasted labels on the boxes.

My job was to run errands, assist Soddington on the guillotine, mix glue, fetch beer for Soddington, and go out with a hand-cart piled high with fancy boxes for delivery to the firms who required them. On windy days the boxes sometimes blew off into the mud, and when I returned with the damaged boxes on these occasions I was the recipient of hearty curses from Soddington.

Soddington was in love with the tall lady. She repulsed him continually, but he persisted, and towards evening, after I had fetched him several gills of beer from across the road, his attentions to the reluctant lady became more insistent. I found this very tedious. He would murmur, his breath heavy with beer and his mustache dripping froth, "You know I like you better than any woman in the world, you know it, yet you give me no encouragement."

"You should be saying that to your wife," she would answer, looking at him in disgust.

"One kiss," the amorous cardboard-cutter would beg. "Come, just one."

"Go away, or I'll fetch Mr. Upchurch," Miss Burr would cry, trying to break from Soddington's grasp.

"What do I care for Mr. Upchurch?" the ardent beer-swiller would say. "A kiss—just one."

This performance was gone through almost every evening and on Saturday mornings, between the hours of twelve and one. Soddington never, to my knowledge, was able to induce Miss Burr to give him one solitary voluntary kiss, but he kept on just the same. To me, the unwilling witness of the daily scenes, they were extremely tiresome.

My dinner, which I brought with me to work wrapped in paper, consisted of two large slices of bread and meat, bread and cheese, bread and jam, and, on Thursdays and Fridays, just bread. I brewed tea in a can which was kept on the premises for that purpose, getting the hot water from the pub across the road. My dinner hour was spent in the free library, which was only a few doors away. I put in a good deal of time profitably in this way. I also procured a lender's ticket which enabled me to take books out and read at home. It was not easy to find my way among the multitudinous collection of books, but I went on reading indiscriminately in the hope that I should get the hang of things in time.

My mother and stepfather thought me very silly for wasting my time in reading. Mr. Soddington took the same view. "What does a young fellow like you want to be always reading for?" he sometimes asked me. "I am trying to get a little education," I once said to him. His answer was: "Look here, my boy, the sooner you get those ideas out of your head the better. Education's not for the likes of you. I had a young brother who drove himself 'batty' with education. Mind you don't do the same. Look after your work and never mind about education." This, I have always found, is the attitude of most working people in England towards book-reading.

My mother allowed me threepence a week spending-money. This was spent on theaters. I enjoyed the performances at the "Metropole," the "Osborne" and the "Junction" theaters, which were given over to melodramas of the most lurid kind. The price of admission to the galleries was three-pence, and for that sum I had my adolescent soul purged with pity and terror. It broke my heart to miss a weekly visit. My favorites were, *The King of Crime* (with Sam Livesay as "Ronjarre") *The Grip of Iron* and *The Face at the Window*. *The Sign of the Cross* was too sloppy.

I endured the job at the cardboard-box maker's for about a year, but a day came when I could stick it no longer. I had learned a little during a year's residence in the cotton capital. The gaping yokel had disappeared. The gloss was beginning to wear off things a good deal. Poverty and hard work were getting on my nerves. There seemed no chance of improvement unless I made a move of some kind. My mother was not pleased when I told her I had given up the job at the box-maker's. But I soon found another, and the new post represented an advance, for the wage was six shillings a week. I became a van-boy at a mineral-water works in Hyde Road. The hours, too, were shorter, from six in the morning until seven at night. But the work was hard, and two months spent in hurling crates of mineral waters about nearly laid me out. The bronchitis had not troubled me since leaving Ireland, but I have never been too robust. So I surrendered the seals of office.

After a week of earnest searching, I discovered a situation at a grocer's. A month among the provisions was as much as I could stand, so once again I handed in my resignation.

Turning my attention to the wine and spirit trade for a week or two, I found that instead of a series of adventures among port and brandy I had embarked upon a job of work far too grievous to be borne, and my weekly wage showed no promise of ever rising above six shillings a week. When I asked the boss for a rise he told me I was not worth the six shillings he was already giving me. I resented this, as I had worked very hard for him. There were accordingly a few nasty exchanges, and finally he told me to put on my hat and coat and clear out. I rushed into the cellar for my clothes and took the opportunity of turning all the barrel taps on before leaving. For all I know or care those taps may be still running.

My next job was a big step upwards. I entered the service of the Great Central Railway as an oiler and greaser in the carriage and wagon department. The pay was nine shillings a week, with prospects of fairly rapid promotion. I remained with the railway company for four years, and had I continued with them I should now be a carriage-examiner, or "tapper." The hours were from six a.m. until six p.m., with night work every third week. The work was not unpleasant, and in any case I soon learned to avoid most of it.

After the first year I became an assistant brake-fitter. My job then was to help in the repair of wagons and coaches. There were four of us employed at the siding where the repairing was done—two brake-fitters and two laborers. We had to book the time spent on each job, a system which gave us scope for the exercise of intelligence. A vacuum pipe, for instance, could be fixed in ten minutes. We would mark it down as having taken two hours. A wheel could be put on a carriage in less than half a day. For a job of that kind we would book two days, or even three. It speaks volumes for the lack of intelligence of the working class that this splendid system no longer exists. Some fool always spoils the job and the others allow him to do it. So it was with us.

The tragedy happened just before I left in 1908. One of the brake-fitters was transferred to Grantham and a new man was sent to our siding in his place. This person, a religious fanatic, teetotaler, non-smoker, and all the rest of it, was known to be a conscientious workman who never stopped working, even to wipe his brow. He was the butt of the cabins, and we knew something would happen when he came among us. We met together to discuss what could be done. It was suggested that we "put him wise" to our system of booking the time taken on each job and leave it to him to do the right thing. But he would have none of it.

"I will book the exact time it takes me to do each job and not a minute more," the snake said. And he did. He ruined our job. He booked the exact time to the second, and he was a quick worker. The result of this sabotage was that we were called before the foreman and asked to explain the discrepancy between our time-sheets and those of the new man. How could we? We were caught like rats in a trap. The exposure was complete. As a result the department was speeded up. Wages remained, of course, the same.

Some idea of the kind of viper we had in our midst will be gained when I mention that he washed his hands and face, not in the company's, but in his own time. Why the creature was never pushed under a train passes my comprehension. Fortunately I left soon after his arrival.

In the course of the four years spent with the railway my wages increased to thirteen shillings a week. I learned a number of things during the period, one of the most useful, to a manual laborer, being the science and art of avoiding undue exertion during working hours. There were many interests to occupy my mind. I worked hard to acquire an education. In this I received no encouragement from any one. There was no one within the circle of my acquaintances who cared a rap about education. I was popular with my workmates, but reading or cultivating the mind was obnoxious to them, and when one of them saw me with a book in my hand he would look at the others and touch his forehead significantly. Perhaps he was correct.

Thirteen shillings a week gave me a limited amount of independence. I asserted myself more at home. Out of the thirteen shillings I paid twelve for my keep. The other shilling was mine to have and to hold, although I did not hold much of it. One half was spent on visits to the theater, and the other put aside to buy boots and clothes. I was always badly dressed. Either my boots let the wet in or my suit was falling to pieces. I resented the fact that both William and my mother were better dressed than I was, but I could not say much. My powers of expression were limited and my knowledge was fearfully inadequate.

But I had ambitions. My prime ambition was to escape from hard work. I had already worked far too hard and far too much. Work and short rations had been my lot as far back as I could remember. Work and poverty were twins, it seemed to me. People who worked hard were always poor, and people who were poor always worked hard. It seemed to me a rotten way of getting a living.

At home, things were not so good. William and I had begun to quarrel more frequently. He had failed to notice that I was growing up. In one of these quarrels my mother took William's part against me, and this seemed more than I could tolerate. I left home in a fit of temper and took up residence with a fellow-worker at the railway shop, who had room in his house for a lodger.

This man was a "tapper" who lived at Newton Heath, a working-class district about a mile and a half from the station. The distance involved my rising at a quarter to five in the morning when I was on day work, in order to get to work by six o'clock. I occupied a small room and took my meals with the family. For this they charged me eleven shillings a week, and I now had two shillings to spend instead of one. As a shilling a week had to be spent on tram-fares, I was nothing in pocket through changing my residence.

My landlord, Mr. Fawcet, was a good fellow. He had a sense of humor and was always merry and bright, a thing I greatly appreciated. His wife was a hard-working woman who, when not busy in the house, was bringing a child into the world. They were a prolific couple who added another to the family each year with methodical precision. They had twelve when I left them a year later, and were preparing for the arrival of another. Years later I heard that Mr. Fawcet had become paralyzed. His wife and thirteen children were doing well.

Mr. Fawcet was a supporter of the Labor Party, a new force which was just then beginning to gain ground and become a factor in English political life. Like most of my fellow workers, I knew nothing of politics. I hardly knew the name of the Prime Minister or the difference between one party and another. Mr. Fawcet aroused my interest a little in labor questions. He took me to a meeting where Mr. J. R. Clynes, one of the new labor M.P.s, was speaking. Mr. Clynes had been returned for the Platting division in the recent election of 1906, and was one of the most promising of the thirty-six Labor M.P.s who held seats in the new Parliament. Mr. Clynes spoke well amid tremendous enthusiasm, but, though I was greatly impressed, I could not grasp the full meaning of much that was said. One statement of Mr. Clynes' struck me as quaint. Speaking with immense solemnity, he declared that most of the public lavatories were cleaner and more comfortable, and far more luxurious, than thousands of working-class homes. This point was voted a good one and loudly cheered.

Before leaving the hall I speculated a penny on the purchase of a pamphlet, of which there were a great number on sale at the door. The pamphlet was called the *Wealth of Nations*. The author was not Adam Smith, but it might as well have been for all the meaning the writing conveyed to me. I was acutely conscious of my ignorance and anxious to learn as much as possible about everything—but the pamphlet beat me. I read it several times with the aid of a dictionary and even tried reading it backwards, but the meaning continued to elude me. My landlord bought a copy of *Unto This Last,* by John Ruskin, which I also tried, but the whole thing was beyond me. Ruskin might as well have written about shoemaking for all I could make out to the contrary. I am happy to say that I have never been able to read anything Ruskin had to say upon the subject of political economy.

The seed had been sown, however. My appetite was whetted by what I had heard. What was socialism? The word had been used many times during the evening by Mr. Clynes and others. The words "socialism," "agnosticism," "determinism" and so on were continually being bandied about by the writers in a weekly paper called *The Clarion,* edited by Robert Blatchford, which I had seen in the reading-rooms at public libraries. I was anxious to know what these words meant. To get a grasp of the subjects was not easy. Nearly every matter discussed by writers and public men was outside the scope of my experience and beyond my intellectual development. Many of the famous books about which I was always seeing references in magazines and newspapers were impossible for me to understand, but I went on plowing through them.

George Meredith put me to sleep pretty quickly, as did Carlyle, Milton, Wordsworth, and several others. I felt ashamed and annoyed at not being able to understand these great writers, but I knew that what they wrote about had some meaning. They were accepted as great. There must be a good reason for this, I thought. So I kept on in the hope that constant association with great writers would familiarize me with literature in the course of time. I am glad to be able to state that a great deal of my reading was done in my employers' time. The hours abstracted from them were devoted to the sacred cause of education—my education. We had things so well organized at the siding that there were sometimes whole days in which we did not do a stroke of work.

I used to lie on the seat in an old railway carriage reading Dickens or Hardy, or perhaps a book of Emerson's or Macaulay's essays. Now and then I would slip out into the city during working hours, to attend a matinee at the old Tivoli Music Hall in Peter Street, where a place in the gallery cost threepence. It was well worth ten times as much. My favorite turn was Bransby Williams, whose *Characters from Dickens* were so well represented. I learnt two of the pieces he recited so effectively—*Devil May Care* and *Fra Giacomo*. Years later I gave these poems at concerts and among friends without suffering any serious injury.

The Tivoli shows finished about half-past five in the afternoon, which gave me nice time to get back to the cabin, have a wash, and book off at six. No one gave me away, as we had these matters arranged between us.

For a time I paid a railway guard sixpence a week for two lessons in shorthand. My landlord, seeing me one evening studying a little gray book on the subject, told me I was wasting my time and money. Although he was a Labor man, he saw no good in education. "If you want to study anything, study your work," he told me. "Education is no good for the likes of you and me." For literature he had nothing but contempt.

One of my great ambitions at this time was to see a big railway accident. I was hungering for some great dramatic event, and a collision between two express trains traveling at sixty miles an hour would have satisfied my craving for drama. But nothing of the kind ever happened. I once saw a man crushed to death between the buffers and the stop-blocks. He was in the act of jumping from the six-foot way on to the platform, but, failing to hear the approach of a train that was backing slowly in, he was caught and killed. I was very much upset by the thought of what his wife and family would feel when they heard the news. But a big wreck, on a grand scale, would not have affected me at all, unless of course I happened to be in it myself.

I have never been able to get excited about the suffering of humanity on a large scale. Political clap-trap about our "bleeding brothers in China," or "starving cousins in India," or our "fallen sisters in Argentine" leaves me cold.

It was while I was on the railway, when I was about sixteen, that I began to take an interest in girls, but I never got very far with any of them. I was so poor that I felt I had no right to make advances, so for a long time I had to content myself with thinking about them.

My first experience of the sexual act came when I was about seventeen. A street girl accosted me with the invitation to go home with her for "a short time." I was surprised to find that she was prepared to charge me only half a crown. This, she said, was because she liked me. I cannot remember how it came about that I had half a crown to spend. I think I must have had my wages with me, as it was a Saturday afternoon and I was going home from work. I went with her to her room at Greenhays, the notorious quarter in Manchester for ladies who carry on the oldest profession. I was diffident and had much to learn, with the result that I came away rather disappointed, but determined to try again when I was a little older.

On Sundays there was little to do. I could not be always studying and reading. I had no money to spend on trips to the seaside or country, and, being so hard up, I could not associate with those who had money to spend. I sometimes went for long rambling walks around the city, and it was on one of these that I first discovered Stevenson Square, the open-air forum for public speaking.

I had never seen anything of the kind before, and was immensely interested by the speakers. It seemed a wonderful thing to me that these men should be able to hold the attention of the crowds in the way they were doing. Practically all the arguments that were being used were beyond my comprehension, but I felt that great affairs were under way. Words and phrases that have since become nauseatingly familiar sounded important and impressive then.

I resolved to attend the Square every Sunday until I had plucked out the heart of the mystery that lay behind the high-sounding phraseology of the orators. I did so and after a time became familiar with the rant and rhodomontade of the rebel and the revolutionary. The arguments about the unequal distribution of wealth made a strong appeal to me. This, I fancied, is what is needed—a complete and radical change in the economic basis and structure of human society. The workers are the people who matter. The rich are plunderers and parasites who live upon what they have stolen from the wealth-producers. I did not formulate the idea in these words—my stock of words was too short and scanty. But that was the substance of my thought on the great question. The revolutionary ideal seemed so new, so bold, so pregnant with redemptive power for humanity. I stood gaping like a political and intellectual bumpkin—which indeed I was—when I first heard it propounded and was able to realize its import.

There was an abundance of revolutionary literature on sale at these meetings in Stevenson Square. It was largely penny and two penny pamphlets setting forth the socialist idea in lurid language. I bought a few of these from time to time and studied them with diligence. Like the pamphlet I bought at Mr. Clynes' meeting, they were hard to understand. Words like "*bourgeois*," "proletariat," "historical materialism," and other heavy phrases gave me a lot of trouble. Heavier works still were available at the free libraries. Soon I was sunk in the study of social questions. I became roughly acquainted, within a short time, with the general theory of revolt. I tried Karl Marx, but that giant bore proved too much for me. He seemed to know very little of the life of working people. His arguments and illustrations were based on blue-books and factory-inspectors' reports.

But the angry passages, in which he wrote of capitalism making its appearance on the evolutionary stage "dripping from head to foot in blood and dirt," appealed strongly to me. It might even have appealed more strongly still, had I had any clear idea of what the word "evolutionary" meant. William Morris and Edward Bellamy were easier to understand. I liked *News from Nowhere,* or what I could understand of it. Kropotkin, Daniel de Leon, and H. M. Hyndman wrote the type of thing which was more easily grasped. Jack London put the socialist theory in a way that admitted of no reply—at least, it admitted of no reply from me. The case for a revolution seemed to be amply proven.

I was rather puzzled to find how the socialist writers and speakers hated each other, and continually referred to other socialists as "fakers," "twisters," and "confusion-mongers." I was informed later that this showed how sincere they were. Every socialist believed so passionately in his own version of the creed that he could not bear to hear any one misrepresent it without being at once filled with overpowering indignation and an urge to explain the theory correctly.

Socialism, however, became too tame for me. I found anarchism more to my taste. Two advocates of that philosophy appeared in the Square. They were both well-read in every direction, and both had a keen sense of humor and a ready wit. Anarchism, I learned, stood for complete freedom. Everything that stood in the way of complete freedom must go. Marriage, which was based on private property interests, and was only "legalized prostitution," must be swept aside. Religion, which was a stupid superstition and a means of doping the masses, must be abolished.

There was no fixed standard of right and wrong. Ruling classes manufactured the concepts of morality which best suited their economic interests. It was wrong to steal, because the ruling classes said so. They said so because they had already stolen the workers' heritage and were determined to hold on to it. Hence their insistence on the necessity for workers to obey the law and keep their hands from picking and stealing. The State must be destroyed as well. Bakunin had "clearly pointed out" that the State was an engine of class oppression and robbery. Marx and Engels had proved this scientifically and historically.

But socialism, said the anarchists, was not enough. Anarchism went further. It went as far as thought could reach. It meant freedom from every kind of restraint. It meant a humanity so highly developed socially that police, prisons, and any punishment would be quite unnecessary. There would be no army and navy. Priests and governments would be no more, and altars and thrones would mingle with the dust. That, I thought, will suit me even better than socialism. I will work for that.

After a while I was able to discriminate between one revolutionary idea and another. In perusing the official organs of the different socialist parties I soon discovered that, while they hated the capitalist class with an undying hatred, their loathing of each other was even more intense. The Social Democratic Party was furious with the Independent Labor Party. The I.W.W. could not contain their scorn for the S.L.P., while the I.W.G.B. damned and blasted the S.P.G.B., and the tiny groups on the last outposts of the left wing, who were more extreme than the most extreme extremists, accused all, including of course the Labor Party and the Fabians, of deliberately twisting and confusing and betraying the workers. My favorite among the sectarian groups has always been the S.P.G.B. (Socialist Party of Great Britain), a small group of academic taxi-drivers who still function in their tiny way. They now have a membership large enough to enable them to hold their demonstrations in a pillar-box near Tower Bridge. They have always claimed to be the only genuine, scientific socialists in the world, and condemn all other parties, whether avowedly capitalist or alleged labor, as confusionists, humbugs, and traitors. When the last member dies, as he should do in the course of nature, the secret of socialism will perish with him. The workers, therefore, are lost.

I soon became aware of the differences and disagreements among the revolutionaries, but I did not allow this to discourage me in the least. I went on reading pamphlets and listening to speakers. Most of these I came later to look upon as mouthers and phrasemongers, but a few were orators of genuine eloquence.

The finest speaker I have ever heard on a socialist platform was a man called F. G. Jones. He had a striking personality, and was handsome and commanding in appearance: a tall, dark man with a dark moustache, long hair, and features somewhat resembling those of the late Frank Harris. His voice was deep and musical, his language distinctive and free from clichés, and he used no gestures. All his effects were obtained through his appearance, voice, and mastery of beautiful language.

Another speaker, whose name was known far and wide as a champion of revolutionary socialism, was William Gee. He called himself "The Socialist Thunderbolt." As a defender of the Marxian position against all comers, he was invincible, and his meetings frequently resembled an intellectual slaughterhouse. His method was to use the verbal bludgeon rather than the rapier, and his opponents went down before him like bags of hay. A stout, rough-spoken man, not easy to get on with unless you knew him, he was hilarious in company, and I have spent many merry hours with him.

Gee was a popular speaker. His gruff manner and straight-from-the-shoulder speech seldom offended–Jones was of a different grain. His manner was cold and aloof. When off the platform, he was seldom known to speak a word to any one. To those who approached him in the usual way of socialists with, "Hullo, comrade, how are you?" he returned a frigid stare. On one occasion a young admirer dashed up to him and gasped, "Am I really speaking to the famous F. G. Jones?" "You are," remarked the master orator, "but not for long."

Jones' aloof and taciturn manner made him feared and often disliked, although he cared nothing one way or the other. I was present once at a Manchester socialist club, when Jones entered without taking the least notice of any one—as usual. He made his way to the bar and ordered a bottle of Worthington. A well-known trade-union official named George Bellamy looked up from his glass and cried,

"Ah, the great F. G." Jones turned towards him and replied, "Ah, the little G. B." The barmaid told him they had no Worthington in the club. "What?" exclaimed Jones in surprise. "No Worthington?" He sank into a seat and spoke no word until closing time, except to mutter from time to time, looking straight in front of him. "No Worthington."

As the result of a chance visit to Stevenson Square, I had been brought into contact with a world of which I had previously been in total ignorance. The things I learned gave me a new outlook on life. Several of the regular speakers there fascinated me to a degree which, in the light of later experience, appears absurdly impossible. I sat at the feet of men who were the veriest ranters and gasbags. But I have always been susceptible to the sound of words. These men were dealers in words. Few of them possessed any real knowledge of anything, but they had the jargon of revolt at their tongues' ends. As the well-worn phrases fell from their lips I imagined myself to be listening to the most wonderful and original thoughts. How could I have known that it was the standardized fustian of half-baked mouthers and half-baked malcontents? It seemed new to me.

Before long I came to an important decision, and one which was to shape the course of my life. I resolved to become a speaker. To sway masses, to dominate crowds, to hear the applause—here was an easy road to fame. More than that, it was a chance to escape from poverty and hard, irksome, badly paid labor. It was the same motive as had driven the labor leaders out of the factory and the mine—the stern resolve to get away from hard manual labor at all costs. It was often said of the late Keir Hardie that he was wearing himself out in the service of his class. It is certain that he would have worn himself out much sooner had he remained down the pit. The labor leaders had left the workshops to toil on the floor of the House of Commons. It was a great racket.

My object was to emulate these men. I would enter the lists as a minister of the gospel of revolt. I had a strongly ingrained exhibitive complex and a keen urge to be at the center of the stage of human affairs. The time had come when I could no longer tolerate being treated as a cipher. At work and at my lodgings I was a nobody. I could not assert or express myself. I had no proper education, no social gifts, no powers of speech. I could not sustain an intelligent conversation. I was a dumb-bell. So that in choosing to become a speaker I was seeking both to escape from hard work and to find a means of exploiting my inborn histrionic talents.

Had I been able to get on the stage I should never have bothered my head about socialism. But I was too shabbily dressed, too lacking in self-confidence. I did not know how to set about it. In seeking a chance to play a part in the melodrama of political life, I did the next best thing.

I realized that to sustain the role adequately I should have to train myself, to acquire a vocabulary, learn to handle the language with accuracy and point, and, if possible, with rhetorical force. I should have to conquer diffidence and develop self-confidence.

I was too well aware of my educational and intellectual limitations not to realize how hard a task I should have to equip myself properly for the new career. My nature had been stifled by a narrow and narrowing environment. I had been cramped, frustrated, and repressed. But I was set on the change.

I had difficulty with my reading, but I persisted. It was dull work wading through the socialist writers and teachers. Most of them are as dull as dull can be, and the gross sentimentality, the sickly whining and cheap moralizing, the bombastic assertion of half-truths as if they were great scientific discoveries, brought me to the verge of vomiting. But I shut my eyes to all this and tried to master the socialist theory and revolutionary dogmas I proposed to advocate.

The socialist contention is that society, as at present constituted, is based upon the robbery of the wage workers by the capitalists; that the difference between what the workers produce and what the capitalist gives them in the form of wages represents that part of the total wealth produced which is stolen by the capitalist in the form of rent, interest, dividends, and profits, that this robbery of the workers by the capitalists creates an antagonism of interests, expressing itself in a class struggle; that strikes, lock-outs, unemployed riots and sporadic uprisings among the workers manifest the growing class-consciousness of the workers; and that ultimately the workers will come together as a class, conscious of their historic task. This is to overthrow the whole system of capitalist wealth production by a social revolution and establish, for the first time in the history of human society, which has hitherto been a history of contending classes, a world-wide socialist commonwealth, in which the wealth that is socially produced shall be socially owned. Class society will disappear and humanity will be free.

This form of social organization would, by changing the economic basis of society, alter the whole superstructure, sweeping away the political and ideological concepts which reflect the underlying material foundation of the present social order, bring into existence a new view of life, a new morality, a new philosophy, and a new ideology. Humanity would, in fact, begin a new life.

An interesting fact about the socialist theory of society is that it came from above. One might have imagined that a doctrine so revolutionary would have its origin among the poor and dispossessed. But, like all revolutionary ideas, it emanated from men belonging to the aristocracy and the *bourgeoisie*. The workers at first would have none of it, but gradually, under the persistent nagging of individuals like Karl Marx, Friedrich Engels (a wealthy cotton manufacturer), Kautsky, Liebknecht, Lafargue, De Leon, Hyndman, and other rich men with subversive ideas, it caught on among the workers. The majority, of course, have always been suspicious of it and remain so to this day. It is in fact admitted now that socialism would be impossible of achievement if left to the workers. It is accepted that it would have to be imposed on them by "an intelligent minority." That minority will not of course be members of the working class but gentlemen like Lenin, who come from the ranks of the capitalist class.

The socialist idea has worn pretty thin now, and only a handful of soreheads and dreamers take it seriously. But at the period of which I am writing it was a force throughout Europe. It had not been in existence long enough for people to have detected its weaknesses and absurdities, and all the yearners and hopers after the impossible dream world conceived and described by Plato, Sir Thomas More and others saw in socialism the realization of their highest hopes.

My own reason for linking myself with the forces of revolt was the very ordinary and natural desire of a dissatisfied underdog to get away from poverty and hard work. I also wanted to be taken notice of. Had I possessed a better education and more sense, I should have attached myself to a more prosperous political party, or, better still, have given the whole idea the go-by. But certain things were hidden from me, one of them being a knowledge of men as political animals.

CHAPTER IV
Finding My Voice

A FTER a while, during which I ransacked many books and
pamphlets for telling phrases and clinching arguments,
which I appropriated without compunction, I had a speech
ready. Every word was learned by heart and rehearsed in my
mind, with appropriate gestures, suitable emphasis, and an
impassioned peroration.

My chance to use it came when, a speaker having failed
to turn up at an unemployed meeting in the Square, I moved
towards the platform and intimated my willingness to say a
few words. The offer was accepted.

With beating heart, and trembling in every fiber, I as-
cended the rostrum and began. As soon as I had uttered the
first couple of sentences, all nervousness left me. I became
saturated with a delightful glow of elation, exultation, confidence, and assurance. The effect on the crowd was extremely
gratifying. A mass of stolid organisms, resembling a field of
blackened corn wilting under the dry summer heat, began
to stir as if life were in it. It rustled and swayed to and
fro as if blown upon by a powerful wind. As my carefully
arranged phrases and prepared impromptus pattered down
upon the heads of the people, the mass awoke and came to
life. The oration lasted half an hour. The end came amid
terrific applause. My debut had been entirely successful.

For some weeks afterwards I felt that any one wishing
to speak to me ought to pay a fee for the rare privilege of
conversing with the greatest orator of this, or any other age.

Soon I became known as "The Boy Orator," and was in
demand at meetings every Sunday in the Square. Unfortunately, before many weeks had passed, my stock of resounding

phrases had worn out and all my golden words were spent. I had not the abundance of subject-matter that would enable me to go on speaking week after week without repeating myself; and I had not that command of words which would have enabled me to ring the changes on the same subject week after week. Nothing makes a man of any likelihood so miserable and self-conscious as the guilty knowledge that he is repeating himself. Such a man, no matter how good his one speech may be, has to keep on the move. If he stayed too long in the same place his hearers might start prompting him when he stopped for breath.

I was not able to say anything on the spur of the moment, or to answer questions of any kind. I could not call to my aid the words that would clothe my ideas in appropriate language. What I said had to be prepared beforehand and learned by heart. It was necessary, therefore, if progress was to be made—and before I lost the reputation I already gained—to go back into training. So I returned to the study of economics, industrial history, and revolutionary theory. It was tedious and unappetizing work. The wearisome assertions and tiresome contentions of the founders and prophets of social upheaval were almost more than I could bear. It was rather exasperating, therefore, to find in after years that I had not only wasted my time, but hampered myself as a propagandist. What was required on that job, I found, was not knowledge and certainly not understanding, but a heavy, dogmatic manner; a copious command of stock phrases; an inability to distinguish between a phrase and a fact; and a firm conviction that all who do not agree with you are either fools or knaves.

In the course of my efforts at self-improvement I visited a famous debating society, the Manchester County Forum.

This society is one of the oldest and best institutions of the kind in the country. It is still going strong. Debates are held on Tuesday and Friday afternoons and on Sunday evenings. Most of the political celebrities have spoken there at some time; bishops, doctors, lawyers, agitators, and politicians of every shade have taken part in the debates. Men now well-known in Parliament and at the bar have used the County Forum as a training-ground.

Among the star turns of the Forum at the time of which I am writing was Mr. Wilkes Barre. He spoke and wrote under two names; sometimes he was Mr. Wilkes Barre, and at other times he was Malfew Seklew; but under either name he was always himself. He was a unique character. Tall, stout, and handsome, he carried all before him in debate. He called himself a Super-Egoist and Intellectual Aristocrat; also "The Man Without a Soul." He made great use of the alliterative style; his opponents were "passionless Puritans on the prowl," "brainless and bloodless bipeds," or "under-done underdogs from the underworld."

Malfew had no time for the working-class. "The working-class," he would declare, "is a mass of moldering matter that doesn't matter." Socialists were "slaves screaming for sympathy and succour"; Christians were "tripe-hounds, placing the flat foot of fallacy upon the trembling toe of truth." He had read a great deal and had been profoundly influenced by writers like Nietzsche and Max Stirner. Their doctrines, however, had been passed through the witty and original mind of a man who possessed certain odd qualities of his own. He earned his living as a market-salesman. His specialty was a tie-frame, a handy little article the use of which he was one of the first to demonstrate in the market-places of this country. His manner of selling the tie-frame was quite original.

After showing how the thing was to be fitted on to the collar, he proceeded to embellish his demonstration in amusing phraseology. "You place it through the clip in this manner, allowing the end to repose placidly upon the palpitating bosom. Should you be suffering with a cold on the chest, it is as good as a mustard-plaster. Should you, on the other hand, be troubled by a cold in the head, you can pick it up and blow your nose with it. Each tie is guaranteed to last for forty years. If, at the end of forty years, it is worn out, bring it back here and your money will be returned."

Malfew kept a sausage shop in Nottingham for a while. On the window he had a notice in large letters, "Democratic sausages annihilated nightly by the struggling proletariat."

He wrote a series of pamphlets which he sold at public meetings in various parts of the country. The series was described as "Haloes hoodooed, or Egoes vivisected." A number of Labor leaders were dealt with in these penny numbers, Blatchford—the Weeping Apostle of Socialism; Philip Snowden—the Uriah Heep of Labor; Keir Hardie—the Twopenny Christ of the I.L.P.; and others.

I became friendly with him and learned a great deal from one who was a distinct and outstanding personality of the market and the public square.

There were a number of crack debaters at the County Forum in those days. One of the most interesting was Mr. Whittle, a Liberal. This gentleman could not speak without working himself into a state bordering upon hysteria. Such a thing as discussing a matter calmly was out of the question with him. He had no sense of humor. Rising once to take part in a debate on the subject of Land Nationalization, he began to pour scorn on a speaker who had suggested putting the unemployed on the land. "It is simply criminal," he shouted, "to take town-bred men and put them to work on agriculture! They would not know the difference between a carrot and a cowl. What, for instance, could a man like me—born and bred in the city—do on the land? What use should I be in a field?" "You would make a good scarecrow!" cried a voice from the middle of the room.

It was Mr. Whittle—in opposing Women's Suffrage— who said, "I warn you solemnly that, if women are ever given the power to vote in this dear country of ours, then the future of England will be a thing of the past!"

I nearly drove him mad once by stating that I had not read much about Mr. Gladstone before I realized that he was a grand old humbug. The more I knew of Disraeli, the greater was my admiration for that statesman; but as soon as I learned more about Gladstone I began to despise him. Mr. Whittle could hardly await his turn to take the floor. He was red with anger and perspiring from every pore.

"He began to deplore Gladstone!" yelled the infuriated man. "Look well at the person who has used that expression here tonight. A schoolboy; a political fledgling; a child not yet able to let go of his mother's apron-strings; a wicked schoolboy; an evil schoolboy; one who already bears upon his brow the mark and seal of moral depravity. And this is the wretched creature who dares to say, 'I began to despise Gladstone!' Better for that youth, gentlemen; better for him—I say it in all solemnity—had he never been born!"

In spite of his odd way of speaking, Mr. Whittle was a kindly soul. Any tale of individual suffering brought forth his ready sympathy and help. He frequently pleaded the cause of the poor. "Take the case, gentlemen," he once said in a debate, "take the case of a poor woman who, having lost her husband, is forced to go out as a charwoman. The

84

breadwinner has been taken from her, her children are crying for the bread that perishes. We cannot but admire the courage and devotion of a woman, nay, a wife and a mother, who, with perhaps a sick husband at home... " The rest of the story was never finished.

Another debater was Mr. Adshead. He had only one subject—the sanitary conditions prevailing in Manchester and Salford. A speaker would open, for instance, on "The Crisis in the Far East," or "Is Germany Preparing for War?" Mr. Adshead would be on his feet as soon as the speaker had finished. "Take the sanitary conditions of our city today, gentlemen. I can claim to know something about it, as a working plumber. There are houses... " And so on to the bitter end.

Mr. Adshead was well known, too, in Stevenson Square, where he held forth on his favorite theme to hilarious crowds every Sunday. He also lectured to various bodies throughout Lancashire and Yorkshire ... once. He spoke on the sanitary conditions in the two cities; but he did not always give his lectures that title. Sometimes he would be announced to speak on "The Rise of Democracy," "The Rights of Labor," or "Science and Religion." I heard him once at a P.S.A. The subject upon which he had been announced to speak was "The French Revolution; its Historical and Philosophical Significance." A large attendance of students of that great historical event was expected, and they were present in force.

"On looking through history, especially those periods which stand out and are of particular interest to us of the present day," began Mr. Adshead, "we find that there are many valuable lessons to be learned. I have had a great deal to do, as a man who can claim to be an authority on this question, with housing. There are houses in your city of

Manchester today which are a disgrace to civilization. Take
the houses in Ancoats alone... " The audience began to
shuffle their feet, blow their noses, and sigh deeply, but Mr.
Adshead went ruthlessly on. He was one of those speakers
who find it almost impossible to stop speaking once they are
started. An outraged audience had to tell him to shut up on
this occasion.

THE County Forum was a good practicing-ground for budding speakers, and I learned a good deal at the debates, in which I frequently joined. It was here that I first heard Tom Mann. He was invited to open the debate, and the building was crammed to bursting-point. I had never heard any one like him. Fire, vehemence, passion, humor, drama, and crashing excitement. There has never been any one to equal him. I have listened to him hundreds of times in all parts of the country. He was, and still is, my ideal of what an orator should be. His personality, in those days, was like a human dynamo. Everything gave way before the tremendous torrents of oratory he let loose upon his audiences. He spoke with terrific rapidity, yet every word was as clear as a bell. It is difficult to believe that any one ever interrupted him. He swept over the crowds like a whirlwind; his mastery of the art of oratory was superb. He was a natural actor, suiting, as Shakespeare has directed, the action to the word, the word to the action. He never repeated an effect, never labored; did not lean with too heavy a hand. Nor, in spite of the vehemence of his manner, did he overstep the modesty of nature. In the very heat and tempest of his passion, he acquired and begat a temperance which gave it smoothness.

Tom Mann is unique, among all speakers of the revolutionary school, in the fact that he is entirely free from any kind of spite or spleen against any one whatsoever. He will have nothing to do, either publicly or privately, with personal abuse of any one, friend or foe. Let anything be said, in his company, of a derogatory nature about any one, and Tom will change the subject at once. He will not have it. In this he is entirely exceptional. Shortly after his opening at the County Forum, he addressed a crowded meeting at the Free Trade Hall. His subject was Syndicalism, of which he was full at the time. Outside the Hall were a number of socialists, anarchists, communists, and the like, selling their literature. A representative of the Socialist Labor Party, a small group of revolutionary Marxians, was exhibiting a poster on which were the words "Tom Mann Exposed." There is nothing exceptional in this, as revolutionaries are continually exposing their best workers. Tom Mann came out at the end of the meeting and caught sight of the poster. "Give me one of the papers containing the exposure, comrade," he said. Having paid the twopence and placed the paper in his pocket, he shook the "comrade" by the hand warmly and said encouragingly, "That's good work you are doing, comrade. I am glad you have actually dared so much."

Tom Mann is today, even in his old age, a giant among pygmies. It is pathetic, however, to think of him spending his declining years in association with a bunch of political nonentities. It is unusual for such a type to become identified with the working-class movement. Tom was never a misery-monger or calamity-howler. He stood up, in a sane way, for a more intelligent form of social organization. He was a virile exponent of workers' control in industry. A manly figure. Most exceptional.

A remarkable individual among platform speakers was MacCutcheon. I found him in Stevenson Square one Sunday afternoon and was struck by his picturesque appearance. A man of sixty-five, bearing a very pronounced likeness to Dickens, the beard streaked with gray, with a wrinkled brow and a severe expression of the eyes, he drew attention at once. He was dressed in a homespun suit of gray, with a sprig of heather in his buttonhole. He preached the simple life. "Back to the land," was his cry. "Grow your own dinners, milk your own cows, weave and spin, hoe and plow, and let each man be his own master. Away with all complex and dangerous machinery."

MacCutcheon was an eccentric. He had never traveled in a train, bus, or tram. He hated motor-cars. He had crossed the Atlantic on a windjammer years before, but refused to travel on a steamboat. He had picked up a living by speaking, and taking collections, for many years. Sometimes he worked for farmers, but seldom for long, as he would not tolerate any one giving him orders. He was very difficult to get on with, and his speeches were always strong and insulting. His public utterances were couched in the most brutal language. He had a rich, cultured voice, which made his observations sound all the more shocking. He disliked the Royal Family, and some of the things he said about them were certainly treasonable. But he looked so threatening, carried himself in such an intimidating manner, and was so ready-witted and sharp-tongued, that no one ever dared to cross him. He was very mean in money matters, due, perhaps, to the fact of his poverty and that he was at war with everything and every one. It was said by those who knew him that he would not give a straw hat away in the winter-time. I got to know him years later, and found him honest, but niggardly to an extreme degree.

James Lister MacCutcheon was a leader of the Manchester unemployed at that time. He led them on several land-grabbing raids. A piece of vacant land would be taken possession of by a party of men, perhaps a hundred or more, with MacCutcheon at the head. They would be ultimately evicted by the police, but not before a good deal of sympathy with the workless men had been aroused by MacCutcheon and other articulate ones.

MacCutcheon maintained that this country should be self-supporting. "Blow up all the big cities with dynamite," he said. "Put the people on the land, abolish machinery and aristocracy. Do away with plutocracy, mobocracy, hypocrisy, and poverty. Make England a garden; build a wall round it. Build the wall thicker than it is high, so that, if it blows over, it will be higher still." He denounced the craze for speed. "Look at those misapplied abortions in mechanics," he would thunder, alluding to motor-cars, motor-lorries, and other vehicles. "A stink at one end and a splutter at the other. Look at the monstrous engines carrying parcels of nothing from nowhere to nowhere, with two men to hold the driver's whiskers on. Away with all that, and learn to milk a cow," he said. He disliked the clergy. Bishop Knox was Bishop of Manchester at that time; MacCutcheon frequently denounced him. "Are you there, Knox?" he would shout, when speaking in the Square. "Come out, Knox; you cunning old fox. Fetch him; bring him here and slay him before me." He often mentioned well-known people in this disrespectful way. "Look at the Chief Constable," he said once, as Chief Constable Peacock was standing in the crowd. "Look at him, the big, hulking clodhopper, standing there gaping like a booby. Look at him scratching his head and thinking of his pension."

On the occasion of a big unemployed demonstration in the Square, at which a number of city councilors were present, having been asked to speak, MacCutcheon, who was chairman of the meeting, spoke for an hour and a half. The other speakers were fidgeting and fuming at having to wait. Just as every one had given up hope, MacCutcheon said, "I notice a number of Town Scoundrels and Members of the Frauds of Guardians are present. Apparently they are bursting to address you. As we do not wish to have an explosion, they had better be allowed to speak their piece. I see Brother Pinfold here, with his hook nose" (Councilor Pinfold had rather a prominent nose) "—he is dying to let you know what a great humbug he is. The hook-nosed Pinfold will now address you." As MacCutcheon was popular with the crowds, poor old Pinfold did not get much of a hearing.

MacCutcheon was as callous as he was parsimonious. Having lodged with a man for some months, without paying a penny for his keep, a time came when the unfortunate man could no longer afford to support him without payment. "Oh, Mr. MacCutcheon, I am afraid I must ask you to leave. Now that I am out of work and with a wife and three children to keep, I cannot do anything to help you. And perhaps you would care to pay something off what you owe?" "No, I cannot do that," said the great reformer, "but I can give you a piece of advice that will be of use to you: Don't stay here and starve like a rat in a hole. Take the wife and brats and go straight into the workhouse. Let the ratepayers keep you."

CHAPTER V

Breaking Into Jail

RESPONDING to the atmosphere of revolutionary ferment which was prevailing at the time, I became attracted by the gospel of "Propaganda by Deed." The Manchester unemployed were active just then. The leaders were in militant mood, calling for drastic action, openly preaching the necessity for the use of unconstitutional methods. The time for talk, many said, had gone; petitions, processions, conferences, demonstrations—all had proved unavailing. Strong action was imperative. Better to fight in the streets, urged the militants, and risk a few broken limbs, than to slowly starve and silently suffer.

This, I thought, is true; patience has been strained to breaking-point. We must fight. Although I was not unemployed, I was ready to play my part. The truth was, I was sick of work; I would have done anything to have become independent of it. Prison—I was almost about to write—had no terrors for me. Of course, prison had as many terrors for me as it has for any one else. But there was no disgrace in going to prison for a political offense. On the contrary, many a man had laid the foundations of a successful public career by going to prison for the sake of his "convictions." It had often been a short cut to a big public position and fortune. It is sometimes necessary, in order to get into Parliament, to go there via the jail. Suffrage leaders, for instance, were getting their names before the public and making their jobs secure, assuring their popularity and making themselves right for life, by going to the cells in a blaze of publicity. The Pankhursts never looked back after they had been to jail. It was a good racket. Why should I not try it? Might it not prove a means of escape from work and poverty?

I was thinking of myself, not the unemployed. I did not, as a matter of fact, care a fig about the unemployed. I saw the chance of getting my name before the public, of becoming such a hero that I should be able to put work behind me once and for all. What a contrast to the modern communist leaders, who sacrifice themselves unsparingly for the sake of the down-trodden masses, toiling and suffering without thought of self, and above all—without fee or reward!

The first step towards the heroic enterprise was to throw up my job at the railway works, a step I have never regretted. Having made this significant gesture, I was bound to go through with the program—I could not stay on at my lodgings.

I joined at once the group of insurgents who were active among the unemployed. They welcomed me with enthusiasm. I was flattered by their cordiality towards one so young in the movement. It did not strike me then that the main reason for the warmth of greeting was my expressed determination to be one of the first to take direct action of an unconstitutional character. It will be seen that I was not only one of the first to rush into danger, but also the only one who did anything deliberately and consciously illegal. I had, as I have already observed, much to learn.

One of the men, who had appointed himself a sort of unofficial leader of the militants, was a gentleman named Arthur Blank (whose name is withheld for obvious reasons). Mr. Blank was a respectable citizen in a small way of business. He dabbled in Labor politics, not suffering himself, but standing appalled at the spectacle of others suffering. His heart bled. He was prepared to help in every possible way—short of actually parting with money. Like many who sympathize with those who have been broken on the wheel of life, he had no patience with moderate methods. "Have you no guts, men?" he had often asked, while addressing the unemployed in the Square. "Are you men? How long will you lie down and starve in a land flowing with milk and honey? You must fight! Better to die fighting than to die starving!"

It was Mr. Blank who suggested a meeting at his house to discuss what action should be taken. He had called for twelve men who were prepared to take drastic action immediately. "No cowards need apply," he had said, at a meeting in the Square. Twelve men volunteered for service, of whom I was one. The historic conference took place at Mr. Blank's house on a Sunday evening. It was in the month of March—St. Patrick's Day, 1908. We sat round a table. Mr. Blank, I remember, did not even provide us with tea; he provided us, however, with a plan. We were to smash a number of windows in Market Street, an important thoroughfare in the center of the city. These windows were to be simultaneously shattered, at the stroke of nine, on the morning of the following day. The shock of this terrific crash, insisted Mr. Blank, would reverberate throughout the land, arousing the populace from its lethargy and causing the Government to tremble like a guilty thing surprised. The scheme was voted upon and unanimously carried.

I had little to say, being young and diffident, although a lion on the platform. Mr. Blank did most of the talking. Two other men spoke from time to time—Joshua Batty and Tom Brown. Both these men were active as agitators among the unemployed. I was known as a young and eloquent spokesman for the bottom dog. The rest were merely "out-of-works" who had developed the habit of attending meetings in the Square. They had signified by their presence that they were ready for any enterprise of "honorable dangerous consequence." We were all ready. We had sworn. We were firm.

When we left, I walked down the street with Batty and Brown. "Why not come home with me?" suggested Batty. "We can all go up to Market Street together in the morning."

Brown and I agreed to spend the night at Batty's place. He lived in Salford with his wife and their two children.

We sat talking until far into the night. Batty was a miner by trade. He was a badly educated man, with an inflamed imagination. Brown was a Tolstoyan tramp who lived in a doss-house and looked as if he did. He had read one or two books, which had gone to his head. He was a bearded, burly fellow, slow of speech and heavy in his movements.

He quoted Tolstoy continually. Sometimes he quoted the New Testament. A favorite saying of his was that of James, "Woe unto ye rich! Weep and howl for the miseries that shall come upon you!" "Scripture says that we should love our neighbor as ourselves," he would often say, breathing heavily. "Now, what does that mean? It means that I should have as good a house as my neighbor, as good a table, as much of the good things of life." As Mr. Brown seldom did any kind of work for a living, I thought it quaint of him to put the position as he did, and with such perfect sincerity. Joshua Batty was as spare and slim as Brown was broad and bulky. He read little, and that not of the best. He worked when he could. He was an impossibilist in matters of work and wages, and had got into the state when a man is proud to be a rebel against everything. Batty was aiming at the same goal as myself—the getting of a living without having to work for a master. Brown had partially succeeded, but was anxious to consolidate his position by shouldering the burden of an unemployed agitator. They were both quite decent fellows, and I liked them well enough.

We sat up till late discussing the task before us on the morrow. We did not, of course, admit the truth about our enterprise, even to ourselves. What we were about to do was for the sake of the Cause. A blow had to be struck, a sacrifice made, a duty done; and we were the men with courage enough to lead the way.

"It will mean going to prison for a month, two months; Perhaps three," said Batty.

"I am not afraid of prison," I said. "It will be an experience."

"I don't think the authorities will dare to send us to prison," said Brown. "The workers would revolt throughout the whole of Lancashire."

"Yes," Batty cried, "if the magistrates are stupid enough to send us down, the whole country will seethe with revolt."

"It may be the match to the gunpowder," I observed. "Our action may lead to a general working-class rising."

"Our names will flash across the country—across the world—as the men who had the guts to do what the whole gang of Labor Members were afraid to do," said Batty, his excitement growing as his mind took fire with the idea.

"I wonder if the others will do their part?" asked Brown. "I don't trust them; their courage will fail them when the moment comes."

"They have sworn to go through with it," I said. "They won't be such cowards as to draw back now."

"Let the others do what they like; we shan't funk," said Batty.

"No fear," I said. "It is the chance of a lifetime."

Before we went to bed, Batty had worked himself up to such a pitch that he already saw himself as a great national leader of the insurgent working-class. "Our photos will be in all the papers," he cried. "We shall be made for life." Upon which the three prospective martyrs did a dance round the kitchen and sang "The Red Flag" before retiring to seek a few hours' repose.

We reached the scene of action upon the stroke of nine the next morning. Batty and Brown were unarmed. Not so I. My pockets were bulging with bottles. As the clocks struck the hour we looked about for the others. There was no sign of them. "They have let us down," observed Brown. "Give them a chance," said Batty. "Rebels are always late. They will be late on the morning of the revolution." Batty often made remarks of this kind, but I had not associated with socialists and revolutionaries long enough to realize how true it was that they were always late. I have never known a meeting of socialists which started at the advertised time. The great demonstrations and mass meetings are the same; always about half an hour, sometimes an hour, late in commencing. The putting of the clocks back or forward, to mark the coming or going of summer-time, throws them completely out of gear. One of the reasons why the revolution has had to be postponed time after time is the lack of punctuality on the part of the leaders and the rank and file. Another reason is that police permission for a social revolution cannot be obtained. And it is not uncommon for meetings to be called to "demand" the release of some class-war prisoner long after he had been let out. The "doziness" and sluggishness and lack of common sense and common capacity for doing even the simplest things properly is almost incredible. Very few of the revolutionary leaders have ever been able to lace their boots, tie a parcel, or post a letter without dropping it in the mud. An eagerness to destroy and an inability to build has been a dominant characteristic of working-class rebels against capitalism. Most of them have been lacking in even the ordinary qualities of mediocrity, while many have been weak-minded or half-witted. The modern communist leaders are almost as stupid and witless as the rank and file; if, indeed, that is possible.

In view, therefore, of the discrepancy between socialist time and Greenwich time, we were not surprised at the absence of our fellow window-smashers. The three of us strolled up and down in front of Lewis' shop. Lewis is the Selfridge of the North; his windows were too good to be overlooked. Six windows were to be smashed, two men for each window. That was the arrangement. Batty and I were to deal with Lewis', while the rest of the party were to deal with five other shops in Market Street. My companions had made no effort to procure missiles. Brown should have been paired off with some one at another window. He stood around without making any move. Batty talked about something else. The minutes flew past; there was no sign of the others. I grew tired of waiting. As the clocks pointed to a quarter past nine, I decided to wait no longer. My hour had come. Drawing a bottle from my pocket, with a vigorous gesture I flung the first stone (ginger-beer bottle). Two more followed in rapid succession. The bystanders stopped in their tracks, wondering what was amiss. Batty and Brown did nothing. I waited. "Give me a bottle," said Batty. I did so, and he proceeded to sling it through another window.

By this time the pedestrians were all agog. Three police officers rolled up. The three of us were taken in charge. Masses of people clustered round, their mouths agape and their eyes apop. The police who arrested us were quite calm. They led us gently along, as though such things were a matter of everyday occurrence. I was not at all excited myself. I felt quite at home, in fact. Everything was going forward quietly and comfortably, including the three prisoners, who were going forward towards the police station. As we reached the door of the police station, Batty yelled out, "Long live the social revolution!" I followed with, "Three cheers for the unemployed!" Brown called on the crowd to get rid of the capitalist system. There was no response. I took a swift glance back at the crowd which had followed us, and was rather astonished to see amongst them not one man who appeared unemployed.

We were charged with causing willful damage to private property. Private property, indeed! The bodies and souls of men and women were more important than private property. In any case, we were out to abolish private property.

Having been charged, we were taken at once before the stipendiary, who remanded us for three days—without bail. This was a blow. We had expected to be treated with more consideration. We were not criminals—we were political offenders.

From the Court we were taken in the "Black Maria" to Strangeways Jail, where we were at once separated and conducted to cells in different wings of the prison. I was rather nettled at the lack of courtesy shown me by the prison officers. "Come on, you," and other disrespectful expressions, offended me a little. But I bore in mind from first to last the fact that I had not been invited. I was a sort of intruder. No one had sent for me. And I hate whining. I had been brought up to endure suffering without showing the white feather, or letting my enemies see that I was in the least degree perturbed by whatever they did to me. "If you win, don't brag; and if you lose, don't snivel," has always been my attitude. So I bore these blows to my vanity without flinching. The prison food came strangely for the first day, but I soon became used to it. I did not like being buried alive for three days, but it gave me plenty of time to think over the whole position. I determined to see the thing through, no matter what happened. I had put my hand, as it were, to the plow, and would not look back.

Three days later we stood again in the dock. A little surprise awaited us. We were charged with conspiracy! This was totally unlooked for by any of us. The word "conspiracy" had a nasty sound. The situation had begun to look grave. And then there entered the witness-box a creature well known to us. He was one of the twelve! He had sat at the table with us, in Blank's house, and voted for the motion. A Judas! A traitor and a spy! A "stool-pigeon!" An *agent provocateur*! This, I thought, is splendid. No conspiracy worthy the name is complete without a spy. Everything was in the classic tradition. The trial began to take on dignity, significance, and dramatic fitness. Yet, a moment before, I had felt afraid. No matter what happened, we were now assured of a big trial and loads of publicity. Our names were made.

We were remanded, reproduced, remanded again, and then finally committed. Our trial was fixed to take place at the Quarter Sessions and promised to be the event of the season. I was well satisfied. I had broken into jail.

For nearly three weeks we lay in prison. I soon became well accustomed to the routine. The solitude gave me a chance to review the situation. A fine speech was prepared in my mind, to which the Court must listen. Three months at the outside was the sentence I had anticipated. I could do it on my head. It would be a small price to pay for the chance of becoming a hero. No more hard work, at pauper's wages. The future looked as bright as one could wish.

The trial made a great stir in Lancashire. Our intention had been to arouse interest in, and create sympathy for, the unemployed, many of whom were undergoing genuine hardship. Between a workless man and starvation there was nothing except the workhouse. What the unemployed of 1933 would say, if they had to put up with real hardship, one cannot say. There is little to grumble about nowadays, but things were very different in 1908. Wages were low, housing conditions none too good, and the poor had a very rough deal indeed. Our window-smashing adventure, although illegal, was held to be fully justified by many who sympathized with the unemployed. The militant suffragettes had, of course, anticipated us, not only by breaking windows, but by acts of a really criminal nature, such as the throwing of lighted torches into pillar-boxes. Most of these creatures were well-to-do women, overfed and underworked, who could think of no other way of persuading an indifferent—and a rightly indifferent—public of the "justice" of their aims than by resorting to these childish and criminal acts. We had some excuse, at any rate: we were fighting for bread, not votes—or, at least, said we were. Batty, Brown, and myself were fighting for popularity and an easier way of living. The "shrieking sisterhood" had no such problem to worry them. They deserved, therefore, no sympathy from intelligent people. They certainly got none from me. A worse collection of snobs and sentimentalists I have seldom encountered.

The papers were full of the "Unemployed Plot." Questions were asked in the House. Labor leaders made speeches in our support, especially Victor Grayson, the ill-starred Socialist member for Colne Valley, who justified our extra-legal action in inflammatory speeches all over the country. Blatchford wrote sympathetically about us in his paper *The Clarion*.

> ## MANCHESTER'S UNEMPLOYED.
>
> ### Plot Leaders Sentenced.
>
> The trial of John Bonar Thompson, Tom Brown, Joshua Batty, and Arthur Smith for conspiring to damage private property was concluded at the Manchester City Sessions last night and resulted in Brown, Batty, and Smith

For three and a half days the Court was crowded with eager listeners, while large crowds gathered outside to await the verdict. We were joined in the dock at the last moment by Mr. Arthur Blank. He had been arrested at Newcastle, where he had gone on business after leaving us to carry on the great work. Mr. Blank engaged counsel to defend him. Batty, Brown, and myself disdained the assistance of any member of the *bourgeois* bar. In any case, we were determined to let the world know that we could speak for ourselves. We permitted ourselves a great deal of latitude in the course of our defense, hurling subversive diatribes from the dock to the Bench with the utmost fluency and impetuosity, denouncing capitalism in the most violent terms, and predicting its approaching end. Batty quoted from Fabian tracts, Board of Trade reports, and other documents in order to show how unevenly wealth was distributed. Brown quoted from Tolstoy and the epistle of James. Both gave stock speeches that had done duty at dozens of streetcorner meetings and were familiar to their listeners in the Square.

My own speech was brief and to the point. I had prepared it in my cell; it took only ten minutes to deliver. I had nothing to apologize for, I said, in ringing tones. My action was carefully considered and justified by the abnormal sufferings of the unemployed. I was prepared to stand by what I had done and take the consequences. In closing, I used a piece of first-class tripe of which I have always been heartily ashamed. "No man with a human heart," I declared solemnly, "can stand by and hear little children crying for bread without doing something—however desperate and unconstitutional it may be—to alter or remove the cursed system which allows such things to exist." Considering that the only child I had ever heard crying for bread was myself when I wanted white—one can see what treacly clap-trap it was. This sentence from my speech was often quoted afterwards as a cry wrung from a soul torn and seared by the sight of human suffering! It certainly was "the bunk." After a long and hotly contested trial, during which excitement ran high throughout the city, my three companions were found guilty of conspiracy and sentenced to twelve months' imprisonment in each case. The police were rather sympathetic to me, as was every one in Court. It was felt by some that I had been led away by men older than myself. The jury found me "not guilty" of conspiracy. There remained, however, the charge of doing willful and malicious damage, which I had not denied. Upon this charge the Recorder sent me to prison for twelve months.

As soon as I arrived in the big room below the dock, where the sentenced prisoners were kept until collected by the van, I heard a police officer's voice call out, "Thompson—some one to see you." It was my mother. She had read about me in the papers. "What is this?" was her first question. "Oh, don't worry," I said. "The time will soon pass."

"But whatever made you do a thing like that?" she asked. "I could have understood it if you had stolen something, but you are going to prison for the sake of a lot of people who won't thank you!" "Well, never mind," I said. "I'm not grumbling." She asked me to write to her as often as I was allowed to, and assured me that I should be welcome home when I came out of prison. Having shed a few tears, she prepared to depart. "Don't worry," I said. "I'm not worrying, why should you?" "I can't make you out!" she said. "I'll explain later—in a year's time," I said. As we were driven through the streets in the van, I observed a *Daily Mail* placard: "Unemployed window-smashers—Exemplary sentences."

THE three of us were separated as soon as we arrived at the prison and did not see one another until our release. After being weighed, examined by the doctor, and fitted with a khaki suit tastefully decorated with broad arrows, I was brought before the Governor. He was a red-faced man with a white mustache and a choleric manner. He asked me, in what I took to be an insulting tone, whether I intended to give any trouble in the prison. As I had shown no signs of contumacy since entering the establishment, I felt exceedingly rattled and said that my conduct would depend on how I was treated. "Who the hell do you think you're talking to?" he shouted, his face going redder than ever. "A pig, presumably," I answered. "Take him away!" bellowed the Governor, his face like the setting sun. "Take him away, and watch him!" Days passed and I heard no more of the incident. One of the prisoners, with whom I snatched a moment's whispered conversation, told me I need not worry, as the old man's bark was worse than his bite.

A certain number of prisoners are set to learn trades during their periods of incarceration. I heard a story of a prisoner who was asked by the Governor if he would like to work at his own trade while serving his sentence of two years' imprisonment. "Yes, sir," answered the prisoner. "Very well. You will be kept at your trade while serving your sentence." "Thank you, sir." "Oh, let me see; let me see... " said the Governor, looking through his papers. "What *is* your trade?" "I'm a sailor, sir."

On arrival, the prisoners are taken into a room called the "Reception." It sounds ironical, like the Army statement that a prisoner has been "awarded" such and such a term of imprisonment. The "Reception" is none too homely. "Stop talking, you." "Stop talking, or you'll soon find this is not a rest-house." "Stop that talking," is the constant refrain. The guests are commanded to seat themselves on rough forms. A warder then calls out in a loud voice, "Now, you prisoners; stand up in your turn and call out your names, your religion, and the amount of money you brought into the prison with you." On the occasion of my introduction the following recital took place. The first prisoner stood up and made answer as follows: "William Pickles, Church of England, fourpence-halfpenny." The next answered in a strong brogue, "Patrick Hogan, Roman Catholic, tuppence." As I was next on the list, I rose slowly and said, speaking in heavy, dramatic tones, "Bonar Thompson, no religion, no money." The warder gave me a startled look, but made no comment. I was duly entered as having no religion. One prisoner announced himself as a Swedenborgian. The warder, who was irritated at these departures from routine, snapped out, "I said your religion, not your nationality."

My attitude towards religion, which changed many years later, was that of an agnostic. Calvinism and Puritanism had brought about the inevitable reaction. Being in no mood to play the hypocrite, I refused to pretend. This, I found, was a waste of time, as nobody in a prison, least of all the chaplain, is concerned about a prisoner's religion, except as a matter of classification. The chaplain at Strangeways struck me as a hard, arid sort of person, lacking in warmth and not too liberally provided with the milk of human kindness. The talks he had with me were irritating to both of us, and he did not attempt to disguise his chagrin at having to pay a monthly visit to one who showed so little evidence of true repentance.

"I represent the advance-guard of a movement of the working-class, which may mean that one day you and I shall change places," I told him once. Instead of taking this youthful remark in good part, he lost his temper and threatened to report me to the Governor for insolence. I refused to speak to him after this, as I was angry at his threat to do such a mean thing. "Leave me alone," I said, on the occasion of his next visit. "I refuse to discuss with a man who abuses his position by threatening to put me on bread-and-water as soon as he is beaten in argument."

On account of my youth, I was put among the juvenile-adults. This meant that the discipline was more severe and the food less in quantity, but we had an hour's physical drill in the mornings, which helped to keep us from rusting away. Civil imprisonment is a lazy life. Hard labor does not mean that the prisoner is compelled to do a lot of hard work; it means fewer privileges, less food, fewer visits, fewer library-books, and no mattress to sleep on for the first fortnight. The latter was no penalty to me.

No doubt such things come hard to those who have been brought up in comfort, but to any one who has roughed it, prison is a home from home. The only thing that really oppressed me was the isolation, the silence rule, and the feeling that one is buried alive. No news comes from the outside, and empires might fall or water start running uphill without us being any the wiser. I was put to oakum-picking and found it rather heavy going, but I soon got into the knack of it. No matter what happened, I showed no sign of displeasure or grief. I realized that if I knocked my head against a brick wall, it would be my head that would get cracked, not the wall.

Prisoners are allowed to write, and receive, one letter a month. I wrote to and received a letter each month from my mother. As I was not permitted to make any reference to prison life or conditions, and she was not allowed to give me any news of the world's affairs, we had to restrict ourselves to personal and domestic matters; but I was pleased to know that she would be glad to have me back at home on my release. I looked forward, too, to the welcome that awaited me from the "comrades." I should be looked upon as a bold champion of the workers, a fighter, one who never turned his back but marched breast forward. It might well be, I imagined, that I should never have to soil my hands with manual labor again. My position as a popular and well-paid leader of the insurgent masses was, I hoped, already assured.

I am bound to confess that I found the existence wearisome and irksome. While it is true, in a sense, that stone walls do not a prison make, nor iron bars a cage, they form an excellent imitation. Youth is not the philosophical period, and the days crawled heavily and monotonously along. But time, as a famous Scotsman said, "runs through the roughest day."

On the twenty-second of March, 1909, at seven o'clock in the morning, having for twelve months worn the broad arrow of a blameless life, the prison gates were flung open to admit me once more into the clear air of freedom.

CHAPTER VI

The Hub of the Universe

W E cannot look into the seeds of time and see which grain will grow and which will not. Had I not been so easily duped by false dreams and shallow illusions about the movement to which I had allied myself, I should have seen very quickly how small a place there was for a man of my temperament among the zealots and fanatics who make up what is called the working-class movement.

The unemployed gave me a fine reception when I reappeared in Stevenson Square. During the months of my durance I had thought out a stirring oration which I unloaded amid scenes of enthusiasm.

My mother thought I was a great man after hearing me speak. She could hardly believe that the calm, self-confident man who held a vast crowd of people, while he talked like a scholar and an oracle, was the shy, inarticulate boy she had known as her son. My stepfather was staggered. He hardly dared to speak to me. He was ostentatiously deferential, subdued, apologetic. For the first day or two I was treated like a tin god on wheels. Friends and neighbors were brought in to gaze upon the prodigy.

This nonsense went on for some weeks, and then the fact that I was bringing nothing into the house, except my wonderful ideas, could no longer be ignored. The atmosphere became slightly chilly. I was making plenty of speeches and receiving salvos of applause, but no money. The prospect of going back to work was too appalling to contemplate without shuddering. I was visited by the foreman from the carriage and wagon department of the Great Central Railway, who asked me if I would care to return to my old job as brake-fitter with full rights. I told him I was not prepared to resume on the old conditions, but would be ready to go back on terms laid down by myself. These were an eight-hour instead of a twelve-hour day, a wage of five pounds a week, and no work on Saturdays, with a guaranteed pension of fifty shillings a week upon retirement at the age of fifty. He could not see his way clear to comply with these demands.

My mother thought I had gone mad to talk in this way, but even now I can see nothing unreasonable in the terms I suggested. I have never made any excessive claims upon society nor asked for anything extravagant or extreme. If any one thinks that five pounds a week for hard, difficult, and skilled work is too much pay, he must have a poor idea of what constitutes a living wage.

My determination never to work unless I got a wage sufficient for the satisfaction of my modest requirements became so strong that it was almost an obsession. Hard work does not frighten me, but hard work at low wages and under conditions inconsistent with human dignity is unthinkable to a man of my temperament. I had more than enough of it as a boy. Who would work if he could raise money in some other way? I made up my mind that I would raise it in some other way.

After the Great Central Railway foreman had refused my terms for being employed, I was unwilling to continue as a burden upon my parents, so I left home and took my chance of survival as a tramp upon the broad highways of England. To set out, inexperienced as I was, needed strength of will, but I have plenty of that where my own interests are concerned.

After a week or two on the road I learned to keep myself alive by speaking in market-places and taking collections, reciting in public-houses and going round with the hat, and by other shifts and devices known to roadsters and wanderers. I was young, hopeful, and confident of success in my ambition, which was to live without working for a master. In that ambition I have been successful. Whether it was worth while I cannot say. I suppose it has been. Whatever we do or leave undone, it's the same in the end. To me life is full of interest, and if all goes well I shall live till I die.

After some months of tramping, sleeping out in haystacks and hedges, exploring ditches and doss-houses, and occasionally even begging from door to door (this was the hardest thing I tried, and a little of it goes a long way), I reached the great city of London.

My arrival in the metropolis caused no interest whatever. Walking in through the Edgware Road from the north, I found myself in Hyde Park. The time was three o'clock in the afternoon, and I found a small meeting in progress at the Marble Arch meeting-ground. The speaker was a religious fanatic whose language was all too familiar to me. After a while he subsided and I stepped forward into the ring. I began to speak about my prison experiences. The crowd grew; no one interrupted. Everybody seemed interested and not unsympathetic. I finished, and a man stepped from the crowd and said: "Well, people, you have heard this young man's story. He is up against it. I need say no more. You can see him outside the gates." He conducted me towards the gate and told me to stand there while the crowd came out. It seemed that collections were not permitted inside the Park, but you could invite those who thought your speech worthy of support and desired to contribute to come outside the gates. I took three shillings.

The man asked me if I had arranged to sleep at any particular place. I told him I was a complete stranger to London. "Come with me," he said: "I'll fix you up." He took me through the streets to a large building called Bruce House. This was a lodging-house on an improved pattern, similar in every respect, I found later, to the Rowton Houses, in all of which I ultimately stayed. Bruce House stands in Kemble Street, off Drury Lane. Close by was the Drury Lane Theater and the Opera House, Covent Garden. The situation was as central as any one could wish.

There are a thousand cubicles in Bruce House, and at that time the cost of staying there was sevenpence per night. This, I hoped, would be a sum within my power to raise. I booked a cubicle under my friend's direction. He then showed me over the building, the library, wash-room, dining room, and so forth. It seemed grand to me. I shall be comfortable here, I thought. He suggested that we should club together and buy a dinner, and he bought half a pound of steak and appropriate vegetables from a shop outside. "The stuff they sell at the bar is muck," he told me. "Always buy your food from outside and cook it here."

We cooked the food on a hot plate in the middle of the dining room, armed ourselves with knives, forks and spoons, plates, etc., which are provided by the management, and enjoyed a good meal. The whole affair, enough for two men with large appetites, cost less than a shilling. "I am doing well," I said to my friend. "Thank you for putting me in touch with such a comfortable hotel."

"Don't mention it," he said. "I've been in the same position as you many a time."

My friend, it appeared, was a Cornishman who had tried his luck in London some years before and, failing to find employment, there being no quarries in the metropolis, had drifted into a hand-to-mouth existence. He kept himself alive by opening cab doors, carrying sandwich-boards, "touching" church people and the numerous charitable bodies for food and clothes, and living on what little cash he could scrounge in one way and another. He was a decent and fairly intelligent man about forty years of age, strong and soldierly in bearing, and gifted with a sense of humor and a cheerful disposition. He put me wise to several things, and I thanked him cordially.

In the evening I spoke in Hyde Park once more, going outside the gates again and collecting about one and sixpence. I was interested to find the great MacCutcheon had been listening to me. He came up to me outside the gate and told me that he too was staying at Bruce House. He and I spoke together for many months, taking the chair for each other alternately. Life was not too easy. It took me all my time to raise enough in collections to pay my "kipp" each night and get something to eat each day. I lived on about fifteen shillings a week, but there was no regularity in the life I had chosen.

Sunday was the best day for meetings. I held three, one at twelve in the forenoon, one at three in the afternoon, and the third at six-thirty in the evening. I took about ten shillings altogether. Had collections been allowed on the spot, I should have taken a great deal more, but London people are not in the habit of running after any one to give them money, whether it has been earned or not. I certainly earned all I received. Public speaking is hard work. Done under my conditions, it was a labor of loathing, but I persevered. Sooner or later, I told myself, I shall be recognized as an orator of more than common gifts.

I knew that I still had much to learn, but in the rough-and-tumble of street-corner and public-park speaking one could not help but learn. I spoke nearly every day, and sometimes twice and even three times daily, until the outbreak of war in 1914. On Sundays I always addressed large meetings, each of which lasted an hour. A wet Sunday washed me out and washed my livelihood away. In the winter the struggle was severe. Park crowds were smaller, and those who came had very little to give away.

The first winter that I spent in London saw me without the price of a bed on many occasions. I walked the streets until daybreak, and in the morning washed in the Serpentine. This is not allowed, and I had to keep a look-out for the policeman while I washed. Often I went without food—but I went on speaking. I had to—there was nothing else I could do.

One thing I never thought of doing, and that was to look for work. I would not have minded a good job, but no one ever offered me a good job. My ambition was to become a great orator—to be well paid for speaking. At the same time I was not prepared to speak unless I had full liberty to say what I liked. My ideas were socialistic and anarchistic. I turned out that sort of stuff because, at that time, I believed in it as much as I believed in anything. I have never been a bigot. There is nothing of the zealot in my nature. I inclined, however, more towards revolutionary ideas than to any others.

At the same time I loved the best things in life—poetry, painting, music, great literature, and the fine arts. I went to the theater as often as my means would allow which, I am sorry to say, was not often. Now and then I was to be seen looking over from the gallery corner of the Holborn Empire. The price of a seat was fourpence, and a very good view of the stage could be obtained from the corner seat. I often went short of a meal for the sake of seeing the great stars of variety, in the days when the music-hall was a feature of English life. I saw all the wonderful artistes whose names are still familiar to middle-aged people all over the country. I saw Eugene Stratton dozens of times, and Chevalier (not Maurice—the great Chevalier), R. G. Knowles, Little Tich, dear Marie Lloyd, Lottie Lennox, Peggy Pryde, Phil Ray, and scores of other fine, gifted performers. During their performances I truly lived. I have even spent my "kipp" money to see a play I wished to know something about, and then walked the town all night thinking about it. Although I am no ascetic,

I have always cared more about these things than food and drink. Many hours were profitably spent in the free libraries.

MacCutcheon held forth in Hyde Park in his usual style, but was looked upon as an eccentric. He lived simply and frugally. As a companion he was highly interesting, always in good spirits, and never complaining no matter how difficult things were.

"Never sink to the level of a grouser, Thompson," he once said to me. "Don't allow circumstances to annoy you. Take everything as it comes and laugh at misfortune." I have always done so. When things go badly with me, I know that is the time to smile.

The longer I lived in London the more I despised the people. I found them suspicious and inhospitable, shallow, empty creatures, puffed up with conceit and full of false ideas about everything. The average cockney, I found, was quite unreliable and incapable of loyalty or generosity. I adapted myself to the mentality of these people, but now and then I burst forth into fits of anger at their meanness and stupidity. Their callousness is amazing. They cannot help being made that way, but I had been brought up amongst people who, whatever their educational limitations, were men and women of strong character. Manchester people had been rougher, but I had found them strong, genuine, good-hearted people, and they had brains.

I felt the lack of these qualities in Londoners, and it often enraged me. After a time, however, I realized that there was no remedy for it and accepted it as inevitable. The few friends I made were Irish, Scotch, or North country people. Sometimes I made friends with an American or a Jew, but I cannot recall any Londoner who was friendly to me at any time. My friends, of course, were as poor as I. I have seldom been able to make contact with a member of the rich classes, and even today I cannot number one millionaire among my acquaintances. Yet I am no snob, and have never passed a man by merely because he had a large balance at the bank.

On Easter Monday, 1911, I was addressing a meeting in the Park, and at the end of my speech I asked if any one wished to ask any questions. This was a mere formality, as I had no wish to be bothered with questions. Questions break the spell of a meeting and do the speaker no good at collection-time. The crowd becomes so interested in the stupid questions—all questioners are stupid—they would not be questioners if they were not—that they forget all about the speaker's need to live. It was this kind of thing that first made me realize how callous and mean the people are generally who take an interest in economic, social, and political questions.

Naturally I did not welcome a question that came, on this occasion, from a young man in the crowd. I cut him so that I could get to the gate and collect my wages. The questioner, however, followed me out. I would have dismissed him as civilly as I could, but his appearance and manner were so likable that I forgave him for asking the question and entered into conversation with him. He was a tall youth about my own age, with fair hair and blue eyes. He had a frank, open countenance with an attractive and friendly manner. He was dressed in rags. We chatted for a few minutes and then parted.

I have met so many people, most of them bores, that ordinarily I am only too anxious to forget fresh acquaintances. The trite remarks, commonplace observations, and the banal and stupid chatter of the thousands of people who have insisted on conversing with me outside the gates of Hyde

Park have contributed substantially towards the ruin of my nervous system. It does not pay to be too ruthless with them when one is dependent upon them for a livelihood, but murder has often rattled through my brain while I have been under the harrow of their maddening conversation.

Above all I have always resented their vulgar and insensitive familiarity. I am never safe from molestation by these hollow-headed bores. In the bus, the street, the café, the train, even in the theater, there is no guarantee that I shall not be set upon. The physical torture of replying to their utterly uninteresting comments upon things quite beyond their mental scope, but upon which they imagine themselves to be authorities, is refined. It is not enough that as a public speaker one must cope with financial insecurity and economic adversity, but one must withstand the bore, the boor, and the blockhead as well.

But the blue-eyed youth with the golden hair had caught my attention. He was certainly not a bore. It seemed from what I had observed of him that he stood out from the common ruck of men. I hoped that we might meet again. We did. He came over to my table in Bruce House the next day. I was drinking a cup of tea and wondering where my breakfast was coming from. There was nothing novel about this. I had grown used to it, and did not worry too much. Something generally turned up, and if not, one had to put up with the inconvenience of going without. Leo—this was the name I came to know him by—turned up this time. "Come and have breakfast with me," he said. We went to a Lockhart's café. "Order what you like," Leo told me. "Are you in funds?" I asked. "Yes—I touched a well-fed parasite of the *bourgeoisie* for a quid last evening," he said.

Unlike most socialists, Leo pronounced the French word correctly. He told me he was half French, but had been brought up in London. His father had taught him to speak the French language like a native of France. At that time his parents were dead, he had quarreled with the other members of his family, and was now maintaining a precarious and harum-scarum existence by "tapping" people in the streets of an evening as they left the theater or the opera. But Leo "tapped" with care and with art.

His custom was to place his arm in splints and to pretend that he had been the victim of an accident which prevented him following his trade. His expression of youthful innocence and sincerity seldom failed to wring the hearts of his victims. As the well-fed ones listened to the sad recital of accident and unmerited misfortune, of the young sister at home starving, the youth's brave struggle to preserve his pride and self-respect, his stern refusal to take anything for himself and to be asking merely for the sake of the little sister, helpless and orphaned, waiting pathetically in their shabby little room, his listeners found it impossible to keep their hands from straying to their pockets.

He earned a pound a day sometimes, but the game was getting risky. He had been warned several times recently by plain-clothes policemen to make himself scarce. He realized that something would have to be done. "One cannot work," he said, and I agreed with him vigorously.

I suggested that he and I might join forces for a while. He accepted this suggestion with enthusiasm, and offered to take the chair at my meetings and help in the raising of funds generally.

Leo soon learned to speak fairly well. We tried every pitch in London—Highbury Corner; Finsbury Park, Brock-

well Park; Victoria Park; Parliament Hill Fields; Peckham
Rye; Clapham Common; The World's End, Chelsea; Jack
Straw's Castle, Hampstead; Jolly Butcher's Hill, Wood Green;
Beresford Square, Woolwich; Golden Square, Soho; Catherine
Street, Croydon; Howland Street, Tottenham Court Road;
and many other places set aside for the use of jawsmiths and
atmosphere printers.

Sometimes we did well and sometimes badly. Sometimes
we drew an entire blank. Either the people would not stand,
or, if they stood, were too stupid or impoverished to meet
their obligations at collection-times. Often the meetings
would be spoiled by rain, or a drunken man, or an outbreak
of fire in the neighborhood, a dog-fight, a horse falling down,
or some similar distracting influence. But we seldom had any
opposition from the crowds. They listened with considerable
interest and sometimes with cordiality.

We held meetings at least once every day of the week
and sometimes twice or even three times a day. We tried all
sorts of places, likely and unlikely. At times when the crowds
became too large or we were speaking at a forbidden spot,
the police would order us to stop. This generally happened
at the most critical moment—the moment just before the
collection was due to be taken. This was annoying, but we
took it as part of the day's work. It was the luck of the game.

Hyde Park, however, despite its disadvantages, was the
best place for our purpose. One never knew who might be in
the crowd, and Leo was keen to hold on to any one who spoke
to him. Once he fastened his claws upon the heartstrings
of a victim all was over. "Make the swines pay for taking
up your time with their silly talk," he used to say. I fully
agreed, but I had no talent as a "tapper." The collection was
payment for services rendered. I had given them a speech,

and the least they could do was pay for their entertainment. But "tapping" meant asking for money I had not earned. I had no moral objection, but it meant humbling oneself, and I could never do it successfully.

Leo had no scruples, and his audacity was astounding. He would try his hand at any one. One afternoon we happened to be standing in the outer lobby of the House of Commons waiting for a Member whom I knew. Suddenly I saw Leo make a swift movement towards a dignified white-haired gentleman who had just emerged from the little office opposite the turnstile. It was the late Lord Oxford, then Mr. Asquith. I crept up to hear what was being said. Leo had dashed forward and grasped the great statesman's hand.

"Oh, Mr. Asquith, you haven't forgotten me, have you?" he said. The Liberal leader looked puzzled. "You remember me in the central committee rooms at Fife," said Leo. "I was with my father, a lifelong supporter of yours."

"Oh yes, I think so," Mr. Asquith said in a dubious sort of way. Leo then began a story of how his father had died, how things had gone from bad to worse, and now he was at the end of his tether. "Is there any work you could give me, sir? Addressing envelopes. Anything."

"I'm sorry, my boy. I'm afraid there is nothing at the moment—but take this and I wish you better luck."

As we hurried down the steps Leo opened his hand and disclosed a sovereign. "You have never been in Fife, have you?" I asked. "Not likely. What's that got to do with it?" he said. Just then we saw a tall man with a monocle passing into Palace Yard. There was no mistaking that figure. It was Austen Chamberlain. "Try him too," I suggested. "Make a day of it." "Right. I will," Leo said. He was off like a flash, and in a moment was speaking earnestly to the Conservative politician. It was not long before I saw Austen Chamberlain's hand go to his pocket. Afterwards he shook Leo warmly by the hand and went on his way. "Guess how much," asked Leo as he rejoined me. "A pound," I hazarded. It was.

Having succeeded with Liberal and Tory, I suggested to Leo that we ought not to leave until he had tried some one belonging to the Labor Party as well. He was quite willing to try, and we went back into the outer lobby. We had to wait for some time before any one worth while passed, and then we saw a dark handsome man making his way through the barrier. It was Ramsay MacDonald. Leo swept down upon him. He talked rapidly and with great fervor for about five minutes. But MacDonald's features did not relax. He peered at Leo with cold steely eyes, and I feared the worst. That man is too much concerned for the welfare of humanity to care anything for any one, I thought. And I was right. There was no handshake, no expression of good will, no wishes for better luck. The great "tapper" had failed. He had broken against the rock of non-conformist socialism. And we went out into the street again. "We might have guessed it," I said. "These men *talk* about poverty and the rights of the poor. That is their contribution to the alleviation of human suffering." The public-houses were open all day then, and we spent the rest of the evening having a good night out.

Gradually Leo became a quite effective speaker. He mastered the platform technique more easily and readily than most speakers do, but he was sadly lacking in mental fertility. His speeches were things of shreds and patches. They were made up largely from other speeches he had heard. He sometimes annoyed me by giving off large chunks of my own speeches. As soon as he had spoken them once he believed they were his own. He even laid some of my brightest gems at my feet as though he had just thought of them himself. But he was a great help. He displayed no lack of invention when it came to telling the crowd about our struggles and sufferings. A pack of lies from Leo at the end of a meeting would often increase the takings by fifty per cent. And he did not antagonize any one. I often did so. I spoke much better than Leo and had a good voice and a dramatic style, but my sentiments were too rabid and too harshly expressed. I trampled on corns in all directions. There was seldom any interruption, but the crowd was not always with me. There was no bond between us. Many years passed before I could see clearly that the wind must be tempered to the shorn lambs of democracy.

I used to wonder, after having denounced and attacked everything and everybody and made game of the pet prejudices of nearly every one in the crowd, why they did not applaud more warmly. I was very young and inexperienced. But Leo always brought them round to a good humor. He would point to me and say: "Here is a man who has suffered capitalism's deepest damnation. He has been persecuted, victimized, and boycotted because he has had the courage to say what he thinks and go to prison for his convictions." It was ghastly. I hate to be spoken of as a man who has suffered, and the word "martyr" makes me sick, but as long as it helped the collections I let him carry on.

As things were looking up a bit, I decided to leave Bruce House and find a room of my own. Leo had planted himself upon an acquaintance and had a temporary security. Bruce House was the negation of home life. The great barracks, with the porters like warders and the keen-eyed inmates ever on the prowl for anything they could pilfer or beg from one another, had begun to get on my nerves. I hated the place, the sound and the smell of it.

There was a man called Charlie Lahr who used to visit our meetings. He was a German with anarchist views who kept a bookshop in Hammersmith, a humorous, kindly chap with an extreme love of literature. He had no time, however, for established writers. They were conventional and bourgeois. Any writer earlier than D. H. Lawrence, who had just come into prominence with *Sons and Lovers*, was out of date. Lahr lent me books from time to time. They were by such authors as James Joyce, who was then being talked about in the coteries because of his novel, *A Portrait of the Artist as a Young Man*, and by Andre Gide and others of the ultra-advanced school.

It was wonderful for me to feel that I belonged to the elect who had read these giants of the future, and Charlie was the means of introducing me to a number of writers of whom I should not otherwise have heard until years later. He raved over a writer called John Travenna largely because that author was not well known. As soon as authors did become well known, Charlie had done with them. He felt, I suppose, that they had been bought over, or had taken to writing for the mob, else why were they popular with the wrong kind of readers?

I told Lahr one day that I was looking for a room, and he offered me one at his place in Blythe Road, Hammersmith. The rent was four shillings a week, and I could read as many of his books as I liked. I accordingly took up my residence with him, and was quite comfortable there for a while. The room I slept in was packed with books. There was hardly room to move. They were all over the floor and under the bed, and a great stack of them was heaped up outside the door. I read and read and read.

Charlie's wife, who was a disagreeable woman, complained about me burning the gas all night. We were always quarreling about it. When money was short, I sometimes took one of the books out and sold it. There was a bookseller near Southampton Row by the name of Tynemouth Shore. This gentleman, who was an exact replica of Samuel Pickwick, bought a book or two from me now and then. I always felt I had been cheated when he offered me sixpence for a seven-and-sixpenny volume. I complained once, but he merely said: "Bring me a first folio of Shakespeare—then I'll talk money to you."

It is an odd thing that Charlie, who has a bookshop in Red Lion Street at the present time, has never known how many of his books I sold in this quiet way during my stay in his house over twenty years ago. Nor does he know that when money was more plentiful with me—which it seldom was—I sometimes brought a girl in to sleep with me among the masterpieces. Or does he?

About that period there sailed into our ken a character who was to give us a good deal of intellectual and emotional stimulus. I first came across him in the middle of a group of people who were arguing in Hyde Park. He was a wisp of a man, conspicuously insignificant, with a light squeaky voice. He was bad on his feet, bad in his teeth, wore a muffler, and a quiff which curled up from beneath a cloth cap, rolled his own cigarettes, and looked what he was not, a "yob." What amazed me about him was the way in which he was dealing with his opponent in argument.

I had just been reading Herbert Spencer, and, having a good memory, I had a very clear recollection of what Spencer had written, especially about education, socialism, and the functions of the State. The seeming "yob" was quoting—at least he maintained that he was—from Spencer's essay *The State*. It is certain that if the eminent Victorian had been alive to hear himself quoted as this man was doing, he would have lost something of his philosophic calm, especially as Spencer appears to have been totally destitute of a sense of humor.

"Spencer was a mystic, as he clearly affirmed in his essay *The State*." This was the first of the "yob's" statements that I heard, and he went on in a casual tone, as if he were saying something so obvious as to be hardly worth mentioning: "He tells us how he prayed for light and guidance even in the most trifling domestic affairs. He claimed to know God by a process of scientific reasoning, and held that the most perfect state was that in which God manifested Himself most vividly." His opponent, who had evidently read Spencer, was foaming at the mouth. "You have never read Spencer!" he cried angrily. "You don't know what you are talking about." "Oh?" retorted the "yob," "let us see how much of Spencer you have read. Have you read his work in four volumes, *The Scientific Aspects of Esoteric Humanitarianism*, or his pamphlets on *The Russian System of Christian Rationalism?*" There are, of course, no such works in existence, either by Herbert Spencer or any one else. But for all the crowd knew there might have been. And the "yob" maintained his attitude with such calm authority and transparent sincerity that his opponent was condemned by the listening ignoramuses.

I fetched Leo and told him what was happening. We edged our way into the crowd and gave the "yob" our full support, taking up where he had left off, and quoting other non-existent writings of the unfortunate philosopher. The "yob's" name was Jack Smith, and he recognized me from having heard me speak. I asked if "Jack Smith" were a fictitious name, but he assured us it was his real name. We spent the rest of the day in a public-house, Leo and I celebrating the arrival of the first original organism we had met for years.

The interesting thing about Smith was that he had read hardly anything. He seldom looked at a book, preferring to invent his own authors and quotations; or, if it suited his purpose better, he invented his own quotations and fitted them on to any author with a well-known name. He had read a little of Karl Marx and only a little, but he quoted things from that bewhiskered bore that would have caused him to turn over in his box at Highgate Cemetery, could he have heard them. Smith was never beaten in argument. He had a mind like a razor. His opponents, even when in the right—in fact, especially when in the right—were invariably put to silence. I have heard him pretending to read out from an author who never existed, fabricating phrases which had the authentic ring of truth, and speaking with intense conviction and sincerity. He always carried his hearers with him on such occasions.

Jack Smith was welcomed into our company with great joy. He was a printer by trade, but more often than not he was out of a job. He hated work with a fine hatred. When he did work he made it a point to turn up at least an hour late each day. After working for about a month at one well-known printing shop in Long Acre, where the hour of starting was eight o'clock in the morning, and rolling in, as usual, just after nine o'clock, he was approached by the foreman one morning. "Here, what time do you think we start work in this shop?" the foreman asked him. "I don't know—you always seem to be at it when I come in," was Smith's answer.

Leo, Smith, and I went everywhere together. We quarreled sometimes, but our friendship was too strong to be permanently broken. We had everything in common, and nothing in common with the prigs who abounded on every hand in the revolutionary movement. Though we preached socialism ourselves, we were not orthodox. As a consequence of this, none of us was taken quite seriously, and for this we were truly thankful.

One evening we went to hear Bernard Shaw speak at the Essex Hall. The meeting had been called to protest against the blasphemy laws. A number of pompous figureheads decorated the platform. The Rev. Stewart Headlam was in the chair, and G. W. Foote, the editor of the Nonconformist organ of pious atheism, the *Freethinker*, was one of the speakers. Foote was an impressive-looking man of the Victorian type, with a splendid voice and a powerful and dramatic style. He lacked, of course, as all freethinkers do, any kind of intellectual distinction or originality. He was saturated with the narrow and grimy morality of the Little Bethel and the Calvinistic conventicle. He slew God in the usual standardized style amid loud applause.

An amusing figure on the platform was that of the late Sir Hiram Maxim, a fat freethinker who appeared incapable of any thought at all. "I am here to join in the protest against the blasphemy" (he pronounced it *blaspheemy*) "laws. We have gone past the stage when we are prepared to bow down before an anthropomorphic conception of hypothetical immateriality," he wheezed. "My religion is the religion of humanity. We must work together for humanity." Sir Hiram's contribution towards the betterment of that humanity he loved so much was the Maxim gun.

We waited for Shaw with some excitement. He made a witty and brilliant speech. "We are not here," he said, "to preach any religion or attack any religion. The purpose of this meeting is to demand freedom for all religions and for those who have none." This statement was not to the liking of the anti-God fanatics who were present in force, but Shaw went on despite several low whines from the bigots. One could not fail to be impressed by Shaw's greatness. He radiated immense spiritual vitality. He appeared to be alive all over. His face seemed to me that of a man who never slept. His whole body was alert, his very existence a challenge to the torpidity, stupidity, and intellectual death which surrounded him on the platform. We were all greatly impressed.

"What about tapping him?" I said to Leo. Leo moved towards the platform. He waited until Shaw was about to leave and then signaled vigorously to him. Shaw turned and asked him what he wanted. Leo shook him cordially by the hand and began a story of how he had addressed a meeting for the Fabian Society in Leicester, decorating his remarks with several witty epigrams culled from one of my recent speeches. Smith and I hung around in the background marveling at our friend's audacity. "He'll pull it off," I said. Smith was dubious. It seemed that Shaw could not get a word in edgeways, although he tried several times. Leo swept the great man off his feet by sheer sustained pressure of eloquence. Shaw began laughing after a while and his hand went to his pocket. The Master had capitulated. Five shillings was the amount of the fine. I have always looked on this as one of Leo's greatest achievements.

Smith was of little account on the open-air platform, but he sparkled like a luminary on the floor. He trapped several self-important socialist pundits into debates and tore them to ribbons. A favorite device of his was to take some well-known statement of obvious truth and make it seem utter nonsense. Only those who were present on these occasions can form any conception of the effectiveness of his methods. His triumphs were all the more to his credit as he was seldom in the right. He made the most preposterous ideas sound true, and he caused truths as clear as champagne to seem like the delusions of a fool. He invented continually: facts, figures, names, instances, theories, everything. I have seldom known Smith to make a statement that was in keeping even with the known and proven facts of the case. He was a genius.

His constitution contained the germs of tuberculosis, of which his abnormal quickness of mind was probably a symptom. He died of consumption in 1924. I miss him badly. Such unique spirits are not often encountered in the dreary world of economic and political mugwumpery and gasbaggery.

CHAPTER VII

Farmer Fish and the Musical Dock-Pullers

O NE day as Leo and I were reviewing the general economic situation in all its multifarious ramifications, we decided that it was time we gave London a rest. Smith had gone to work at a place near Woolwich and was not available at the customary haunts. I owed rent at my lodgings and an eviction was imminent. Leo was becoming restless, and so was I.

Things were getting stale, and money was scarce in our pockets. "Let us strike out for adventure upon the open road. There is wind on the heath, brother, and we can't raise it here." So we packed our belongings into a small brown-paper parcel and hit the trail.

At Luton we set up as fortune-tellers. Leo stood blindfolded in the market-place while I addressed the crowds. "This is Professor Zoma," I assured them. "His mother was world-famous as Gypsy Lee. She was only a gypsy, but Heaven had gifted her with second-sight and magic powers only given to a select few of God's creatures. Her son, who stands before you today, is the only living person to whom the great Gypsy Lee has bequeathed her marvelous secret of thought-reading and second-sight. He will read your character by the hand or by the eye. He will tell you your good points and your bad ones, your faults and your failings. He will sketch your future and tell you what time holds in store. The charge is three copper coins. Step forward and learn your destiny from Professor Zoma." It was good to see the honest toilers stretching forth their horny hands and submitting their work-worn faces for a "reading." We took about twelve shillings before the police ordered us to clear off.

At Bedford I addressed the multitudes in front of the Town Hall. For some reason or other, the police were present in large numbers, headed by the Chief Constable, who stood through my speech with a threatening expression upon his face. I felt annoyed at this display, and launched a ferocious attack upon the police force as a whole. The crowd grew and grew. The atmosphere was full of tension. I took advantage of the situation to arouse sympathy and a record collection.

"Why are the police here tonight?" I asked, with a rhetorical sweep of my arm over the huge mass of people. "I challenge the whole of Scotland Yard to produce a scrap of evidence that I have ever committed any crime involving moral turpitude. I challenge the Home Secretary to furnish a tittle of evidence to the effect that I have ever forged a check, robbed a bank, rifled a gas-meter or even committed a murder. He cannot and dare not. These helmeted hooligans," I thundered, getting into my stride, "these brutes in blue, these flat-footed emblems of a vile capitalist tyranny, these hired bullies of the brutal boss-class, are here because they have been sent here by a scoundrelly Government" ("Hear! Hear!" from a couple of doss-house dwellers) "to watch me, to harass me, to crush me because they know that I represent an awakening proletariat." (Cheers from two or three local I.L.P.ers.) "But they shall not intimidate me. I defy them. They may imprison me, shoot or hang me, but as long as there is a drop of blood in my veins I shall fight for the poor and the needy, the downtrodden and the oppressed."

Several of the younger police officers began to fidget, but the older ones continued to stand gazing stolidly at me. I finished with a terrific peroration and left the platform to the accompaniment of some cheering from a sympathetic but bewildered audience. The Chief Constable stepped forward and asked me if I intended to take a collection. I said I did. "Then I shall arrest you if you do. I warn you."

Leo immediately mounted the orange-box and informed the crowd of what the Chief Constable had said. "We are starving," he said, with an expression of deep pathos. "We have walked forty miles today without a scrap to eat. For myself I care nothing," he said, with simple dignity, "but to think that my friend, my great leader, who has sacrificed everything for the sake of his principles, to think of this heroic working-class fighter having to sleep in a ditch, suffer hunger and cold, when he might be drawing his twenty or thirty pounds a week as a Liberal or Tory hack if he cared to sell his principles—that hurts me. That cuts me to the heart. We are outcast and starving, men and women of Bedford. But we dare not take a collection. Well, good men have suffered for their principles before. John Bunyan, whose bones lie rotting a few yards from where I stand," (Bunyan's bones, if there are any of them left, lie in Bunhill Fields, London but Leo was no stickler for accuracy of detail) "lay in your jail for thirty years" (twelve) "rather than give up his principles. And we are prepared to do the same. We are only starving. That is all. But we are not permitted to take a collection. Good night, fellow workers. The meeting is at an end."

The crowd was thoroughly sympathetic by this time and looked upon us as a couple of heroic figures. They rolled up in dozens and pressed money into our itching palms. The police took no action.

After the crowd had cleared away, and while Leo and I were counting the spoils, which amounted to about fifteen shillings, the Chief Constable came over to us and said: "You will hold no more meetings in Bedford unless you wish to go to prison." "How is that?" I asked. "It is not allowed, that's all." We thanked him and walked away.

"This is money for jam," I said. "We ought to take pounds at Northampton."

We spent the night in the best doss-house I have ever slept in. The beds were clean, the walls were dry, the roof did not leak, the air was relatively pure, and there was no sign of vermin.

Next morning we set out for Northampton, which we reached in the evening. But our Bedford success had been a flash in the pan. The Northampton meeting was flat and unsatisfactory. The crowd was poor and apathetic. The collection came to something like three shillings. We stayed in the town a couple of days, holding meetings each evening, but the results were about the same.

Leo took it into his head that we should return to London. I opposed this at first, but only half-heartedly. We were both tired of the road, and the prospects looked no brighter as we went further north. We did go as far as Leicester, but the meetings were no better there. A fortune-telling attempt at the market-place was stopped by the police, and, knowing that fortune-telling is illegal, we decided to give it up. We could do as well by speaking on social questions, so why bother to tell fortunes and run the risk of getting fined? There was no money for such things as fines.

As we touched Northampton again on the return journey, we ran into a couple of men we had known in London. They, too, were on the road. Leo and I agreed, rather rashly as it turned out, to join them on the way back to London. Four men on tramp together are too many. It resulted in Leo and me having to carry the others as passengers. They were a helpless brace of incompetents, and this soon became apparent. One of them developed bad feet, and this irritated me extremely. Being a good walker myself, capable of tramping forty miles a day without feeling the strain, I had only contempt for muffs who got blisters on their feet. Leo agreed with me. People whose feet won't stand plenty of wear-and-tear ought not to go on long walks, they should stay in the towns and be carried about in trams and buses.

By the time we had passed Bedford, things became rather gloomy. We were all broke. One of the cripples suggested that we should ask a farmer for work. I gave Leo a significant look. We could have murdered the two wretches and left their bodies to rot in a ditch, only it was too much trouble.

"We could earn enough in a few days to see us on our way again," one of them said. "As things are now, we shall starve by the roadside."

"So your only alternative to death by starvation is work?" I said in acid tones. "I suppose you set out on the road with the object of finding work sooner or later?"

They admitted this was so, and seemed to see nothing wrong in it.

Leo butted in at this point. "Why not try it, just for fun?" he said. "We need not stick it for longer than we care to."

I was disgusted, and we walked in silence for a while. Then Leo beckoned me to hang back a few yards. "Listen, Bonar, old man," he said. "You know me better than to imagine I should make such a suggestion seriously. But let us pretend to go in with these fellows. We can accept a job if one comes," he said, "and while we are supposed to be sweating and moiling, we can look round for what we can lay our hands on, and be off. And it will be an experience."

Now Leo was a youth of considerable personal charm. He had an extremely persuasive way with him, and won me over at last.

Not long after this we met a farmer driving a cart along the road. Leo, who nearly always took the lead in these matters, called on him to stop. "Can you find us a job, mister?" he asked.

The farmer, a cunning-looking old fellow with a beard, plied us with many questions. Leo told him that we were four music-hall artistes from the London Hippodrome. "The Four Favorites," he said. "You have heard of us, of course. We were left stranded at Leeds and have had to walk back to here. We want work, any kind of work as long as it is hard."

I felt apprehensive, but my fears were a tribute to Leo's powers of simulation, for he had no intention of doing any work, either hard or soft. I ought to have known him better, and I apologized afterwards for having doubted him. The farmer, whose name was Fish, set us on to pull up docks in a field. As it was then about three o'clock in the afternoon, we should not suffer too horribly, even if we had actually to rive one or two reluctant docks from the challenging soil.

Leo offered, on behalf of us all, to provide a first-class concert on the village green in the evening, if Mr. Fish would pass the word round among his neighbors in the meantime. He agreed to do this, and we then entered a large field to commence operations. I knew all about pulling up docks, but I kept my knowledge to myself. We spent the rest of the afternoon discussing our forthcoming concert and arranging the artistes in the order of their appearance. Leo would sing, I would recite, and the other two would then sing. At this point we stuck. "What about a sketch?" I suggested. So we spent the next two hours writing and rehearsing our sketch. This gem of comic art was a jumble of odds and ends from the sketches we had seen at music-halls. Our thanks were due to Messrs. Lew Lake, Ernie Lotinga, Wal Pink, Joe Elvin, and many other gifted writers and players, from whom we borrowed the best and brightest quips and japes, and the most telling situations.

At the end of our half-day of intense labor in the field we were called into an outhouse by the farmer's wife and given several slabs of bread-and-butter and a pint of beer amongst the four of us.

We felt as full of sparkle as a glass of ale that has been standing for a couple of days. But our hearts leapt up when we beheld the crowd that awaited us on the village green. There must have been a hundred people. Fish had ridden on his bicycle all over the countryside, it appeared, and rounded up the lads and lasses for the great event which was now about to take place.

Our arrival was not greeted with applause. The local chawbacons eyed us stolidly. The opening number was provided by one of our group, who had been rehearsing all the afternoon. It was a recitation about a man who sat watching a hole in the road. The thing is not without humor when recited by a person with a good flair for character and some knowledge of elocution. The distinguished first-night audience received it in deathlike silence. The artiste was about to begin on another piece, when Leo pulled him back. "Save the other one till later," he whispered. "We must warm them up first." They looked to me as if they ought to be warmed up in hell. I did not like the look of them at all. Leo then burst into song. He had a pleasant tenor voice, and rendered "Friend o' Mine" in a most touching manner. The congregation remained dumb. Nothing, it seemed, could touch them. Then the other man sang. He was a bass-baritone. (He was other things as well, but there are truths that are better left unspoken.) The listeners held tight. "No signs of mutiny yet," I remarked to Leo. "It is the calm before the storm, I'm afraid," he said anxiously.

At this point Leo took the situation in hand. He addressed the crowd. "I am now going to call upon the greatest dramatic actor of our time. One who is well known in all parts of Great Britain and who was Sir Henry Irving's leading man for many years. He is famous in Europe and America."

I began with "The Dream of Eugene Aram." As the well-known (but not to them) verses fell from my lips, the audience stirred for the first time. "I've got them," I said to myself.

I had. Unfortunately I did not want them when I had them. I have seldom seen a crowd enjoy itself so much. They laughed until they ached. To say that I was pleased to see their happy smiling faces would be a gross misstatement of the facts. I could have murdered them. I could have butchered every man, woman, and child in front of me. As I gazed around in fury I noticed that the two members of our group who had let us in for this were laughing too. But not Leo. He was an artist. He knew what it meant to have one's work misunderstood and misjudged. I carried on to the bitter end. "Drew the midnight curtains round" (loud giggles) "with fingers bloody red." At the word "bloody" the whole gang rocked with laughter for several minutes. And so on to the end.

After a few more songs and a comic recitation from Leo, which were received in gloomy silence, we put on the sketch. It was entitled "Sausages," though why so I cannot remember. This was a success. But the jokes that had caused London theater-audiences to fall sideways with laughter aroused no smile upon any of the fatuous faces before us. It was the physical things which made them heave with merriment. Every time one of us fell down or was pushed down, they yelled. So we omitted most of the dialogue and spent half an hour hitting each other over the head, kicking and biting each other and stamping upon each other's prostrate bodies. Every now and then one of us would yell out the word "Sausages!" which never failed to get a big laugh from the big saps who watched us. We could have kept the sketch on for quite a long run, but physical exhaustion forced us to finish it after a while. That concluded the grand concert given by "The Four Favorites" on the village green at _____ on Monday, the fourth of June, 1911. It was a ghastly scene.

Farmer Fish took up a collection on our behalf, which realized the handsome sum of two shillings and one halfpenny, in coppers. He then suggested that we stand treat to himself and several of his friends in the local boozer. This meant that the two shillings were soon gone. We were very pleased to hear that Fish was prepared to let us sleep in a stall in the stable. "But first you must have supper," he said, as though he were conferring a favor upon us. He had paid us nothing for our toils in the fields, had robbed us of a hard-earned collection by a scurvy trick, and was now doing us a favor by letting us sleep in a stable, so that we should rise refreshed for the hard day's dock-pulling that faced us on the morrow. He was also inviting us to sup with his family into the bargain. A philanthropist, evidently. The supper was a horrible stodge of some kind, a sort of mixture of bran and pork, badly cooked. It tasted like chewed string, with a flavor of old boots. Farmer Fish was in high spirits and rallied us on our moody expressions and downcast appearance. "What you chaps need is a few months' work in the fields. That will soon pull you together. I've got plenty for you to do this week. You'll soon grow to like the work, I know."

"What wages were you thinking of paying us?" I asked.

"Wages?" exclaimed the jolly farmer, as if he had not thought of such a thing before that moment. "I'll tell you what I'll do. I'll give you half a crown a week each and your keep."

"That's very generous of you Mr. Fish. I hope we shall prove worthy of your trust," I said.

"I think it's really magnanimous of you to offer such a figure to inexperienced men like us, Mr. Fish," said Leo warmly. "Thank you."

The farmer gave us a sharp look, and said it was time to be getting off to roost. "Up at five in the morning, you know; don't forget."

We got out just in time to prevent me from exploding and crept into the stall that had been so kindly provided for us.

For an hour or so the "Four Favorites" lay cursing in the darkness. Just outside the stable Farmer Fish's bicycle was resting against the wall. "We ought to pinch the old hound's bike," said Leo. "He owes us that, after the work we've done." "No," I said, "it's not valuable enough to steal. But I would like to take it out into a field, dig a hole, and bury it. Justice demands some act of that kind. By God, I'll do it! I'll do it early in the morning before we leave this accursed farm."

At that moment a harsh voice broke upon our ears. "Oh you will, will you? You may think you will, but you won't. You'll clear out of here at once. Come on, you pack of impostors. Artistes from the London Hippodrome, are you? Well, get back to the London Hippodrome as quick as you like. Get to hell out of here!"

It was the voice of Fish. He had been eavesdropping, and had probably heard all we said about him. I hoped he had.

We rose from our stall to find Fish with a lantern in his hand and leading a villainous dog on a chain. Behind him was one of his sons, a leering rascal called Sam, who had sat staring at us during supper. But for the dog, we should have stayed to tell Mr. Fish our opinion of him in full, but the animal looked thoroughly vicious, and we left with as much dignity as possible, Fish taunting and slandering us as we went. He followed us down the path to the main road, accompanied by his son and dog. As soon as we touched the road, we turned and cursed him to all eternity.

"You are a scoundrel of the worst type!" I bawled. "I shall report you to the police for blacklegging, blackmailing, starving your laborers, getting money by false pretenses, and keeping a dangerous dog!"

"You dare to send that dog after us," cried Leo (Fish looked as if he were going to do so), "and we'll cut his guts out." As he spoke he produced a large knife which he had picked up somewhere the day before. Fish thought better of it and returned to his house.

Here we were at midnight, miles from any town, tired and penniless. After dragging our weary bodies along the road for a while, a farmhouse presented itself, standing a few yards from the road. A large cart of hay stood uptilted near by. Into this we proceeded to climb. Leo and I settled down to a night's rest, while one of the others, unable to find a snug enough place where he was, began to work his way farther up. In doing so he succeeded in bringing the cart down with a terrific noise and breaking one of the shafts. While we lay sprawling on the ground, a dog started barking furiously. It barked loudly enough to wake the dead. I love animals, but I could have shot that dog. There was nothing for it but to clear off, and as quickly as possible. Once more we were on the high road, with small chance of finding repose for our protesting bodies and overwrought nerves that night.

We were still walking at dawn, but it was some hours after sunrise before the grass was warm enough for us to lie down and sleep.

At midday Leo awoke and shook me out of a dreamless slumber. "Let's be off before they wake," he whispered. I climbed out of the long grass to greet the sun. Our fellow travelers—the authors of our present trouble—lay snoring a little way off. "Sleep on and take your rest," I said softly, "and may you wake to find your hearts' desire—work!"

Leo foraged for food at the farmhouses along the way and we fed well and drank too. "I wish I could ask for things as you do, Leo," I said to him. "But I can't." It was no effort to him to ask for food or money, or anything. I believe he enjoyed doing it. To me it was gall and wormwood to beg for anything, even a cigarette. Perhaps I should have learned to do it, but I was never long enough on tramp at one time to get into the way of it.

A sharp warning of the risk we ran by telling people we wanted work, in order to make it easier to get money, was forthcoming that very day. As we drew near the town of Watford, Leo tried to "touch" a man who was making his way towards the town on some business of his own. "Can't you two chaps find work?" he asked.

"No–I only wish we could," said Leo. "We have been trying for weeks. It is heart-breaking to have to do this. We would be only too willing to work at anything, if a chance offered."

"Well, I happen to know that men are being taken on at Boulters', the builders just near here. I'll show you where to go."

He took us right to Boulters' entrance. "Go to the office on your left and ask for Mr. Samuelson. Mention my name.

He will start you at once, as I happen to know that he needs laborers immediately. I'll wait here till you come out, to hear how you've got on."

Both Leo and I had got rather sunburnt through exposure to the burning rays, but we paled under our tan. "This is terrible!" I said, as we neared the office. "Let's run for it."

The man was watching us from the front entrance, so we dared not go out the way we came, without telling him the truth, and this would have been too disagreeable. The man was acting in good faith: how should he know that we did not want work? To hurt his feelings was more than either of us could bring ourselves to do. I knocked on the office door. "Can you tell me where Mr. Lovell is working?" I asked the person who answered the knock.

"Mr. Lovell? I don't know anyone by that name who works here."

"He is at work somewhere around the back, I think. He only started this morning," I said.

"You had better go round and ask for Mr. Halliwell," said the door-opener. "He'll tell you where your man is."

When we told our would-be benefactor that we had been told to go to Mr. Halliwell, he said, "That means you will be started at once." Started at once! We dodged round the back of the building and ran for it. "You must never say that again, Leo," I said as we hurried down the High Street. "Say we are on our way to join the Navy, or something like that."

"You are right," agreed Leo. "That was a close shave. I'll say in future that we are walking to some distant place to see a dying relative."

CHAPTER VIII

Round About the Marble Arch

Back in London, I resumed my speaking at the Marble Arch meeting-ground, Hyde Park, with Leo as permanent chairman. I got my room back at Charlie Lahr's, and things went on as before. Existence was always precarious, and sometimes food was scarce. It was seldom I could get a decent meal. Sometimes Leo had a stroke of luck, and sometimes I had a record collection. A beanfeast followed as a matter of course. But these celebrations did not take place very often. We had, on the whole, a thin time.

It irked me to be badly dressed, and I could not afford good clothes. As soon as I had enough money to buy a pair of boots, I found that my suit was falling to pieces: when I did manage to buy a new suit, my boots were letting water in. And so with everything. One could never get beyond poverty. There was no chance of any kind of security. But I enjoyed life in spite of these things. It detracted from my feeling of confidence to be badly dressed; it lowered me in my own esteem, and held me back from doing things. But I found satisfaction in the things of the mind. I read and studied continually, and I observed human character as I encountered it in many forms. I often argued with people at meeting-places, not because I enjoyed arguing or wished to convert any one to anything, but because it was good practice: it helped me to develop mental alacrity and verbal dexterity. And when I made a speech, I learned something, if my hearers did not. Ideas came to me on the platform that I should not have thought of had I not spoken. The physical effort of speaking stirred up the brain and caused thoughts to emerge from their hiding-places in the subconscious. I have never made a speech without learning something, so that the platform has been a kind of university to me. I taught myself, even if I could not teach others.

Although I preached revolutionary ideas, I avoided the stereotyped phraseology of the socialist ranter. I managed to give the well-worn theme of social revolt a certain freshness in statement by the avoidance of standardized shibboleths and the crude jargon of the barren-brained mouthers who infested the speaking-pitches. Because of this, I was always suspect among the "class-conscious comrades of the working-class movement." They disliked my humor, and they hated my way of living. Scratch a socialist, and you find a Calvinist. These creatures, who pretended to have emancipated themselves from "bourgeois morality," were as full of copybook ethics and chapel codes of morality as any Sunday-school teacher or local preacher. The more advanced were the worst in this respect, as they were in all other respects. The anarchists, communists, revolutionary Marxists, and extreme non-compromisers were shocked and scandalized by the fact that I would not work in a factory. These humbugs, who claimed to be out for the abolition of the wages system, were full of righteous indignation because I would not participate in that wages system they said they wanted to destroy.

It is no exaggeration to say that some of the worst types of humanity I have ever encountered were men and women who belonged to the "working-class movement." To romantic persons, who look at the movement from outside, or who are incapable of facing reality, the movement appears quite interesting; the people in it sincere, genuine, self-sacrificing, and above the average of the working-class in general intelligence. The impression is wholly false, for the truth is entirely otherwise. The average socialist is not sincere in anything; he possesses nothing more than bigotry and intolerance, which he calls sincerity. He is not the kind of person who is made for sacrifice, and is certainly not above the average in intelligence. In every quality that goes towards the making of a sane and intelligent human being, he is considerably below the average.

The modern communists, of course, are recruited from the world's intellectual and moral riff-raff, but the old socialists were not much better. I am speaking of the extremists. The moderates are of a higher moral and intellectual grade. No doubt this estimate will seem monstrous to the outside sympathizer, and wildly prejudiced to those who never look below the surface of human personality; but I know socialists and the socialist movement through and through. I can speak of them authoritatively, after years of experience.

Those who are doped by words and hypnotized by fine-sounding phrases have a horror of reality. They dare not face the truth about anything. I have always tried to look truth straight in the face, and my experience of reality has been too sharp and deep-cutting to permit me to drug myself with shallow illusions and facile generalizations. In writing of socialism and socialists I am dealing with what I know. I have no longer any reason to hide the reality of things, either from myself or from others. I spent over twenty years in the movement, and have learned to regard with deep suspicion all those who begin their correspondence with "Dear Comrade" and end with "Yours Fraternally." I have seen every form of detraction and calumny of the basest description practiced. I have seen the worst forms of hooliganism carried on by socialists, anarchists, communists and others of a like stripe and kidney. And these types are not, as sentimental fools so often maintain, a mere minority, who admittedly bring disgrace and discredit upon all great ideals. They are, and always have been, an overwhelming majority of those who profess and call themselves opponents of the capitalist system. It is utter nonsense and the most blatant hypocrisy to pretend otherwise. I challenge successful contradiction, and can furnish truck-loads of evidence to substantiate what I have written.

Although I knew all this before I had been very long in the movement, I continued to advocate the socialist ideal in my own way until long after the war. I might, and certainly should, have attached myself to some rich political party, where my gifts of speech would have been suitably acknowledged and adequately rewarded; but something held me back—love of personal freedom and intellectual liberty, a dislike of intellectual restraint and spiritual domination, a strong love of having my own way and traveling along my own path. I preferred to pick up crusts in the gutter as a free-lance rather than sit at a rich table as the well-fed servant of any political party. I was thoroughly stupid in this attitude, and I am just as stupid now as then.

I have already said that I was never very sincere about the ideas I propounded on the platform; but my insincerity was of a different kind from that of the others. I was not a bigot or a blackguard. I have never interfered with any one, no matter what views they held or expressed. I minded my own business. I refrained from evil-speaking. In that I differed from the "comrades," and it is one of the reasons why I was not respected by them. I could not descend to their level.

Here and there I met decent and intelligent people whose friendship I valued, but these were decent in spite of being socialists, not because of it—never because of it.

There is something in the theory and philosophy of socialism which appears to turn quite good people into swine. I have noted it over and over again. It is sometimes said that other movements are just as bad. It may be so, though I doubt it. It is certainly true, in almost every case, that as soon as a man takes it upon himself to preach a new political creed of human emancipation, equality, justice, and brotherhood, he begins to lose his manly qualities and ends as a pest and a rotter. Or perhaps it is because he has those potentialities in him to start with that he is attracted by these movements for human "betterment." It is a fact of common experience that the best people from the human point of view—the kindest, the most helpful, the most tolerant and the least spiteful—are those people whom the reformers and revolutionaries stigmatize scornfully as "reactionaries." What benefits mankind has received in the past have come from these "reactionaries." It would take a book of many volumes to record the cruelties and crimes of the idealists, the reformers, and the rebels against the established. Most of them, in whatever way they manifest themselves, are disturbers of the world's peace, enemies of beauty, and a deadly menace to the highest qualities in man. They reduce everything to its lowest common denominator.

Although I reacted against religion for a while—as a natural result of my Puritan upbringing—I soon discovered the hollowness and hypocrisy of atheism. I could find no intellectual sustenance in this barren creed. I found the freethinkers unable to think at all; they were merely Calvinists with a different label. Leo and I used to visit their meetings now and again. One could not fail to observe the utter intolerance of the average secularist. If God had not existed, they would certainly have invented Him in order to attack Him. The narrowness, the mental rigidity, the low bigotry of these smug blockheads were incredible. One felt the chapel atmosphere at all their gatherings. And the lack of scholarship, the haphazard and ramshackle way of handling great subjects, the literal interpretation of the Bible, their foul attacks on the most noble and beautiful sentiments of the human heart, their brutish ignorance of the arts, their poverty of intellect, absence of imagination and lack of any kind of culture—were so appalling that one could hardly believe it.

Yet my years in the revolutionary movements were not unhappy. I knew that stupidity and evil had been in the world far longer than I had, and did not delude myself with the facile belief that there would be any less as a result of my arrival in it. I was not a prig, and had no desire to be a saint. I expected to vibrate and sensate as other people do, and I asked for no sentimental considerations from other people. I certainly expected none from the "comrades," nor have I ever received any. I was poor, often destitute, a prey to hunger and cold very often. But there were many compensations. I recalled the saying of Epictetus: "The happiness we receive from ourselves is greater than that which we obtain from our surroundings." The inner constitution of my spirit was strong enough to prevent me from taking anything too seriously; I had a quick eye for the detection of humbug and a rich capacity for enjoying the absurdities of human life. What, therefore, had I to complain about? Only lack of money. And to complain about that was worse than useless.

I was born with a nature which quickly responded to beauty, but without any scrap of sentimentality. The calami-

ties of life did not move me, but sorrow in certain manifestations—the unmerited suffering of dumb beasts, the strong in
the toils of the weak and cruel, the pathos of everyday life,
the mystery and strangeness of the world, certain things in
art—these affected me profoundly. I read a great deal, but
was never a victim of book-learning.

Leo and I visited the music-halls as often as we could.
In these places we truly lived. The music-halls gave us a
reflection of life, proletarian life, its gusto and humor, its
vulgarity and rude vitality, its drama and farce. The theater
was, as it has always been, a craze with me. I should have
been an actor. Here was life, more real than the life it
portrayed. I had the gifts that would have brought me to the
front as an actor: a melodious voice of considerable range
and volume, power of facial expression, style, the capacity
to throw myself into any mood at a second's notice. But I
let it slide, as I have let so many things slide. And it does
not matter. Nothing matters. But we have to assume that
something does, so that life can be made more thrilling and
endowed with a show of significance. As Voltaire might have
said, had he thought of it, "If nothing mattered, we should
have to invent something that did."

As time went on Leo developed into a platform speaker
of considerable facility. But the humor and liveliness which
made his conversation so stimulating were not reproduced
in his speeches. These were intended to appeal to the sentimental and facile types who love to hear of human suffering
and oppression. "So long as there is one man, woman, or
child who lacks the best that civilization can provide; so long
as there is one man prepared to plunge a bayonet into the
stomach of a brother-man; so long as there is a sister of ours
who is forced to sell her body in order to live; so long as such

things are permitted in a so-called civilized country: then I say that civilization stands condemned before the bar of enlightened public opinion." This stuff wrung cheers from his listeners, and I suppose that is why he turned it out.

"You certainly give them bucketfuls of the tripe, Leo," I said to him at the end of one of these diatribes. "It is rather awful to have to stand by while you are a-sobbing and a-sighing. Do you think it is really necessary for you to do it?"

"It is–for me. It suits my personality. Look!" He brought a half-sovereign out of his pocket. "A dear old lady pressed that into my hand as I left the platform. She was all worked up over what I had been saying. She really ought to have made it a quid—she enjoyed herself so much."

The jargon of the "rebels" was the same then as it is today. There were always "thousands starving;" the workers were always being "batoned down;" there were always hundreds and sometimes thousands of our "heroic comrades" either being "mown down" or else "rotting in jail." Capitalism was, of course, collapsing rapidly. H. M. Hyndman, the Polonius of Social Democracy, had a lecture which never failed to arouse fervid enthusiasm among his listeners. It was called "In the Rapids of Revolution." Hyndman's speeches were always interesting. He spoke with eloquence and force, and was fond of reminding his hearers that he was a person of importance, who mixed with the great as a matter of course.

"As I gaze round this hall to-night," he would say, as he rose to address a meeting, "my mind travels back to a similar gathering held in this building in the early eighties. I remember that upon that occasion there sat by my side my old friend and comrade Karl Marx, whose ideas I made more easily understandable to the great English working-class.

There was also present my old friend Jack Williams, whose speeches I often wrote for him in those early days" (this was a sop to the proletariat—Jack Williams was a working-man and of no account intellectually). "I remember, too, my old friend Clemenceau, who listened eagerly to my speech that evening. And I remember, if my memory serves me right, my old comrade William Liebknecht," and so on. Mr. Hyndman never failed to bring in the name of some one like George Meredith or Lord Beaconsfield, giving the audience to understand that he was on terms of the closest intimacy with these famous ones. And he was.

George Lansbury was active at that time. His speeches were the same as he gives now: a plea from the heart for the abolition of capitalism and the building of a better society for all. I always found him a good-hearted and genuine man, free from any kind of affectation. As he stood for kindness to every one and the principle of fraternity among all sections of the Labor and socialist movement, he was continually denounced by the "scientific" socialists and the "class-conscious" revolutionaries as a twister and a traitor. Hyndman was suspect, too, as he was a member of the bourgeoisie, but he was fairly popular on the whole, as he never had much good to say of any one; or, if he had, there was always a sting in the tail.

Keir Hardie was at the head of the Labor Party in the House of Commons, and a rare bore he was. His brand of socialism was a queer mixture of Trades-Unionism, Fabianism, Collectivism and Primitive Christianity. "I take my socialism from the 'Sermon on the Mount,'" he used to say. This sort of political-cum-religious haggis has always been very popular with a large number of people in England. It sounds well and may mean anything or nothing. Fortunately, it means nothing.

During the year 1913 there was a big strike in Dublin in which Jim Larkin flashed into the limelight as the champion of the docker. I attended the first meeting he addressed in London. It was held in the Holborn Hall with Ben Tillett in the chair. Larkin's appearance on the platform—he arrived late—aroused extraordinary enthusiasm. He spoke with a rough eloquence which made a profound impression. He was a man of overpowering personality; grim, virile, and passionate, and embodied in his person the struggle of the laboring-class for life and freedom. He was tall, manly, and handsome, with fine features and dark hair streaked with gray. His eyes and mouth were of a man of great sensibility and great personal power. In all his speeches–which were often too long, a common fault with men who care more for the thing said than the way of saying it—there were passages of true eloquence and poetry. Larkin struck me as a man of fine character and immense courage. There was a strain of poetry and nobility in him. He was difficult, almost impossible, to get on with; he would brook no opposition, and felt, perhaps too deeply, the wounds of life. A lovable character, and a giant among little men with little minds and little ideas, his career has been a kind of tragedy.

There was a loud outcry when Larkin refused to speak at Grimsby because the chairman was a man who had figured in the divorce-court. The freethinkers foamed at the mouth and all the toleration-mongers and other touts were scandalized almost to death, but Larkin was implacable. I admired him tremendously for his attitude in the matter, especially as he refused to discuss it with any one outside Ireland.

A group was formed at that time of which I became a member. There were about twelve of us, and we talked as if the revolution was actually at hand. This group was the British section of the American organization, "The Industrial Workers of the World." It seemed to me that this was as healthy a bunch of lads as I had struck so far. Their object was to overthrow the capitalist system by the organized might of the revolutionary working-class, united into one great world-wide Industrial Union. I was with them for about a year. They appointed me "National Propagandist" for a while, at a salary of a pound a week, but the salary was seldom forthcoming, as our funds were obtained through collections taken at outdoor meetings. The meetings were addressed by myself and an American named Swasey. He had been sent over from Detroit to show us how to achieve the revolution in Great Britain. He was a good speaker, with a racy style and a sprightly personality; and he beat me at taking collections and selling literature. I did not like this, but I had to admit that when it came to separating the crowds from their cash, he had the better of me. It was a fine day for me when I became as efficient as he was at collection-time.

Swasey was arrested once, at Leeds, for inciting the unemployed to steal. "There are dummies in a shop-window in Briggate wearing good clothes—warm overcoats, thick boots. Yet you stand shivering in rags!" he told a meeting of unemployed. He was taken before the magistrate, who remarked as soon as Swasey appeared in the dock, "Anybody can see you're guilty," and fined him—after a trial lasting less than five minutes—the sum of thirty shillings. We in London had the utmost difficulty in raising the money to pay the fine. Yet we had no doubt about our ability to overturn the capitalist system.

I was arrested myself about this period. My language was often extremely violent; but in order to find some way of laying me by the heels the police were obliged to employ a trick and to commit perjury in a wholehearted manner. It was largely my own fault for getting on the wrong side of them, but I had a great deal to learn then. Like many others, I did not know the strength of things, and I believed—until the folly of such a belief was driven into me by many experiences—that if I got into trouble other socialists would forget any differences of a sectarian nature and stand by me against the common enemy. Although I was not "sincere" in their sense, that is to say I was not solemn or orthodox in my terminology or in my way of life, I handed out the revolutionary dope as well as any of them and better than most. And I had at least gone to prison for my "principles;" neither had I ever sold out to the other side, nor betrayed the cause. I imagined that this would be counted unto me for righteousness. I had much to learn.

The Hyde Park police had decided to put me "where they could find me." The blow fell one afternoon as I was addressing a meeting. I had a heckler in the crowd—a rare thing for me. He became a thorough nuisance. The crowd were hostile to him, and told him several times to shut up or clear off. "Perhaps the gentleman has had a drop of drink!" I suggested. As he was a well-known temperance advocate, this observation raised a laugh. I was immediately arrested. The crowd followed to the door of the Hyde Park police-station but no farther—a habit of crowds. I was charged with using "language likely to cause a breach of the peace," and bail was refused.

When the case came on next morning, the police swore that my language had been most provocative, the crowd thoroughly resentful, and the situation so threatening that I had to be arrested for my own protection. I denied this, of course, but, as I had no witnesses, the case went against me. The magistrate gave a short lecture on the enormity of the offense and bound me over in the sum of five pounds to be of good behavior for twelve months or go to prison for twenty-one days. I could not find a surety, so I had to serve the time.

At all my meetings after this I made a big noise about the police perjurers. The police very naturally lay in wait for another opportunity, and a few weeks later, when a similar incident occurred, I was arrested again. The police took the same line as previously—there was hardly a word of truth in anything they said. The magistrate fined me forty shillings or a month's imprisonment. As I had no money and no one came forward to help me with the fine, I went to prison for a month.

I could have left London after this and returned to Manchester for a while—my mother had written asking me to do so—but I was determined to stay and fight the police. I denounced them in vehement terms at all my meetings and was arrested again. The same charge was brought forward, and, as in the previous cases, no bail was allowed. Everything possible was done to make it appear that I was a dangerous character. This time the police had made everything up out of their own heads. I felt that the thing was getting past a joke, and asked for a remand so that I could collect witnesses and secure legal assistance. The police opposed this, but the magistrate agreed to the case being held over for a week. I was released on condition that I found a surety in the sum of ten pounds. I had some difficulty about this, as I did not know any one who would stand surety for me. The police gave me no assistance. Fortunately a man who had heard me speak happened to be in court and came forward as surety. It was a lucky accident, otherwise I should have had to spend the week in prison, which would have prevented me from getting witnesses together, or doing anything else.

In the course of the week I secured thirteen witnesses. Quite by accident, I was also able to get a counsel for the defense. A society then in existence called the "Free Speech Defence Committee" supplied me with a lawyer, Mr. du Parcq, now Mr. Justice du Parcq, to conduct the defense. It was beginning to dawn upon one or two persons that there was something queer going on. The case was reported in the Press. People who read of my insulting language and the hostile crowds from whom I had to be rescued by the police could not make it out. Every one who knew me as a speaker knew that there was never disorder of any kind at my meetings.

As a consequence of the publicity which had been given to the case, the court was crowded when my case came on a week later. This, together with the presence of a counsel and such a host of witnesses, threw the police into confusion and dismay. They had hitherto looked upon me as a person of no account; poor, unfriended, and unattached to any important political party. In consequence, they became as obsequious as they had before been contemptuous, and looked extremely perturbed and self-conscious. The two constables gave evidence in the same words, almost the same intonations. The first constable, a man of about fifty years of age and very stupid, swore that my meeting had been disorderly. He stated that the disorder was caused by the nature of my language, which was insulting and offensive to the majority of my hearers. He claimed that I had been arrested for my own protection, as the incensed crowd was on the point of throwing me upon the Park railings, so stung were they at my aspersions upon God and Government, King and Empire. He said I had stated that all kings and queens, from the time of Cromwell, had been rogues, thieves, liars and fornicators.

He said that I had described the Kaiser as a criminal lunatic who ought to be in a mental home. His last statement was correct. I had said that the Kaiser was not "all there."

The esteemed magistrate took a grave and serious view of the case. He looked graver and graver as the second constable corroborated what his comrade had said. Mr. du Parcq had no difficulty in shattering this farrago of rubbish with a few well-aimed questions. "Is Mr. Thompson an ignorant man?" he asked the first constable. "No," was the grudging reply. "Is he likely to know who were the kings and queens of England?" "Yes." "Then why should he describe Cromwell as a king?" No answer. "Was Cromwell a king?" "I don't know, sir." "The officer is not an historian," interposed the magistrate sharply. "Get on with the case."

I then entered the witness-box and took the oath. The constable was asked by the magistrate if he had any questions to put to me. "Yes," said the officer. "Is it not a fact that you have been convicted of a similar offense twice in this court before?" Mr. du Parcq protested against this highly improper question being asked. "The constable cannot be expected to know the law on a matter like that," said the magistrate impatiently. "We are wasting time. Do get on." "Did you mention Cromwell in the course of your speech?" asked the magistrate. "I made no reference whatever to Cromwell," I answered. "But both the officers say you did." "Both the officers are stating what is not a fact." "Be careful, for goodness' sake," exclaimed the magistrate. "There is such a thing as perjury, you know." "I am fully aware of that," I said, looking significantly at the two constables. "Did you say that the German Emperor was a criminal lunatic?" asked the magistrate. "I did, and most of the audience seemed to agree with me. No one objected." "You admit to calling the

German Emperor a lunatic?" asked the magistrate. "Yes, the statement was made on good authority. The audience were in agreement. There was no disorder of any kind, except that caused by the police when they arrested me." "Remember what I told you about perjury, and be careful what you say," was His Worship's comment on this.

After calling five witnesses, my counsel intimated that he did not think it necessary to call any more, as the case against me was an obvious distortion and mishandling of the facts. This, he went on to say in an excellent speech, had been clearly shown in the evidence. He submitted that the case against me had entirely broken down.

"There is no difficulty about this case," began the magistrate. "It is perfectly clear to me that your language was grossly insulting, that the meeting was thoroughly out of hand, and that but for the timely action of the police you would have been in serious danger of physical injury. I have listened to the evidence for the defense and find it entirely unconvincing. Against it we have the evidence of two trustworthy constables, one of whom has been attached to this court for upwards of fourteen years. I believe the evidence of the police. The case against you is well proven. This sort of thing has got to stop. You will pay a fine of forty shillings and five shillings costs."

Mr. du Parcq was astonished when he found the constables' discredited evidence calmly accepted by the learned magistrate. I cannot say that the magistrate's decision was any other than what I fully anticipated. His ways are not our ways.

I was interested to note how the magistrate seemed to enjoy his work. It is love of his work, I think, which keeps him young and renders him proof against the attacks of time.

My fine was raised outside the court by a large crowd of sympathizers, who had at last awakened to the facts of the situation. Mr. Baker, of Baker, Baker & Company, who had been present in court, was so sympathetic that he auctioned his walking-stick for fifteen shillings among the crowd and put it towards my fine. A clergyman gave ten shillings. The rest was easily raised. A cheer went up as I reached the street. Many strangers shook me warmly by the hand. Every one was certain that I could not have used the language attributed to me by the police. It was so silly. I certainly did not use any such words and expressions as I was accused of. But when I thought of the three framed-up charges that had been brought against me, and the wholesale lying of the police on each occasion, I used language–in the tea-shop with Leo and Smith–which would, had the magistrate heard it, have assured my committal on a charge of blasphemy.

From that day onwards the police left me entirely alone; many of them, indeed, became quite friendly. The two constables were not seen again near the meeting-ground. I was told afterwards that some disciplinary measure was taken against them, but whether this was so or not I cannot tell. Against the force as a whole I have no complaint to make. Many of these fine upstanding men are among my most interested listeners.

NOTE: Many readers will find the account of the court proceedings incredible. Everything is exactly as described. Whether the court records have been preserved or not I cannot say, but the clerk was scribbling as usual while the witnesses were giving evidence, and appeared to be taking careful notes of all that was said. The magistrate's name is not given for reasons which will be obvious, but what he said was so vividly stamped upon my mind that I recall his words and expressions quite clearly. I do not contend that the matter is of the slightest real importance, but it is, I think, sufficiently interesting to be set down. I could relate many incidents of a far stranger nature, but there are so many interests involved, and so many innocents abroad who would imagine that I was exaggerating, that I have decided to leave them—for the time being at any rate—unrecorded. Fact is so often so much more incredible than fiction that one hesitates to put it down in a work of this nature. If I mention that I was nearly lynched by an angry crowd in Piccadilly in 1911 because I neglected to remove my hat as the Kaiser drove past, it will hardly be believed. Yet this happened, and was the cause of my allusion to that monarch Kaiser as a criminal lunatic. I spoke too soon.]

LEO made more money than I did, not in collections, but by exploiting the well-to-do sentimentalists and social uplifters who clustered round the humanitarian platforms. All these people—suffragettes, anti-vivisectionists, divorce-reformers, pacifists and other bores—were extremely useful, though it must have been horribly tedious to listen to their chattering and prattling about the rights of this and the wrongs of that. I could not stand it, and missed many chances because I could not suffer fools gladly. Leo was made of sterner stuff, and could simulate a keen interest in the most absurd ideas if there was anything to be gained by it. I envied him and wished I had been made differently, but I suffered agonies as it was from the chatterers and babblers who insisted upon entering into conversation with me at the end of my meetings and at other inconvenient times. Over and over again I declined invitations to join these persons at tea, even though I could have done with a meal, because I knew the tea was only a bribe. They wanted to make me the victim of their stupid conversation, to unload their views of the political situation, the future of mankind, the non-existence of God, or the need for a revolution, or something equally ghastly. I vowed to myself that, if a time ever came when I could afford it, I would engage a bodyguard and no one would be allowed to approach me unless they came with money in their hands. It never seemed to enter the heads of these bores that I had to work hard enough, tearing my voice and nerves to pieces on the platform, without having to listen to their chatter afterwards. It was, is, and always will be, as long as I have to lecture under such conditions, a problem more important to me than any other—how to avoid the bore.

One day, as I was settling down to the study of Mr. Hilaire Belloc's splendid story *The Girondin*, which I had picked up from a shelf outside a bookshop in Charing Cross Road, I was interrupted by a voice saying, "Hello, comrade" (I loathed the word even then, how I abhor it now!) "I hear you have gone over to the Conservative Party." "Is that so?" I said, without looking up from Mr. Belloc's absorbing story. "Oh yes," said the voice. "You have sold out all right. A man I know saw you standing outside their offices one day last week." "Thanks for the information," I said. "Good-by." I began to meditate later upon the system of reasoning which concludes that one has joined a certain political party because one is seen outside the offices of that party. I ought to take up my stand, I reflected, outside the House of Commons or Westminster Cathedral, or, better still, outside Buckingham Palace. The word would soon go round that I was an M.P., a cardinal, or a member of the Royal Family. It would not do, though, I could clearly see, to be observed standing outside a prison, a lunatic asylum, or a cemetery.

The person who made that remark is a representative type of the kind of vicious half-wit who makes up the rank and file of all communist and revolutionary parties in this country. It has been argued that other countries produce a better type of rebel. The facts, however, do not square with this contention. All that I have encountered, and I have met some pretty specimens in my time, are of the same brutish and boneheaded breed. There is only one sight more pleasing to me than that of a dead communist, and that is the sight of two dead communists.

CHAPTER IX

Land of Our Fathers

THERE has never been a central hall or any kind of general meeting-place in London where revolutionaries could forgather under pleasant conditions. They met in little holes and corners in certain districts, but these places were neither central, easily accessible, nor well known. One place where a number of us used to meet and talk together was a café at the back of the Shaftesbury Theater. There was a sandwich-bar with a long form to sit on, and a hall downstairs for meetings. This place was a rendezvous for rebels and revolters of the more extreme kind. It was a sanctuary for syndicalists and single-taxers; one could have a snack with a secularist or an assignation with an anarchist.

One Sunday morning just before the war, having roused the proletariat at Jack Straw's Castle, and the collection being sufficient, I took a bus from Hampstead and alighted near the café. I noticed upon entering that a stranger was present—a queer-looking individual dressed in a queer style and speaking in a queer way about the simple life. He stood in the center of a group of eager world-builders, expounding the beauties of the natural life, urging his hearers to throw off the trammels of the town and return to the simplicity of rusticity. We were wasting away in the city, he insisted—rotting and withering on the stalk. Back to the land, to the bosom of the earth, our mother and our nurse. This was the burden of his tale, as he stood with hand upraised and whiskers swaying in the breeze from the electric fan.

He was a tall man, wearing a dark-gray suit, white scarf, a long raincoat reaching to his feet, and a cloth cap with flaps covering his ears. His face was half hidden by a large tawny-colored beard, shot with red in the glow of the February sun. His eyes were hazel-colored, large, and melting like a ruminant's, and with too much white in them. He spoke in a low, rumbling voice, with a kind of evangelical earnestness and solemnity. A freak, I concluded.

There were plenty of that kind in the labor and socialist movement; simple-lifers, fresh-air cranks, banana-biters, nut-eaters, milk-drinkers, male suffragettes, free-lovers, dress-reformers (who wore the ugliest kind of clothing), anti-God fanatics—all sorts of intellectual, moral, and political fungi. Red-Beard was one of the many pieces of intellectual flotsam and jetsam which flowed past us from time to time. I was not anxious to hear much from him about the simple life. Nature I loved, and next to nature art; but persons of this sort were neither natural nor artistic. I noted, however, that Leo was listening to him with apparent appreciation. (He intends to "touch" him for what he can, I thought. That is good, but there is small chance of even Leo extracting money from a man who loves humanity as much as Red-Beard says he does.) "It is the duty of every one of us to do what he can to ease the burden which rests so heavily on the shoulders of suffering humanity," he was saying. That sort of talk is a sure sign that the fellow is an arrant humbug, I thought; but Leo was nodding and smiling in approval.

When Red-Beard left the café, Leo followed close on his heels. Half an hour later, while I was drinking my well-known cup of tea, he came skipping in with an offer to pay for tea and sandwiches all round. As there were a dozen of us hanging round the corner or sitting on the form, I knew he had been successful in his mission. He had fastened on Red-Beard like a leech and sucked ten shillings out of him.

"Come on, Bonar," he said. "Let's go mad." We whipped up three other boys and gorged ourselves to surfeiting on steak-and-chips at the offices of that powerful organization, the S. P. & O. (sausage, potatoes and onions). After which we went into conference. There were five of us, and, as it transpired, we were about to start upon a great adventure, the issue of which none of us could foresee, else we might have paused—or we might not, I cannot say.

First of all there was Leo, the king of tramps, young, good-looking, daring to the extent of foolhardiness, resourceful in all emergencies, ready-tongued, plausible, pulsating with nervous energy: the juvenile lead of our strangely assorted company. Next in rank came John Ramage, Scotch, level-headed, calm, hardy, well educated, and of irreproachable character: a tower of strength on any expedition of honorable and dangerous enterprise. Then there was Jack Smith, diminutive, unstable, quarrelsome, a mixture of the merry and the melancholy, stimulating in conversation, full of fantastic and preposterous wit, and with a brain like quicksilver: he was a good companion and helped to make existence tolerable in good times and bad. There was Fred, a raw fellow, lacking in intellectual attainments and knowledge of the world, but physically strong, and useful in a fight. Last of all, myself, of whom the reader has already heard.

It appeared that the bearded land-reformer had money–so much Leo had already discovered. He was willing to finance a party of willing workers who were prepared to make the experiment of living on the land by their own exertions. He was mad on this land question. It was Leo's suggestion that we should take advantage of his land-mania and turn it to our account. We agreed. Leo saw the bearded one again, and, simulating a keen interest in land reform, invited the old boy to call a meeting in the hall below the café bar.

The meeting came off a few nights later and a weird affair it was. Red-Beard took the platform, while we sat on chairs near the front, to hear him expound his scheme. There was a large tract of land, he explained—over two thousand acres in extent—going begging. This land was in Wales, not far from the town of Carmarthen. It was arable, fertile, and capable of sustaining the five of us and as many more as we cared to bring with us. It was free land; belonged to nobody; and was outside the jurisdiction of any government or any court. Only the King of England could lay claim to it, and not even he until a conference had been held at The Hague. The first person to claim it had it for good. By the act of claiming it he had established his right of possession. That right none could dispute. It was a case of first come, first served.

"There is a house standing on the land," said Red-Beard. "That house is yours, as soon as you effect an entry. Should any one try to evict you, don't hesitate to shoot, and shoot to kill. No law can touch you, because you are extra-territorial. Should a policeman come with a warrant for your eviction, you should shoot him dead, and don't bother to bury him—let him lie until he rots or the birds have picked his flesh away. Your feet are on your native heath. No matter who you are or what you do, none can call your power to account."

This, we thought, is the finest idea the world has ever known. It is better than socialism. It is the best kind of anarchism. We are made for life. And yet—there must be a catch in it somewhere. Who was this man? Were his intentions wicked or charitable? Brought he airs from heaven or blasts from hell? He came, too, in such a questionable shape. The curious clothes, the queer-looking eyes, the beard, and this rigmarole! We feared some foul play, yet hoped there might be some basis of truth in his story.

Assuming a sincere interest in his talk, we asked questions. Was there any one living on the land, or was it derelict, waiting for spade and plow? Yes, there was some one living in the house—a woman. "A young woman?" asked Leo, the pre-war Don Juan. "No," said Red-Beard, "an elderly woman." "Oh, to hell! A bogy in the hedge," some one murmured. "No, no," said Red-Beard, "she will give no trouble. She is insane, quite insane," he went on, "and her distemper takes a curious form: she imagines, poor weak-minded creature, that the land belongs to her." Ha, ha, can you beat that? We roared with laughter. The land belonged to her, the silly, demented thing! What next? That was a joke, that was! Well, well, well. "Why don't they take her away?" we asked. "Surely it was not safe to have a maniac like that living there by herself?" "Oh, no," said Red-Beard, "she's harmless enough: just ignore her; she won't give any trouble when she sees that there are five of you and that you mean business."

"There is everything you need on the farm," he went on to say. The farm! So it was a farm. "And there is plenty of livestock," he said. "What sort of livestock?" asked Smith. "Oh, there are cows, sheep, horses, a bullock or two, pigs, hens and chickens, geese and turkeys, and a couple of Welsh goats. Should you find yourselves short of anything, the neighboring farmers will help you."

Red-Beard, we found, was a great stickler for legal forms. He read a number of letters that seemingly had been rolled in the mud and then dried, which gave them an appearance of age. These were communications from himself to the King, in which he quoted liberally from law-books and historical documents dealing with the holding of land under the Crown. He read from these at great length until we fain would have thrown something at him. His Majesty's replies to these missives were left unread. He did not have time for those.

Having cleared the issue from all dubiety and ambiguity by the reading of these State papers, he then asked us to append our signatures to a long roll, upon which a number of red seals were affixed. We complied with the request and signed names—not necessarily our own names, but we signed names. He then borrowed a match from Ramage, and, setting fire to the roll, watched it burn to ashes. "And now, gentlemen," said he, "those names are of the past; they do not belong to you or to any one now; they have gone up in smoke. Your name from this time forward is Baron Edmunds. Henceforth you take on the personality and identity of Baron Edmunds. You are all Baron Edmunds. You can arrange the numerical order amongst yourselves. You can call yourselves Baron the first, second, third, fourth, and fifth, as you may decide. You are Baron Edmunds now, gentlemen, and as Baron Edmunds you will take possession of the house and farm." He then bade us good night and promised to see us next day, to make final arrangements for our journey to Wales.

As soon as Red-Beard had gone, we called ourselves together in conference to review the situation. Ramage suspected a trap of some kind; Fred was certain the old man was pulling our legs. "No," I said, "that man is not the sort that plays practical jokes; he is not intelligent enough, he is a crank." "Yes," broke in Leo, "but he is a crank with money. He is a gift from heaven. We must exploit him. Leave him to me and I will drain him dry as hay." "But can't we separate him from some of his wealth without all this trapesing about the country?" said Smith. "We can't go to Wales, even to acquire land—the thing is impossible. Let some one bring the land to us, while we remain here in touch with civilization." "Yes," said Fred, "it's money we want, not land. Who wants land?" "Let us take possession of our estates, gentlemen," I suggested. "We need not stop on the farm once we have established our claim in person. We can rent it out or sell it for a large sum." We debated the matter for some time, and ultimately agreed to adjourn the sitting until the morrow, when we should have gained further information about Red-Beard's financial resources and his readiness, or otherwise, to part with the "necessary."

The first thing that Red-Beard proposed on his appearance next morning was that, as the house might not be large enough to accommodate all of us, a tent should be purchased and sent on to the railway-station nearest the farm, there to await our coming. Red-Beard and Leo went down to Houndsditch and bought a tent, which was immediately dispatched to the station at a place called Nantgaredig, a couple of miles from our prospective demesne. Baron Edmunds was to follow immediately. The tent cost Red-Beard thirty shillings, and Leo touched him for twenty, so that all our fears were set at rest on the question of supplies. We consulted briefly in a doorway and agreed to set out at once.

On a cold Saturday morning at the beginning of March of the year 1914, therefore, five young men might have been seen talking together on the platform at Paddington Station. We were loaded with brown-paper parcels containing books, boots, collars, and other impedimenta. In the shabby parcels were all our worldly possessions. We were saying good-by to London and to city life for a long time—at least, so we believed. We had worked ourselves into this frame of mind

by constant brooding on the drawbacks of our miserable city life and the free future that was opening out before us. We were landowners in our own right, and rich landowners; or soon would be.

Red-Beard arrived to bid us *bon voyage*. To each of us he bequeathed the sum of thirty shillings, a sum sufficient to pay our fare to Carmarthen and a little over. Before the train left we asked him to tell us his name. "You will learn my name later," he said with a wintry smile, "but not now. You must not expect me to send you any money, and nothing will be sent to you unless you ask for it to be sent direct to the house on the farm. You will easily be able to sustain yourselves by your own exertions as land-cultivators, and in the course of time you will become expert farmers and your fortunes will flourish like the green bay tree. Write and tell me how you fare, but do not ask me for money. It will not be sent." He gave us an address in Red Lion Street, Clerkenwell, which would always find him, he said, and after shaking us all by the hand, wished us good-by and good luck.

After a long and hilarious journey, with many changes and flying visits to the beer-shops—for we had cast dull care aside—the expedition touched port at the ancient and sleepy old town of Carmarthen. We spent the night at an inn and rose next morning in high fettle. As no trains were running, the day being Sunday, we decided to walk to the farm, a distance of fifteen Welsh miles. Now Red-Beard had been very insistent upon one thing—we must not divulge our purpose to a living soul, we were to keep our own counsel, and on no account were we to inquire the way to the farm. He had drawn out a chart or plan of the spot, containing explicit instructions and directions how to find the way. We were to look out for a forest, a shop kept by a man named Jones, and a chapel with a red-brick roof. We tramped along the road on that quiet Sabbath day, care-free and merry, full of life and hope and the wild irresponsibility of youth; singing I.W.W. songs and waking the echoes and the villagers as we passed.

It was nearing six o'clock when we reached the shop, the chapel, and the forest, and took the path as Red-Beard had directed. As we made our way through the thick wood, it became more and more evident that we were losing our way. Something was wrong with the plan, or we had read it amiss. There was not a soul to be seen, no sound but that of our own voices, which we lowered unconsciously as the light faded. The atmosphere was eerie, strange, and boding. As we pursued our way one thought was in our minds: how much better it would be if we turned back and made the journey in daylight. But no one liked to speak his fears or admit defeat. Smith was beginning to exhibit signs of distress, Fred was complaining of foot trouble; but Leo and Ramage were pushing on ahead, and, as we were in mortal terror of losing them, we quickened our weary steps and plodded on through the gloaming.

And then we saw a man, a little man with a black beard and a Bible under his arm. He was evidently on his way to the chapel. Should we ask him the way to "Hillside?"–for that was the name of the house, so Red-Beard had instructed us. A hurried consultation was held. We decided to cast discretion to the night-winds and inquire of the stranger if we were on the right way to the house. We swept down upon him, and Ramage put the fatal question. The chapel-goer regarded us with obvious suspicion. "Yes," he answered, "you are indeed on the way; keep straight on, look you, until..." He gave complicated directions. We thanked him and resumed the journey, leaving him standing gazing after us with a curious and cynical expression on the part of his face upon which hair had not encroached.

On and on we trudged, and the house seemed farther off than ever. By this time I had lost all sense of reality. My Celtic imagination had peopled the forest with fearsome forms. The silence, broken only by the pad of our feet upon the ferny ground, the dreary murmur of the wind through the trees and along the grass, and the sense of isolation from civilized humanity, filled me with loneliness and dread. I have always been afraid of the dark, but this was the very heart of darkness, of night and the creeping terrors that infest the soul of my race.

At length I could no more. "We will proceed," I said aloud, "no further in this business." My voice awoke mocking echoes that seemed to extend for miles. The Shakespearean phrase, so awe-inspiring in its original relation, rang jeeringly across the hills. My companions did not answer. An uncanny silence had fallen upon us, and though there were five young, sophisticated, modern men there together, each man felt alone. The whole atmosphere of the place was sinister, alien, and charged with menace.

Then the moon came out and the darkness was cut into strips of black and white. Our senses began to clear, and Ramage, who had felt the horror no less than I, was the first to throw it off. "That looks as if it might be our house," he said, his voice quite normal, as he pointed to a large building set in a hollow. We pressed forward, our confidence returning with the sight of a home and smoke ascending from the chimney. We had a feeling that this was the house. Creeping quietly towards it, we reached the door and knocked. There was no answer. We knocked again. No answer. Again. No answer. We tried the door. It was locked. We looked through the window. There was no sign of life: yet smoke was coming from the chimney, there were clothes on the line outside, and a cat was seated on the window-sill. "Let us break down the door," said Ramage. "After all, it is *our* house." "No, lift the window," suggested Leo. "Let's see if there is any one inside; perhaps the madwoman is afraid—we must set her mind at rest." The window was raised while each in succession had a peep into the room. There was a kettle simmering on the hob, a table laid for one; there were books in the bookcase near the fireplace, as Red-Beard had told us there would be—but no signs of the madwoman.

This was the house, then. But would it be wise to force an entry? After all, we were not quite certain. Supposing we had been misled by Red-Beard? To make our way into a strange house without being sure beyond doubt that the house was really ours was to court trouble—serious trouble. What could we say if charged with breaking and entering? We had visions of penal servitude. At least I had, and Smith

and Leo. But Ramage had worked himself into the belief
that the place was ours by right, and cursed heartily at the
door being locked. So had Fred. "Open," he called, "in the
name of Baron Edmunds!" Despite our scruples the idea
appealed to us. "Open!" I shouted. "Baron Edmunds is here.
It is himself in person. Open!" There was no response.

We retired for a space and began to explore every avenue,
in the hope of finding some one who could confirm our belief
that the house was the one we were seeking. But we found
no one. Although it could not have been later than eight
o'clock in the evening, there was no sign of life anywhere
in the vicinity except the cat and the smoking chimney.
The moon sank and our hearts sank with it. All our fears
came back again, and Leo, who was half French and highly
strung, began laughing and joking to ward off his gathering
terror. Smith stood beside me trembling a little, rolling a
cigarette with shaking fingers; Fred suffered less, though
even his mind was troubled by the peculiar atmosphere of
the place and his tough nerves were shaken by a feeling
he could not escape. Ramage had grown more angry, and
cursed frequently—his way of showing how much he felt the
pressure of the mysterious unseen. I felt like choking, and
the company of my companions gave me no comfort.

How long we stood about there I do not know, but we were
brought to a sense of sanity and reality by the sound of feet
tramping up the narrow road towards the house. Voices smote
the night—human voices. Our fears fell from us at once and
we walked forward to greet the strangers. Heavens! There
were thousands of them, or so it seemed at first; actually
there were about a dozen: dark, dour, dangerous-looking
Welshmen. They came at us with curses and loud cries.
Smith and I retreated. Leo climbed a tree. Not so Ramage

and Fred: strong, hefty men, a fight was just what they needed to restore their fretted nerves to normal.

"Come on, boys," cried the hardy Scot. "let us charge them"; and Fred and he dashed forward to the fray. "Right!" called Leo, descending from his tree. "Charge into them. Down with Wales!" Smith and I rallied to the call, and shouting, "Three cheers for Ireland, France, and Caradoc Evans!" sprang madly at the perfidious aborigines. We swayed to and fro for some minutes, hitting, biting, and cursing, until a voice shouted, "Stop!" A tall Welshman who appeared to be the ringleader of the gang commanded cessation of hostilities and suggested parley. "What the hell do you chaps want here, at this time of night?" he demanded. "You have frightened the woman of the house out of her wits. She came to us for protection, and we're here to see that she has it. If you can't explain your presence here, we'll beat the lot of you to a jelly."

Leo, whose volubility and personal charm have got us out of many a warm corner, explained the position briefly, supplemented by confirming evidence from Ramage.

"We should have gone on fighting," remarked Ramage to us in French. "We had them on the defensive. Why the devil did you stop like that?"—but he continued, for our sakes, to discuss terms of peace. He was a bitterly disappointed man, though, and has never ceased to regret our failure to prosecute the struggle to a conclusion.

"Who sent you down here?" demanded the gang leader. Leo gave him a description of Red-Beard. "I thought so," said the chief of the tribe. He then told us something about Red-Beard which threw a great light on the situation.

It appeared that Red-Beard's name was Edmunds, and he was a bit of a lunatic. He had been separated from his wife for some years, and had been ordered by the courts to pay her two pounds a week maintenance money. Instead of making any payments, however, he had made the poor woman's life a hell by every kind of petty annoyance and persecution. He had sent her threatening letters, and had on several occasions sent parties of men to the farm on the same fool's errand as he had sent us. The Welshman told us that a few days before she had received a letter informing her that a body of men were arriving at the house armed with revolvers. The unfortunate woman had not liked to apply for police protection, so the neighboring farmers had formed themselves into a Vigilance Society, keeping a look-out for just such people as ourselves. Hence the presence of the gang.

We thanked him, apologized for the trouble we had caused, and upon giving our word that we were returning to the nearest village at once, and that he should see no more of us, he called off his men, and with good feeling on both sides we bade each other good night.

It took us nearly two hours' heavy tramping back through the forest, during which Smith—who was a town-bird and unused to such jaunts—fell into streams, cut himself on sharp stones, got stung by nettles, and developed sore throat. It was close on eleven o'clock when we emerged upon the village green at Brecfa, tired, hungry, unstrung with the odd adventure through which we had passed. A group of the local lads was gathered on the green, watching us out of the corner of their eyes. No doubt they had learned all about the invaders from London and were having a laugh at our expense. We were not the first they had seen on the same mission! We may not have been the last.

We spent the night at the village pub. Next morning we were up early, and after doing ourselves handsomely at the egg-and-bacon struggle, set out for Nantgaredig, where the tent was waiting for us. We erected it in a field adjoining the station. As our money was running short and we were nearly two hundred miles from London, we were faced with the problem of getting back as quickly and cheaply as might be. First we decided to obtain, if possible, some money from Red-Beard, or Edmunds. A telegram was dispatched from the post-office as follows:

IN POSSESSION OF HOUSE NEIGHBORS HOSTILE
MONEY RAN SHORT PLEASE SEND
£5 IMMEDIATELY

We decided to allow two days for a reply. If nothing came by that time, we should have to be off. The day was spent in the taproom of the local pub, where we talked and played darts with the patrons.

As the weather was extremely cold, we took some coal from the wagons which stood at the siding, discovered an old pail, in which we lit a fire, and placing it in the center of the tent, closed the flap and settled down to seek repose. We soon fell asleep, but were awakened later by sulphur fumes from the slate-coal which nearly choked us. We were forced to open the flap of the tent to allow the fumes to escape. They did, and were replaced by the sharp, biting March air, which froze us to the marrow. The arrival of morning was a welcome relief.

A visit to the post-office disclosed no news from Edmunds. No news was bad news, so we decided to sell the tent. Leo and I made a visit to Carmarthen, found a scout-master, and offered him the tent for twenty-five shillings. He arranged to come down the following morning and view it, with a promise to buy if satisfied. Next morning brought no answer from Edmunds, and the tent was sold to the scout-master for twenty-two shillings. After all expenses had been met and our total wealth ascertained, we found ourselves in possession of eight shillings per head. To return to London by train was out of the question. Our only course was to walk back.

CHAPTER X

The Return

WHEN the retreat began, a number of natives, including the village constable, who had been told off to see us safely out of the district, assembled to witness the evacuation. They were not friendly, but we were not loathe to go. We bade them farewell without tears. They were glad to be rid of us and we were delighted to be gone: our stay had been brief, eventful, and unfortunate. The journey homeward promised to be long and unpleasant; but we were young, vigorous, and not averse to any adventure that might befall, disagreeable though it might turn out to be.

We burst into song again as the farm, with its strange, weird, and inexplicable atmosphere, was left farther behind. We had never seen the lady of the house, who had been so cruelly slandered by the rascally Edmunds, and whom we had been too ready to misjudge. We should have liked to explain our position to her, but we felt a little ashamed, and an interview might have been embarrassing to us all. Should she be still in the land of the living, and should these lines meet her eye, I hope she will accept this, the only public apology we have ever been able to make, and forgive us our trespasses as she would hope to be forgiven.

At Llandilo the expedition halted, and, as a few shillings still remained in our pockets, we paid for accommodation at a pub and spent the evening in discussion of our plans for a speedy and comfortable transit to the great city we had been so delighted to leave, and to which we were now so eager to return. We decided to pursue the journey on foot until some one could be persuaded to give us a lift or until Leo's fertile intellect evolved some scheme of salvation from the plight we were in. The morning brought no happy inspiration to that master-mind, while the rest of us, although fully qualified to solve all the baffling problems of mankind, remained incapable of solving our own! The dreary journey was resumed.

A tramp of twenty-seven miles lay before us ere the town of Brecon, which was to be our next stopping-place, would be reached. We had not gone far beyond Llandilo, however, when Leo saw a man whom he had met somewhere before. This person turned out to be a dentist who had settled in the town and was in need of a traveling-salesman to advertise and sell his—the dentist's—toothpaste. He offered Leo a job on the spot. "And I could do with a smart young man to do odd jobs at the surgery. What about your young friend?" he asked. The young friend was Fred.

Now Leo was, and is today, a man thoroughly sound on the question of work. However, on this all-important question there are certain occasions when the bravest and best of us have to compromise. Just as Cardinal Manning told the London dockers, during their historical fight for the famous "Dockers' Tanner," that, if a poor man was denied bread, it was no sin but a duty for him to steal bread; so we must recognize that if a man is faced with starvation and there is no course open to him, if he wishes to live, except to go to work, then to work he must go. It is regrettable, but, human nature being what it is—frail and weak—we cannot blame the man who works if no other means of earning a living is presented to him. "Shall I do it?" asked Leo, turning to us with pain in his eyes. "You must please yourself, Leo," I said. "Our situation is dire. There are too many of us on tramp together. Sooner or later, unless a miracle happens, we shall have to split up, for economic reasons. Your immediate problem is solved, and so is Fred's if he goes with you on this job. You will not stick it long, of course," I continued, drawing him aside and lowering my voice. "Get what you can and 'scarper' [leave]; we shall meet in London later."

Fred was ready to accept. Ramage, as befits a member of an industrious race, was all in favor. "Och ay, mon," he said callously, "take it and see how you go on."

"I will take the job, then," said Leo; and he, Fred, and the dentist went back to Llandilo. Smith, Ramage, and I stood for a while and watched them go, then went on our way. Brecon was reached late in the evening. The three of us were very tired, and sought our beds early at the inn. The next day's program was the tramp to Hay, the last town on the Welsh side, after which we should be on English soil in the county of Herefordshire. In the course of our travels a certain amount of dissension arose amongst us. Ramage was a member of the I.L.P. Smith and I were prepared to overlook that as long as he did not obtrude his *petit-bourgeois* reformism into arguments with too much seriousness. It soon became apparent, however, that he had a reactionary side to his nature and was saturated with reformist ideology. He was not only not prepared to use any and every weapon in the struggle against capitalism, but he argued strenuously by the roadside in favor of reformist measures and the voting of the capitalists out of power by constitutional methods.

He would not countenance sabotage, for instance, nor was he in favor of removing the world's tyrants by physical force. The man was simply reeking with *bourgeois* morality. The maintenance of such heresies neither Smith nor I was prepared to brook. High words ensued, and insults filled the air. Smith was a nasty and unscrupulous debater at all times, and his taunts and jibes got on Ramage's nerves. Smith accused Ramage and Leo of plotting behind our backs in French, a language the rest of the company could not follow, to leave the party in the lurch at the first opportunity. This accusation, which was quite absurd, stung Ramage to the quick, and he denounced Smith in strong terms. "You are the meanest man I have ever met," he said, "and what is more, I can't stand this dawdling; it will take us years to reach London at this rate." "Well," answered Smith, "you had better walk on by yourself; you are rotten company anyhow." "I shall be glad to do so," said Ramage, who was a self-reliant person and also a quick walker. Now I am a quick walker also, and can tramp miles without feeling the strain. But Smith, who was a Cockney and bad on his feet, was a slow walker.

Yet I was anxious to stay with him, as he was a stimulating and lively companion and an old friend; we understood each other perfectly, too, and were not willing to be separated if it could be helped. I was sorry to part with Ramage, who was a right good fellow despite his I.L.P. outlook. "Carry on, then," I said; "we'll catch you up later. Send for us if you have any luck. In any case, we'll meet in London in the near future." So Ramage walked on by himself while Smith and I continued at a slower pace.

By nightfall we reached Hay, having tramped for twenty-one miles or thereabouts, and we were in a distinctly penurious condition. After booking our beds at a fourpenny doss-house, we had sixpence left between us.

Our next stage was Hereford, which we got to early the following day. At this town I sold my overcoat for half a crown; and, having dined sparingly upon "faggots" and tea, we engaged a couple of beds at a lodging-house, reserving a shilling and sixpence for the morrow.

The next day being Sunday, we found everything very quiet and the air filled with Sabbath peace. Our journey was no more than fourteen miles across the country to the ancient town of Ross. This quaint old-fashioned place was as dead as a cemetery. Smith and I walked into it at about two o'clock in the afternoon and had difficulty in knowing what to do with ourselves. The shops were all shut; the inhabitants were all asleep, or dead. We walked round the town hall, a queer-looking structure standing up on four slender pillars, for an hour or so, whistling the "Dead March" in *Saul*. Nothing happened. At six o'clock a model lodging-house opened. We paid our fourpence and secured two cubicles for the night. A little later we found a shop open at the corner of a street and bought half a loaf costing three-halfpence, a packet of tea costing a halfpenny; a halfpenny-worth of sugar and a farthing's worth of milk, in a cup kindly lent by the lady of the shop on our promise to return it within half an hour. We also purchased a portion of corned beef for twopence. Thus, for a total outlay of $4\frac{3}{4}$d, we partook of an excellent meal—excellent, that is, for us in our condition.

The "deputy" at the lodging-house was also the general hairdresser by special warrant. Smith, who needed a shave more than I did, decided to submit himself to his ministrations. The man was not a barber, however, he was a butcher. Realizing that whiskers cover a multitude of chins, and that even "kipp-house" residents need shaving sometimes, he took advantage of their poverty to ply his razor upon their faces at cut prices. For mutilating the face beyond hope of recovery, he charged a penny. It was worth less, but Smith's poverty, if not his will, consented. In the course of his work on Smith's face, the barber enlivened the proceedings by a running accompaniment of facetious comment and emitted many a merry quip and side-splitting sally as he hacked and slashed his way along. Every stroke was a cut, which seemed to excite his mingled amusement and sympathy. "Your friend," he said, addressing me, "has a remarkably tender skin. Some people might think I was cutting him, but it is the skin, of course, which is exceptionally sensitive"; and he chuckled musingly. Smith's face, at the conclusion of the ordeal, resembled a piece of raw meat. I decided to allow the hair to remain on my chin until next day.

The day following we made our way to Gloucester, a distance of sixteen miles. It was a cold frosty day, with a biting March wind cutting us to the marrow. The spire of the beautiful cathedral glittered in the winter sunlight as our two woebegone figures entered the historic city. Our pockets were empty, as were our stomachs. We were cold and famished. The first thing to be done was to find some one connected with the socialist movement who would stretch forth the hand of fellowship to a couple of starved and penniless comrades. Had Leo been with us, the position would have been readily and successfully dealt with, but neither Smith nor myself was much good at telling a tale of woe, however true the tale might be. But something had to be done—our state was desperate. Having made inquiries we learned that there was a well-known socialist in the city—one Bell, a pillar of the local Labor cause. This Bell was a natural philanthropist, we were given to understand, whose heart was open to every story of human suffering and want. As a socialist, his heart bled for all who were downtrodden and oppressed, and his purse was at the disposal of the poor and needy at any hour of the day or night.

It was cruel of our informant to pull our legs, but he was evidently a person with a keen sense of irony, for Bell was not at all a man of hospitable impulse, as we soon discovered. We were obliged to hang around in the bitter blast until six o'clock in the evening, as Mr. Bell did not return from business until that hour. We stood shivering on the doorstep while the great humanitarian attended us. He came at length, and his appearance was not inspiring. The waxed mustache, the cold gray eyes, the pince-nez, the alpaca jacket and stand-up collar, and the air of austere probity and incorrigible rectitude bespoke the petty moralist and the pontificating skinflint.

He listened to our story in chilly silence, and, after putting a number of questions to us in magisterial tones, he handed out the frozen mitt—he wore mittens, by the way—in the most decisive manner. "I do not know you," he said; "you have no credentials. If I knew you to be deserving cases, I might assist you; but I have only your word that you are genuine, and, frankly, I don't believe your story." "We are anxious to avoid sleeping out tonight," I said. "A shilling would enable us to secure beds. You might let us have that, even if you don't know us." "'Twere good you do as much for charity.'" "I don't approve of charity," he said sharply. "But we do," asserted Smith. That did it. The door was slammed in our faces and we turned disconsolately away. To say that we were angry would be putting it far too inadequately. We surged with fury, not at having been refused help, but at the disgusting smugness of the fellow, the Pecksniffian unction, the condescending air and patronizing manner.

"There is only one thing for it," I said to Smith. "I must cast a few pearls among swine. Let us go into this public-house and I will recite something."

I approached the landlady. "Have you any objection, madam," I asked, "to my giving a recitation to your guests and passing the hat round at the end?" "Do so, if you like," replied the good lady, "but I don't think you'll do much good." "One can but try," I remarked. Addressing the whole room collectively, I announced my intention of rendering a dramatic poem entitled *Fra Giacomo* by Robert Buchanan. I stood upon a little platform and let it go. Hunger and desperation helped me to impart the proper wildness and dramatic frenzy into the character of the unfortunate victim of woman's frailty. In vain. The sturdy artisans sat at their tables in supreme unconcern. Not a muscle of their faces moved. No one, to use a proletarian phrase, took a "blind" bit of notice. The hat went round, and returned—empty. For the second time that day my heart thumped with rage. I could hardly see my way out of the accursed tavern, so blinded with anger was I at the callous insensitiveness of that room full of wooden images. My vanity was hurt, too. I had always prided myself on being able to hold any audience, no matter how rough or uncultivated, spellbound by my art of declamation. It was humiliating and infuriating.

"Let us try another pub," I said to Smith. "By God, I'll force them to take notice!"

The next house was full of laboring men. My request was granted, "But I don't think you'll get much," said the landlord encouragingly. "They've no money to spare, those chaps." "One can only do one's best," I said, and began. I offered two pieces for their delectation. "The Story of Jonah and the Whale," written by myself, which would make a cat laugh, and "The Dream of Eugene Aram," by Tom Hood, which had made Mr. Gladstone weep and would make a dog howl. No notice whatever was taken of my histrionic achievements by the occupants of the tap-room. I went round with the hat amid a dead silence. No hand was extended to drop a coin within that piece of ancient headgear. For the second time within half an hour, I had drawn a blank.

As I staggered through the doorway, a man selling laces said to me, "You did no good, did you?" "No," I muttered, hardly able to speak with disgust and distress. He went on: "Here's a penny, then. You look dead-beat: don't take it to heart, nobody does any good here." I thanked him warmly, and was for refusing the coin, but he would take no refusal, assuring me that he had enough and could easily spare a penny and wished it was more. I wanted to take his address and send him a present when things bucked up, but he laughed and said, "Nonsense! What the hell is a penny?" "A lot to me, just now," I said, as Smith and I wished him good luck and departed.

"There is something queer about this town, Jack," I said. "Too bloody right, there is," agreed Smith. "No more reciting in the pubs here," I swore. "They are all dead people, it seems." "Try Mark Antony's oration, in the graveyard," suggested Smith. "You might do better there." I could do no worse, I thought, unless I tried the mortuary. "Singing might move them—if only to murder you." "No fear," replied Smith. "I'd rather walk about all night than face the ordeal." "Well, we must do something," I said. "Old town tonight."

As it chanced, there did happen to be a Socialist lecture at Ruskin Hall that very evening. Having made this interesting discovery, we directed our steps towards the Hall immediately. A man with an I.L.P. button in his coat was standing at the door. To him we poured out our tale of misery and sorrow. He responded with sixpence, which was all he could afford.

The meeting was about to commence, and we sat in the Hall for a while to listen to the speaker. The chairman, however, wore us down with an introductory speech, which is probably going on to this day. His opening words were sinister to a degree. "I do not wish," he said, "to stand between you and the lecturer for this evening." This is a well-known method of chairmen, and it means just the opposite of what the words imply. "You can hear me any day," he went on to remark, "but it is not often that we have the opportunity of listening to one who needs, I think, no introduction to a Gloucester audience." Then followed twenty minutes of reminiscence, followed by half an hour on the political situation and "turning to this if I may," and "time," and "if I may trespass for a moment," and all the rest of it; until at last Smith and I broke under the strain and stole quietly from the room.

We were starving, but dared not break into the sixpence. Shelter comes before food in these cases. As it was, we were a penny short of our "kipp." To raise the penny was as difficult as it would have been to raise a thousand pounds, unless we begged in the street, and that we could not bring ourselves to do. There was nothing for it but to return to the meeting-hall, which we did. In the end we raised another threepence, and with that we had to be content. Our beds were booked at the nearest doss-house, and the extra twopence went in food. We bought two-pennyworth of bread, and one of the doss-house members gave us a drink of tea—an uncommon act in these places, but we looked done up, and the man's heart was touched at the sight of our obvious distress.

The next day's jaunt took us to Cheltenham, a short distance which we covered in a few hours. We had not breakfasted, and the sharp March air made us hungry. Hunger troubled us all the time. I am not worried much about food nowadays, as the wear and tear of the years has destroyed my digestive processes; and neither is Smith, for he is dead; but eighteen years ago I was younger and healthier, and to go short of food was no joke. A copy of the socialist paper *Justice* in a shop-window caused us to ask if there was a socialist party in Cheltenham and, if so, where? "Oh yes," answered the newsagent. "You should see Mr. Bradbury—he will tell you all about it." Having obtained Mr. Bradbury's address, we sought him out with all speed. He lived in a poor street and had the bailiffs in when we called. We spun him the yarn and he was sympathetic, but bereft of funds. "Go to these people," he said, giving us the addresses of three socialists in Cheltenham who would be likely, he said, to aid us in our hour of need. He wished us better luck, and we wished the same to him. Upon which we left poor Mr. Bradbury to battle with the bailiffs, and departed.

The first man on our list was a rich boot-merchant with socialist leanings. He turned us down at once. They always do. But he did it without patronage or the insult of offering us a moral lecture. He just said, "No, go away; I can't help you." We apologized for troubling him, and took ourselves off. The next victim was a miller, who worked, naturally enough, at a mill. His heart bled for us to the extent of one shilling net, for which he earned our loud applause. With the precious coin in our possession we felt almost solvent—and almost fainting with hunger. Our first call was at a fourpenny doss-house, where we excused ourselves from booking a night's lodging until later in the day, the appeasement of the pangs of a terrible hunger taking precedence over all other considerations. The "boss" of the house kindly allowed us to make use of the kitchen in which to cook a meal, and trusted us to book our beds later in the day if we had any luck. We bought a piece of steak from a butcher, costing fourpence; half a loaf costing three-halfpence; a penny packet of tea and sugar mixed and a farthing's worth of milk from the small grocer's at the corner of the street. I had not acquired the cigarette habit at that time, which was just as well, but Smith was a heavy smoker of "shag" tobacco, which he bought in packets and made into cigarettes himself. Twopence, I think, was expended by him on tobacco. I do know that, after dining to repletion and covering the lodging-house table with grease and stains, we left the establishment with threepence-farthing to spare.

It was early in the afternoon, and we had some hours to pass before the third victim could be interviewed. He was, Mr. Bradbury had told us, a trade-union official whose office was some distance from the town, and he would not be at his home until half-past six. We hung about the streets, read the papers in the Free Library, and passed away the time as best we could. The weather remained cold, and since parting with my overcoat it had become, of course, much colder. It always does. The third man was our last hope. If he failed us, it was the streets for us that night—unless, as I have said before, a miracle happened.

Six-thirty found us on the doorstep of the union official's house. He came, in answer to Smith's faltering knock. I began the story. Having heard it through, he gave out the following disquieting statement. "I am sorry; what you say may be true—I do not say it is not—but I must decline to help you. I have been 'done down' too often, and have sworn never to assist any one again. You may be suffering through the fault of others, but the innocent must suffer with the guilty. I have been made the victim of impostors in the past, and now I make it a rule never to help any one."

These ominous words chilled us to the very soul, but we stuck to him with the courage of despair. He looked a decent kind of man, a good type of the artisan class. Despite the adamantine phraseology, a warm heart, we felt, beat behind his waistcoat. Smith took up the tale, producing his trade-union cards. He was a fully paid-up member of the Platen Machine Minders' Association. "I am no beggar," he said indignantly. I could see the union official beginning to weaken, and began where Smith was leaving off. For over a quarter of an hour we wrought upon him. We were desperate and would not be denied. At long last he broke down, left us to consult with his wife and family, and reappeared with a shilling in his hand. "I don't know if I am doing right," he said, "but my conscience would not let me rest if I let you go unassisted and found later that you were genuinely in need." Having taken the shilling, we thanked him and withdrew. We were saved.

We put up, not in the doss-house, but at a (more respectable) commercial hotel. We talked the landlady into giving us a room for the price of one shilling for the two of us. The threepence was spent on two cups of tea and half a loaf. Before going to bed we sat for a while in the Commercial Room. There were several guests smoking by the fire, who did not fail to observe our dilapidated appearance. One of these, a commercial traveler from Birmingham, exuded sympathy from every pore. "Ah," he said, "I can see you chaps are up against it. I know what it means to be stranded and out of employment. I have a wife and five children and know what a struggle it is to keep the head above water." The others nodded sympathetically. One of the company was the driver of a motor-lorry, who was going to London, we learned, the next morning. Good, thought Smith and

I; we may get a lift right into London. We are all right for breakfast here, they are all full of sympathy. Probably they will have a "whip-round" to help us on our way. We went up to bed full of confidence. Breakfast was to be on the table at eight o'clock the next morning. Smith and I arranged to get down in time to be invited to join the guests at their morning meal. At half-past seven we had risen, having shaken off downy sleep, death's counterfeit, and by eight I had reached the dining-room.

The company were seated at the board, absorbing eggs, bacon, ham, sausages, kidneys, tomatoes and other delectable comestibles with enthusiasm and extreme gusto.

Seating myself on a sofa some distance from the dining-table. The lorry-driver looked up with his mouth full of buttered-toast and nodded curtly. The rest remained attentive to the viands and made no response to my fraternal greeting. A few minutes later Smith arrived. "Good morning," he observed, looking round with a cheery smile. "Good morning," replied the commercial traveler, as he struggled with an egg. No invitation to join the feast was forthcoming from any of the guests.

We sat for a few minutes, hoping that something might develop, that some gesture of hospitality might be made. Nothing except the low murmur of conversation, above which rose the noise of chewing, crunching, and lip-smacking indicative of hearty appetite and powers of keen enjoyment of food, reached our ears. Smith rose slowly; I rose slowly. We both rose slowly. We moved to the door which led into the living-room of the family. "Good morning, missus," called Smith, expecting that the landlady would emerge and say, "Oh, you're not going without something to eat; sit down and I'll bring you some breakfast." Not so. A woman's voice replied from the kitchen: "Oh, you are off? Well, good morning; good morning." Turning again towards the guests scattered at the table, I said, "Well, good morning, all." "Good morning," answered several, as they continued their repast.

We walked slowly through the door into the street; slowly we ambled along the sidewalk, looking back now and then in the hope that some one overcome with pity and remorse would come running after us with a bag of gold, or a handful of silver, or at least a parcel of food. No such person came after us. Realizing that our anticipations of hospitality had been premature and our hopes of assistance vain, and that the cheerful sympathy and *bonhomie* of the guests the night before had proceeded, not from a genuine desire to help their brother-men in adversity, but from the drinking of too much spirituous liquor, we cursed ourselves for a couple of trusting simpletons and walked on in angry silence. Why had we let Leo leave us? We were not fit to bear the name of roadsters. No genuine tramp would have acted in the ridiculous way we had acted. He would have asked for what he wanted; he would have made himself a nuisance until those people at the hotel would have given him anything to get rid of him; he would have shamed them into helping him. We were a couple of ninnies, that was certain. Had Leo been with us he would have left the hotel loaded with food and money.

The next stop was Oxford, a distance of forty-three miles. I had a friend at Oxford, the secretary of a socialist society for which I had lectured several times. He was a boon companion, and had often invited me to visit Oxford and spend a day or two at his house. To reach Oxford that day was our aim and object. After tramping until about one o'clock, we struck the town of Northleach, where we landed half dead with

hunger and fatigue. Or, at least, Smith did. I can stand a
lot of hunger, and am not easily fatigued by walking. What
fatigues me is working, not walking. But Smith was not so
good. His feet troubled him, and in order to accommodate
my pace to his I was obliged to shuffle and crawl, which left
me miserable with exposure to the cold, biting wind and
stinging air. Had I been alone I should have kept on at a
pace of five miles an hour. With Smith as companion, I
dragged along at the rate of three or less.

However, this could not be helped, and I made no reference
to the matter. At Northleach Smith got a job holding a
horse's head while the driver of a lorry-wagon had his midday
meal at a pub. The efforts of the diminutive and town-bred
sociologist to control the irritable quadruped were futile.
Although he had been so eager to take up gentleman-farming
a few days before, he was curiously ill-fitted for agricultural
pursuits. It is doubtful if he had ever touched a horse before.
His attempts to manage the animal did not indicate that
he had. Several times the beast nearly ran away, and each
time Smith narrowly missed being trampled underfoot in his
preposterous attempts to restore its confidence in his ability
to manage an unruly jade. I stood on the pavement laughing,
until the gallant rough-rider lost his temper and nearly lost
the horse at the same time. "Let it gallop to hell, if it likes!"
he yelled, letting go the reins; and the disgruntled mustang
strolled leisurely along the street, its eyes alone betraying
its disgust and dudgeon at being left in the guard of such a
master. I strolled quietly after it and returned the animal
to its original position outside the pub. "You had better
keep out of his way," I said to Smith. "You annoy him. This
beast is horse-conscious, and resents the proximity of men
like you." "I hope he bites you to death," said my friend,

with a venomous expression. At the end of half an hour the driver returned. He paid no money for the service rendered, but told us that some food was waiting for us in the yard. We found a large teapot filled with that delicious fluid and a large chunk of bread-and-cheese spread on a large table. The food was appetizing and sustaining, but insufficient in quantity. Nevertheless we were glad of what there was of it and resumed the journey in good spirits.

The road from Cheltenham to Oxford is high, lonely, long, and exposed to every wind that blows. It is the loneliest road within my experience of roads, and I have traveled many. There is not a house to be seen; nor, when we tramped it, did we meet a soul after leaving Northleach until close upon Witney, which is six miles from Oxford as the crow flies, if the crow does fly in that area, which is open to question.

As the slow hours wore on and the evening shadows crept over the fields, our hearts turned to lead and our spirits fell to zero. Smith's distress made him irritable and snappy, while the maddening slowness of his pace exasperated me extremely. We snapped at each other like a pair of dogs; once we came near to having a stand-up fight in the middle of the road. The ostensible cause of our acrimony was an argument about something utterly absurd; the real reason was weariness, lack of proper food, anxiety about the immediate future, and disgust with ourselves for having embarked on such a wild-goose chase.

"Why don't you lie down in the ditch here and quietly pass away?" I suggested to my friend. "The world is already overpopulated with the wrong kind of people, yet you hang on in a mean, selfish desire to add to the misery of mankind." "What I want to know," exclaimed my dear old pal, "is why your parents did not think a little before allowing you to grow up into human form." We grew tired of recrimination and squabbling after a time and fell into a miserable silence. We lost count of time and almost let go our hold upon reality. Darkness came, and we walked on and on and on and on. I began to imagine that we had been walking since the beginning of eternity and were doomed to continue until the conclusion of time.

At close upon eleven o'clock we trailed slowly and sadly into the town of Witney. A clock struck the hour as we passed along the main street. We had not spoken for hours. Things were too much for us. There was nothing to say. We crept on like sloths, leaving the town behind. Another eternity rolled by. At last—at last, the lights of Oxford came into view. Snail-slow and feeble, benumbed with misery and cold as we were, it seemed as though the city of dreaming spires, our Mecca and our goal, was receding instead of getting nearer. Smith spoke. "Your friend," he said, "won't be up at this time of night. He has probably shifted from Oxford by now, anyhow, or at least moved to another address. Take my word: you won't find him tonight. We shall have to go to the casual ward, or try the police-station." "One thing I will say, Jack," I remarked, "you are certainly an optimist through it all. You naturally look on the bright side. You are too good for this world really; you ought to be in heaven, above the bright blue skies."

It was only to be expected that my friend's house was at the other side of the city, not at the side at which we arrived. But we reached it in the end. We reached it in the end, and it turned out to be the end of all our troubles. The door was opened immediately by the master of the house himself. "Good heavens!" he exclaimed. "Where the devil have you come from? Come right in. Is that Jack Smith with you?

You have landed just at the right moment—the supper is on the table. You are both as welcome as the flowers in May. You shan't leave Oxford until you feel like going. You must stay for at least a week." And, talking in this strain, he led us into a room with a roaring fire blazing up the chimney and a table loaded with food for life. Our Odyssey was at an end.

We stayed a day at the great seat of learning, resting and recuperating at my friend's expense, allowing the beauties of the lovely old city to soak into our souls and heal the wounds of battle and pilgrimage. We had, that is to say, a rest and a good time. In the evening I gave a dramatic recital at Ruskin College, at the conclusion of which a collection was taken up, which realized about fifteen shillings. Our luck was in.

The following day we walked, for pleasure, to Reading, where I gave another dramatic recital at the Socialist Hall. A collection of twelve shillings was recorded.

Feeling like gentlemen at large, we sauntered into London the next afternoon, calling, as we reached Shepherd's Bush, upon a notorious blood-red revolutionary, to whom we gave a full account of all that had befallen. He was amused, but expressed disappointment that we had not won Wales for the social revolution. We stated as our considered opinion that Wales ought to be wiped off the map, and if that delightful consummation could be achieved by means of a social revolution we promised our active support for the scheme. But we asked to be excused from taking any personal part in it, other than directing the enemy forces from a quiet office in London.

We entered the café at about six in the evening and found everything going on as usual. This was disappointing, as we anticipated, for some absurd reason, that tremendous changes would have taken place during our absence. We had been away exactly a fortnight, but it seemed to Smith and I that we had been away for half a century. Ramage turned up the same night. He had got through more easily than we had, having secured a lift for the greater part of the distance. He had visited Edmunds' address in Red Lion Street and discovered that nothing was known about him, as he only used the place—which was a rag-and-bone store—as a postal address.

Leo and Fred rolled along some weeks later, dressed fit to kill. It seemed that they had worked for a gramophone company, as a side-line to toothpaste salesmanship, and had made away with a few gramophones as compensation for unpaid wages. More gramophones than were equivalent had been confiscated, hence our pals' appearance of extreme, almost bloated, solvency. "I have that within," said Leo, indicating his breast-pocket, "which passeth show. Come along to the head office of the S. P. and O. Let's go mad!" Of the man Edmunds none of us has heard a whisper from that day to this.

CHAPTER XI

Caviar to the General

I often think there is as much to be said against war as there is to be said for it. While the last war did good to so many, it brought ruin to many more.

The greatest argument in favor of war is, I suppose, that so many people like it and enjoy it. It is, without doubt, the greatest unifying force in the world. I found that to be true when it burst upon us in August 1914. I found myself in a hopeless minority when I reacted against it immediately, indignantly, and violently. The Labor Party leaders fell over themselves in their eagerness to get on the recruiting platforms. Blatchford and Hyndman, Victor Grayson and Ben Tillett, H. G. Wells and Jack London, Prince Kropotkin and Gustave Herve—nearly all the prominent personalities in the international socialist movement threw their weight into the struggle for allied supremacy. The workers of every belligerent country sprang to arms like grayhounds slipped from the leash. The trouble with the working-class was not to get them into the trenches, but to keep them back. They had been spoiling for a fight for so long. The opportunity was too good to miss.

It was the universal unanimity on the war question that put me right off. Had the majority been opposed to it, I should probably have been one of the first to volunteer. But if all these masses of duffers and pinheads were in favor of it, I thought, there must be something wrong. I do not dislike my fellow creatures, but I have no faith in them. I distrust their judgment, hate their attempts at interference, and loathe the idea of being dictated to by them. *Odi profanum vulgus et arceo.* Even if I were in the wrong and knew it I should stand out, for the love of having the great big blubbering, bullying, chuckle-headed mob against me. My experience of crowds had taught me to despise them, and a few years in London had destroyed my faith in the masses and almost convinced me of the probable ultimate collapse of the human mind.

The war of 1914 was the most popular event within living memory—but not with me. While others cheered I cursed both loud and deep and made enemies in every direction. I was denounced by rich and poor alike, as a coward, a slacker, a shirker, and a pro-German. I enjoyed this so much that the war was half-way through before I began to realize the tragic aspects of it. I fell into the error of hating the men who caused it and some of the men who were fighting in it. It was not easy to keep a sense of proportion in the midst of a world given over to hate and slaughter. "Your King and Country need you!" announced the recruiting posters. "You can keep on needing me," I said. "You have never needed me before, why do you want me now? To make use of me as a bullet-stopper. To send me out and let the enemy make a cockshy of me. No."

Yet there were times when I wanted to be out in it. I nearly joined up several times, just to see what it was like. Had I been approached in the right manner, I should have gone. But I was not going to be bullied into going. I resented the attentions of the self-appointed recruiters, the unofficial whippers-in and those heroines of the home-front, the ladies of the "white-feather" brigade. I was approached one day in the Strand by one of these creatures. It was during the early period of war hysteria, when nearly every one in the country was throwing their weight about in a thoroughly objectionable manner. The streets were thick with these hags with white feathers, who were permitted to molest every man they saw with their odious attentions. "Young man, why aren't you in khaki?" asked this overfed lady in a curt and nasty tone. "Because there is a war on, madam," I answered. She said: "I suppose you think that's very clever, but I'd like to know what you would do if the Germans came here." "I should volunteer for foreign service. What would you volunteer for?" I replied.

For the recruiting officer I had a special formula. "Well, young man, have you thought about it?" he would ask. "Thought about what?" "Joining up!" "Yes." "Ah, then you are going to join now?" "No." "No?" he would say, surprised, a shadow crossing his face. "How's that?" "Because I've thought about it," I would answer sternly.

The way the Press referred to the prospective cannon-fodder was highly flattering. "Rounding them up," "Roping them in," and "Combing them out" were favorite slogans. The cute manner in which the politicians, the Press lords, and most of the well-known people in influential positions kept out of the firing-line while inciting others to go was also quite diverting. The way persons like Bottomley and others used to visit the back of the Front and rush home again to tell stories of having been under fire was one of the most interesting features of the period. Most of the fire-eaters who went about the country preaching "bloody murder," as Mr. Ben Tillett put it, were, of course, too old to take part in the actual fighting. Curiously enough, they were too old during the Boer war also. And then, during the Crimean war they were too young.

The activities of the civilian population is so much a part of history, and so like the conduct of civilian populations at all times and in all countries, that there is little need to dwell upon their absurdities. The splendid efforts of the Society crush to win the war can be summed up in the answer of a well-known lady who, when asked what she was doing to help, said, "I've cut down my servants' supply of meat. What more can I do?"

There were, of course, the old man and the young woman. "Would to God I were ten years younger, I'd be doing my bit with the brave boys at the Front," said the old man. It was not without interest to note that when the age-limit was raised, towards the end of the war, most of the "Would-to-Godders" developed asthma, lumbago, or heart trouble. There was no rush to join the brave boys at the Front. The young women who sang, "We don't want to lose you, but we think you ought to go," nagged and scolded and would not take "No" for an answer, until the young men were either crippled for life, or blinded, or laid under the earth for ever.

Nothing made the old men and women so angry as to see a young man not in khaki, and nothing would satisfy them until the young men were either maimed beyond all hope of repair or killed entirely. "Why aren't you in khaki?" asked a stout red-faced lady of a man I knew, who had been sent home with only a few weeks to live, as he walked down Charing Cross Road in civilian attire. "I have been out already and done my bit," he answered. "But you look all right. You can go again, can't you?" asked the red-faced one severely. "Why aren't you dead? Why didn't the Germans kill you? You must hurry up and get better and get back to the trenches so that the enemy can finish you off next time." It was not put quite so bluntly. The old geysers who pestered the soldiers in the hospitals would say, "Now you must hurry up and get well quickly so that you can get back to the trenches and have another go at those dreadful Huns."

5. Reasons in support of the application. (These should be fully stated, and any documentary evidence in support of the application should be forwarded herewith.)

I have been a revolutionary Socialist for ten years. I am an Anti-militarist. I believe in the International Brotherhood of the workers. I believe this war to be a capitalist war. I am a Socialist Lecturer & Labour organiser & have been in prison several times for expressing views hostile to those of the Capitalist Class. I have opposed this war from the start & would suffer any penalty—prison, torture, or death rather than take part in it. I claim absolute exemption on these grounds.

6. (a) Signature of person by whom application made — *John Bonar Thompson*

(b) Address (if not already stated) ...

It speaks well for the restraint and patriotism of our brave fellows on the Home Front that when they made a raid on a German shop, turning the family into the street and wrecking the premises, there was not one case of their ever interfering with a shop belonging to a rich German. The poor alien who kept a pork-butcher's, or a baker's, or hairdresser's establishment would have his place smashed to the ground and receive a good hiding into the bargain, but the plucky lads who did such noble deeds knew better than to lay a hand upon the person or property of any rich alien. Thank God the heart of our people was sound on that matter at any rate.

Public-speaking became impossible in Hyde Park very soon after the outbreak of war. Only religious and patriotic gatherings were permitted by the mob. The heroic revolutionaries, the Marxian rebels and the scientific class-struggle merchants scuttled like rats into the munition-works, where they lived like aristocrats until the nasty business was well over. As soon as the armistice was declared these brave

fighters came slinking back to the usual pitches and began
bellowing about the need for a working-class revolution, and
denounced Lansbury, Philip Snowden, and all those who had
borne the brunt of anti-war agitation for over four years as
"traitors," "fakirs," and "Imperialists." Among those who
helped to make shells at high wages while preaching revolution were the Smart Alicks who later became the leaders
of the great communist racket. One of these, who made so
much money out of it that he could think of no other way of
spending it than drinking himself to death on brandy, was
the man who was secretary of the communist party during
the big period of communist ferment just following the war.
The Russian revolution may have done no good to the people
of Russia, but it was a Godsend to scores of British agitators
who lived on such a scale of magnificence that many of the
middle-class parlous Bolsheviks joined up, in the hope of
collaring a good share of the swag. Some of them did very
well, until Stalin turned the tap off. It was the biggest thing
that ever happened to any revolutionary party in the history
of the world, and I deeply regret that I was fool enough not
to dip my hand into the till while the going was good.

But such goings-on were not even dreamed of until after
the war was well over. A few of us carried on meetings in
Finsbury Park every Sunday. I spoke there regularly and
got away with the most vigorous anti-war propaganda until
the middle of 1916, when I was arrested under the Military
Service Act for refusing to respond to the call-up notices I
had been receiving for some time. I had appealed before
the local tribunal and actually persuaded them to grant me
a certificate of total exemption, on conscientious grounds.
They put me through a severe examination in order to find
out if my objection to war was genuine or not. I answered all

the questions with fluency and art. George Lansbury, who was the editor of the *Daily Herald* at the time, backed me up in every way with leading articles testifying to the fact that I had been a socialist and anti-militarist for many years and was one whose sincerity had never been questioned.

The tribunal were convinced of my sincerity and gave me a certificate of total exemption, but the military representative, who was no fool, appealed against their decision on the ground that my objection to joining the Army was political, not conscientious. He won. When the appeal came on at the Middlesex Guildhall a couple of months later, the first tribunal's decision was reversed, my certificate was withdrawn, and I was ordered into the Army. I refused to go. I was arrested and handed over to an escort, taken to the barracks at Mill Hill, medically examined, passed fit for active service, and cast into the guard-room.

"So you are a Conscientious Objector, eh?" remarked the sergeant of the guard in a sneering voice. "Well, you'll soon find out that we tame lions here." "So I have heard," I said; "only you're not dealing with a lion this time, you're dealing with a man." "A man! I'd have you put up against the wall and shot, if I had my way. You're a coward; you ain't got no heart. I'm old enough to be your father, but I've got a good heart, see," and he slapped his chest vigorously. To him: "It's your bloody brain that's wrong." He made as if to strike me, and I got ready to strike him back, but he thought better of it and desisted. "I thought you didn't believe in physical force, you 'Conchies.'" he said. "Don't call me a 'Conchie,'" I protested. "I have no conscience and never had, but I've got intelligence, and my intelligence tells me that I don't want anything to do with this bloody war, and what's more, I'm not going to have anything to do with it. Get on with your lion-taming, but if you or any one like you imagine that you can bully me into doing what I don't want to do, you'd better think again." "You're a queer customer," said the sergeant, and left me to myself.

He returned later and tried to talk me into joining up. "A smart chap like you would rise to be a General, if you used your nut properly," he said. But I was deaf to flattery and remained unshaken, so the hardy soldier suggested a game of cards to pass away the time. I played poker with him and two others until "lights out," and we all became good friends.

The following day I was taken to Aldershot and attached to a battalion of the West Kent Regiment. As soon as I received my first order I disobeyed it and was conveyed to the guard-tent forthwith. A great buzz of excitement went round the camp when it got about that a Conscientious Objector had arrived among them. My fellow-prisoners—absentees, deserters, and men charged with the glorious crime of half murdering a "Red Cap"—were on my side from the start. I spent one of the happiest fortnights of my life as a prisoner awaiting court martial in the guard-tent. There was nothing to do but read and write and eat and drink and smoke and tell stories.

I addressed the court martial at great length, and made a deep impression by such a statement of my reasons for refusing to be a soldier as they had never heard before. "Are you not prepared to fight your enemies?" I was asked. "Yes, certainly," I answered. "But all my enemies are in this country. I've no need to go to France to find them. Give me a gun and I'll start fighting them right away. Right now," I said, looking at a sergeant who had given evidence against me.

This attitude, coupled with the fact that I was an Irishman, made me quite popular amongst the troops, and I very nearly joined up, especially as the Regimental Sergeant-Major told me on the quiet that if I gave in and took the oath he would see that I got a good job as postman and would never be sent overseas. I was fool enough to decline this offer, and gave myself a lot of trouble by allowing scruples to stand in my way. The sentence of the court martial was read out a few days after the trial. I was "awarded" fifty-six days' hard labor. I left Aldershot with regret, having enjoyed my stay and made several very good friends among the soldiers.

At the conclusion of my sentence, which was served in Wormwood Scrubs prison, I was brought before the Central Tribunal, found to be genuine, and offered work of national importance under the Home Office scheme for the employment of Conscientious Objectors. Had I chosen to refuse this work I should have become automatically liable again for military service under the Conscription Acts, which would have meant going through the whole business again. There seemed no sense in doing that, as I had already experienced what it was like to refuse service, be court-martialed, sentenced, and all the rest of it. There was nothing more to learn by such an attitude, so I accepted work under the scheme. The conditions were that I should go where the Committee sent me, perform such tasks as were allotted to me—which were guaranteed non-military in character—and observe the rules laid down as to discipline and so forth.

The Governor of Wormwood Scrubs gave me a ticket for a place called Dyce, near Aberdeen, put me upon my honor to proceed there without delay, and wished me good luck. I left the prison, caught a bus to Fleet Street, visited the office of the *Daily Herald*, saw dear old George Lansbury—always a very present help in time of trouble—touched him for ten shillings, picked up a couple of the staff who were friends of mine, had a few drinks, and caught the midnight train for Aberdeen.

I reached the village of Dyce at about eight o'clock in the morning and found that a Conscientious Objectors' camp had been erected in a field near a granite quarry. There were two hundred and fifty of us lodged under canvas, and a rare time we had. The work was hard, very hard indeed—digging granite out of a quarry and wheeling it to and fro on to the roads. The work was so hard that we refused to work for more than five hours daily, in two shifts of two and a half hours. The food was good, however; there were hardly any restrictions; and we could lie around half the day, go blackberrying, visiting, making love to the village girls, or anything else that took our fancy. It was money for jam.

There were all sorts among us—socialists, anarchists, altruists, Christians, atheists, theosophists, spiritualists, and a member of the Salvation Army. We held lectures in a large marquee and arranged concerts, mock-trials, football and cricket matches and drinking-parties. The drinking-parties were made up of a small group of paganized non-militarists, who were not representative of the Conscientious Objectors as a whole. The majority were men who objected on moral or religious grounds—severe, self-conscious, rather puritanical types. They were all decent fellows enough, men of strong conviction on the war question; but my own temperament was different, and I sought the society of the less serious types—the Rabelaisian, singing, merry-making fellows who took life lightly and gayly.

I spoke several times at the Socialist Hall in Aberdeen and painted a horrible picture of our sufferings at the camp.

Deen people were most hospitable, as Scotch people are, and nothing was too good for us. I had the time of my life, and was sorry to leave, as we had to do at the end of ten weeks. The work in the quarry being finished, we were transferred to Wakefield Jail, which had been converted into a work-center for Conscientious Objectors.

The conditions here were not so good, but we set to work to improve them by constant agitation. Although the food was excellent, we complained about it, and a speedy increase in the quality and quantity of the rations was effected. There was hardly any work to do, but we objected to it, and the burden of toil—sewing mail-bags mostly—was lightened considerably. There were about six hundred men in the prison, representing every grade and shade of opinion, political, ethical, and theological. The restrictions were few. The locks were removed from the cell-doors, and we could come and go as we thought fit. In the evenings, from six till nine-thirty, we were free to go out and wander where we liked. At week-ends we went over to Leeds and saw the sights of the city.

The work-center was a little world in itself, and a delightful world it was. Many of the men complained bitterly and posed as martyrs. It was fantastic to reflect that, while the flower of the nation was being passed through the hopper of war like the rubbish of the fields, and half Europe was becoming a cemetery, we, who refused to lift a finger in the national cause, were sheltered in this quiet retreat, well housed, well fed, well cared for, and even paid a wage of eightpence a day—for failing to fight. The thing became farcical, when one thought of papers like the *Daily News* and the *Manchester Guardian* getting all hot and indignant about our harsh treatment by a brutal Government.

The stupidity of the Government in not only tolerating us, but pampering and protecting us into the bargain, was Gilbertian. And the more we were petted and indulged, the more rabidly did we exclaim and protest at the ruthless persecution to which we were being subjected. Many of our friends outside actually believed that we were subjected to unnamable atrocities. Questions were continually being asked in the House—by Philip Snowden, Ramsay MacDonald, Mr. Pringle, Mr. Hogg, and Joseph King—about our terrible treatment. The patriots and the public wanted to have us shot, and could not understand why we were not taken in front of a firing squad. Neither could I. I often asked myself what I would do if I had to face death rather than give in and join the Army. Would I have had the courage to stand my ground and refuse? Yes. I would not do it today. I don't think it worth while to die for any cause, but I would have done it then. Self-respect and pride—that is, vanity—would have sustained me even unto death.

There will be no "Conchies" next time; that is certain. In the event of another big war breaking out, the man who becomes a "Conchie" will at the same moment become a corpse. The only countries which tolerated conscience in the last war were England and America, and they have learned their lesson. If England goes to war again, the Government will have more serious work to do than to consider the objections of persons who will not fight. Martial law will be proclaimed on the first day, newspapers which are not wholeheartedly in support will be suppressed at once, and any one, either in or outside Parliament, who lifts his voice against the war will be put to silence. Street meetings and demonstrations will be forbidden, and fleets of aeroplanes loaded with death will hover over the areas where disaffection or reluctance to respond are known to exist. The communist-peddlers who prate of "armed insurrection and heavy civil war" as a counterblast to national war will be the first to creep into bed and stay there, or, if not, they will creep into the grave pretty quickly.

During my stay at Wakefield I got into touch with a man who turned out to be a great friend of mine, and still is. He was a socialist speaker who held large crowds every Saturday and Sunday evening at Victoria Square, Leeds. My friend is now well known as a leader of English communism, T. A. Jackson. He is, in fact, the intellectual head of the communist movement in this country; so much so that if he dropped out of the movement the intelligence which remained would not be discernible without the aid of a powerful microscope. Mr. Jackson was, I found, a student of literature, a man of catholic taste and wide culture, a fluent and illuminating writer, and a witty and eloquent speaker. Unfortunately for Mr. Jackson, he has been endowed with a powerful sense of humor, which has done him no good in a country where humor is regarded with suspicion in nearly every department of public activity. He did me many a good turn in those days, and has done me many a good turn since. His company has stimulated and inspired me on many occasions. I regard it as a pleasure to have known him; and, despite the fact that our political opinions no longer correspond, it is not unlikely that, if and when the revolution comes, our heads will roll into the same basket.

I am of the opinion, however, that there ain't going to be no revolution in this country. The working class are finished. They have had their day, and the machine is making them a superfluous quantity. The next hundred years will probably see their total elimination. A few specimens will no doubt be kept in museums, to remind posterity of the period when men did the work that will then be done by machines. I shall be sorry to see them go, for I like the workers; they are very decent people on the whole, and not without intelligence. It is rough on them that they should be done away with just when some of them are beginning to think that there will be more room for them on the planet, but it cannot be helped. They are the victims of modern progress, and their doom is written. I think, however, most of them will be needed for another war. The next big holocaust will use them up, and then some fresh arrangement will have to be made for the distribution of commodities and so forth.

I hope to be too old for the next war, as I was too intelligent for the last. It is unlikely that I shall be able to see my way to take part in it, unless I am offered a job as a General or Air Marshal. I shall probably be living in a cottage on Dartmoor, reading Shakespeare and cultivating my garden.

As the next war is almost certain to be fought in the air, the best thing to do will be to get away from the big cities as speedily as possible. The man who wishes to save his life should—as soon as war is declared—proceed at once to an outfitter's, buy a pair of running-shorts and a pair of running-shoes, and start running right away. Let him keep on running swiftly until he is out in the country, far from any town, village, or house. He should then get under a hedge and stay there until hostilities have ceased. He can take a supply of sandwiches, potted meat, and tinned fruit, and a few hundred packets of cigarettes. Let him lie low and say nothing for a month. He can then emerge from his hiding-place and make his way back to the city, if any. The war will be over by that time, and so will most of the population.

CHAPTER XII

Working the Markets

AT the conclusion of hostilities I was thrown upon my own resources and turned to the old problem of getting a living without working. Whether it was the result of the strain of the previous four years, or a touch of sunstroke, or some mental aberration, I cannot say, but I did a thing which lowered me in my own esteem for many a long day and left a scar upon my soul which time cannot efface. I went to work. I mean to say that I actually took a job. The job only lasted for a week, but the principle was the same. I had betrayed myself, and shame and moral ruin should have ensued. I took a job as a kitchen-porter at a restaurant near the Haymarket. The man who led me into it was an old friend I had known in pre-war days. He was a dope fiend. His name will be known to many, no doubt, as he has recently had a book published called *The Hundredth Man*. In this book he tells how he cured himself of the drug habit after a tremendous struggle lasting for many years.

Cecil Lenoir was a drug-addict at the time he and I went to work at the restaurant near the Haymarket. I had known him in the days before he developed this habit, which he had acquired in the United States. He was a fine chap, good-looking and intelligent. He and I worked together in the kitchen, Cecil as dish-washer and lift-man, myself as porter. The hours were from eight in the morning till eleven at night, with two hours off in the afternoon; seven days a week. We slept in. The wage was eighteen shillings a week and board. One week sufficed. The chef was a big red-haired man, an Italian who looked a typical Englishman. He left the first

day and was succeeded by a Frenchman with an enormous
mustache and hair standing straight up on his head, who
looked a typical Italian. Like all chefs, he burst into a fearful
temper at about two o'clock every afternoon. To all questions
he made one reply, which I had better put down in French,
lest I should offend. "The manager is waiting for the ice,"
Cecil would say to him across the room. "Take him my
answer! Take him my answer now! My answer is, 'Merde.'
That is my answer hear. 'Merde'—that's the word: 'Merde.'"

Poor Cecil suffered terribly if anything happened to prevent him securing a daily supply of cocaine or heroin. Every
morning at ten o'clock he slipped out to a chemist near by
for his daily dose. It cost him a shilling a day. Failure to
get it caused him to double up with terrible pains in the
stomach. I have said that one week sufficed. It more than
sufficed—we drew our wages and shook the sawdust of the
restaurant-kitchen from our feet forever.

Cecil left for America soon after and I looked round for
some way of making money. It was Leo who suggested that I
should go on the markets as a pill-vendor, or medicine-seller.
He had been discharged from the Army for about a year,
having got his ticket, after a keen struggle, on the grounds
of ill-health. Upon leaving the Army he had gone on the
stage and done fairly well, playing parts and making himself
generally useful in a repertory company. At the time I met
him he was touring the music-halls in a sketch, in which
he played the juvenile lead, at a salary of seven pounds a
week. "Try the markets," he said. "Political speaking leads
nowhere. You have all the natural and technical equipment
for a successful career as a quack doctor." I took him at his
word and became a market-worker, starting modestly as a
vendor of tooth-powder—one stone of precipitated chalk and

a sixpenny bottle of scent made enough powder to clean the teeth of half the population of London. The heaviest expense was the tins in which the powder had to be enclosed.

My first pitch was in Leather Lane, a well-known street-market near Holborn. I explained to the crowds that my preparation was made from a secret remedy bequeathed to me by an African chief while I was touring in the jungle. The crowd bought a few tins at sixpence a tin, but there was something unsatisfactory about the sales. The truth was that tooth-powder had been flogged to death on markets by negro sellers and many others. I realized that I had better try something more original. For a week or two I tried boot-polish, without much success, but then I came across a man who put me on to something that was to prove a small gold-mine for nearly three years. This was a book on the subject of birth-control. "You are the man to sell these by the hundred thousand," he said. "With your voice and powers of oratory you will have no difficulty in making yourself ten or twenty pounds a week."

I did not welcome the idea at all. Birth-control was not an attractive subject to speak about. Many people were opposed to it. It was not the sort of thing generally sold on market-places. But the man urged me to give it a trial. "If you sell the books at a shilling each, you will have a profit of tenpence on every copy. Take a hundred copies and try it out. If you sell them, pay me; if not, return the books. I am so confident of your success that I will gladly trust you with a quantity." On these terms I agreed to have a shot at it. With a hundred copies of *How to Avoid a Large Family!* I made my way to a market at Brixton, took up my stand and commenced to speak. I had no plan in my mind of what kind of lecture I should give, but I began by reminding my hearers

222

that the two most powerful instincts in human nature are hunger and sex. From that I went on to draw a harrowing picture of the hard-working mother, with a large family, a small husband with a tiny wage, and the fearful struggle they had to provide for their numerous progeny. "And don't forget that the rich limit their families. Take the case of the Bishop of London, who is enthusiastic about large families for the poor. One would think that a public man who is so keen on the need for increasing the population would set an example, would lead the way by having an extra-specially large family of his own. Not so!—the Bishop of London is a bachelor. He has no children of any kind." The big stiffs yelled their heads off at this subtle and side-splitting thrust.

"If a poor woman goes to a doctor and asks him to give her the information that will enable her to prevent the arrival of another unwanted child, he will refuse to help her; but the wealthy lady, who can afford a big fee, will be told exactly what to do. Now this book which I hold in my hand contains that information which at present is only available to those who can afford to pay an enormous sum of money for it. I am the first man who has dared to come out into a market-place and offer this precious knowledge to the people at a price which is within the reach of all. I would gladly give these books away, but I am not a millionaire. Remember that I risk my liberty every time I sell one of these books. In France, Germany, and America there are men and women serving long terms of penal servitude for daring to sell this same book to the poor people who so badly need the information it contains. The price is not one guinea, not half a guinea, not even five shillings or half a crown. The price is so small that I am almost ashamed to mention it, in case you think I am mad. The price is one shilling."

I sold out. The crowd fought for copies, and I could have sold another hundred. All my scruples disappeared immediately. A hundred shillings for twenty minutes' work. Tenpence profit on every copy sold. This was money for old rope. I dashed back to the gentleman's address and bought five hundred copies. He was delighted, but not more than I was. The next day being Sunday, I pitched in Petticoat Lane, where between the hours of eleven and two I disposed of nearly two hundred copies. For weeks I worked the London markets as hard as I could, taking money every time I opened my mouth in public on the subject of family limitation. The joke about the Bishop of London never failed. Poor old Bishop! It was a shame to use his name for such a purpose, but the temptation was too great to be resisted. I used it thousands of times, in all parts of the country, and it never failed once.

My earnings while in London never fell below five pounds a week, and often reached as high as ten. I lived well, dressed like a duke, and drank like a fish. The more I drank, the more eloquent I became. I sought and found female society and left a trail of broken hearts in every direction. It was a great life.

When things became stale in London I went to Glasgow. Glasgow was a perfect Tom Tiddler's Ground. I spoke twice a day, and seldom took less than two pounds a time. Two pounds for twenty minutes' work, twice a day. On Sundays I worked Glasgow Green, speaking six times a day. I was earning over twenty pounds a week. One day, wanting a change, I took the train for Aberdeen. In one week at the granite city I took twenty-seven pounds. I got drunk every afternoon. The more I drank, the better I spoke and the better I felt. Strong drink agreed with me physically and mentally. Alas, those days are gone. After laughing at milk-drinkers for thirty years, I am now reduced to drinking pints of it to keep my strength up. And I dare not touch spirituous liquor in any form. There is tragedy here.

After working Scotland to death, I went on to Newcastle-on-Tyne, where I worked the Bigg Market and the Quayside with great success for many months. I found the Tynesiders rather reserved at first, but when they got used to me I made friends of them in large numbers. I lived on Tyneside for over two years and ultimately—having allowed myself to take up propaganda work for socialism again—became a famous figure throughout Northumberland and Durham. I took to the socialist platform again for the sake of a girl. For the first time for many years I fell desperately in love. She threw me over in the end, but it was a glorious romance while it lasted.

While in Newcastle I joined the Clarion Dramatic Society. This group of amateur players have done many years of good work in promoting and sustaining interest in the works of Ibsen, Strindberg, Tchekof, Hauptmann, St. John Hankin, St. John Ervine (my brilliant and distinguished fellow-countryman), Stanley Houghton, Noel Coward, and all the big noises in the European theatrical world. They greatly honored me by giving me extremely good parts to play. During the time I was in the city I sustained many roles—leading and misleading—with, I believe, considerable success. I played the leading part in *The Admiral Guinea*, by Stevenson and Henley; "Dr. Flisher" in *The Beaver Coat*, by Hauptmann; "Hilchrist" in *The Skin Game*, by Galsworthy; and "Sartorius" in *Widower's Houses*, by Bernard Shaw. Shaw visited a performance of his play *Man and Superman* when it was done by the Society in their hall in the Royal Arcade. At the end of a grueling evening, during which the famous dramatist and field-preacher exhibited traces of acute discomfort, the actor who had played "John Tanner" walked over to him and asked, "Well, Mr. Shaw, what did you think of our acting?" "Oh, perfectly abominable, of course," Shaw replied.

Although I have every respect for my fellow-actors of the Clarion Dramatic Society and played with them myself under excellent conditions, I am of the firm opinion that most of the amateur groups in the country should be declared illegal and the members put to death.

I became heartily sick of the birth-control racket before I finished. After the miners' lock-out of 1921 there was a big drop in the workers' wages. My takings went down considerably. And the subject bored me. I dislike talking about sex. Only freaks would make it the major subject of their jawing and scribbling. Birth-control disgusts me, anyhow. The idea of starting married life cluttered up with a collection of mechanical implements and other devices for the frustration of the natural procreative process is revolting. The popularity of birth-control with the cretins and morons of today is alone sufficient to condemn it. Contraception is an excellent thing for people with the mentality of slaves. It is turning thousands of men and women into nasty, unwholesome perverts. I repudiate my former support of it. Only the fact that it was an easy way of making money ever induced me to have anything to do with it; and I had not studied the subject at that time, and have no desire to study it now. It is enough that there is no longer any money in it for me, and that I regard the whole matter with distaste.

I gave up the markets in 1922 and returned to the platform as an advocate of revolutionary socialism. It was a big comedown economically, but I had to adjust myself to a lower standard of living. So the dog had returned again to his vomit.

CHAPTER XIII

The "Crocus"

THE "crocus" is the name market-people give to a man who sells pills or medicine on market-places. The public call him a quack doctor. He is often a picturesque figure, sometimes a grotesque figure, but always a figure. He lives entirely upon his personality, his appearance, voice, tongue, and gift of convincing oratory. All he needs is a bag of pills, a case of bottles filled with colored water, or a few packets of herbs "my famous herbal remedy." He lives by his tongue as a lawyer does, or a clergyman, politician, or public speaker; and unless he is possessed of more brains, more resource, more personality, and more knowledge of human nature than most of the professional gentlemen I have mentioned, he will not last very long at his difficult and highly skilled profession.

In market work the article sold is of small importance—it is the tale told about it that sells it. You might be trying to sell the Elixir of Life, but unless you could tell a good story you would not sell one bottle. You might be trying to sell cold water. If you tell your story well, you will sell out and they will come back for more. The purchasers will swear your medicine has done them more good than any doctors' drugs. They will recommend you to their friends, and you can stand on the same market-place for the rest of your life and do a roaring trade.

There is a technique of market salesmanship. It has to be learned on the job by practice and experience of crowds and their ways. The "crocus" business is traditional, like the actor's, the vaudeville artiste's, or the circus worker's. It is a craft, a science, and an art. I am proud to say that I am a master of it. I could go on any marketplace in Great Britain and take myself a pound or two in a couple of hours, without any trouble at all.

Some men I have known, who have left the political platform to take up market salesmanship, have imagined that, because they were able to hold large crowds as political speakers, the same ability and drawing capacity would insure them success on the markets. They were speedily disillusioned. Market work requires a different method of approach, a different style, a different and far more difficult technique. Some men are born with it, some acquire it by study and practice, many are incapable of learning it at all.

I had this mistaken idea when I first went on the markets. I imagined that because I was a practiced speaker in another sphere I should have no difficulty in attracting large crowds and persuading them that my tooth-powder was the best in the world. It was a chastening experience to find that such was not the case. I did not, however, do what many fatheads do—blame the people for their ignorance in not listening to me or buying my commodity: I looked for the cause of my failure and found it in myself. Realizing how much I had to learn, I set about learning it, and, as I am a quick student, it did not take long. In a short period I was able to "bat" as well as the next man, and better than many. "Batting" is the most difficult part of the market-worker's business. The art lies in "coming to the bat," and if you lack it, or cannot acquire it, or neglect it, you may be as eloquent as Demosthenes, but you will never do any good for yourself as a market-worker.

"Batting" is selling, or rather announcing of the price of your article to the crowd. You must know—either by experience or instinct, by scientific study of crowds or by divination, or a mixture of both—the exact moment to announce the price of your world-famous cure. You must not strike too soon or leave it too long. You must be able to gauge the psychological moment. You must then strike hard and strike home. If you can do this you will have a good "hand-out;" if not, you will draw a blank and your labor will have been in vain. You will not "break the hedge" (hedge and ditch: pitch).

There used to be half a dozen "crocuses" working the markets of Great Britain and Ireland who were geniuses. There was the great "Sequa," of whom countless stories are told and whose name has become a legend. He was long before my time, but I have heard his name spoken with awe by market-men in all parts of the country and even by members of the general public, or "fingers," as the public are called in market language. Sequa worked big. He drove a carriage-and-pair into the fairgrounds and pitches, and he carried a brass band. It is said of him that this band played loudly under his instruction during the extraction of aching teeth from the jaws of his credulous clients. He was a Master.

I was well acquainted with John William Cox, a powerful and eloquent "crocus" who died in the workhouse a few years ago. This veteran pill-seller stood at the head of his profession and possessed amazing powers of spellbinding and selling. He had one great fault—he loved the sound of his own voice, and often went on talking long after he should have "come to the bat."

I never practiced as a "crocus," though a "book-worker" is almost a "crocus"—the style and methods are similar. But I was greatly flattered by men like Cox and Douglas Reid and Lloyd of Portsmouth pressing me in my own interests to become one. I tested myself once or twice at places where

I was not known as a "book-worker," and had no difficulty in inducing the "hedge" to accept me as a learned doctor. I pitched once from Cox's stall at Newark and took more money than the great professor himself, which impressed him so much that he appointed me his successor in perpetuity.

All sorts of lines are worked by market-men. A versatile worker will be a doctor in the winter and a racing-tipster in the summer; though street-tipsters are not genuinely of the market, nor are they popular on the pitches, as they have the reputation of being "narks." A "nark" is a man who spoils other workers by illegitimate methods of working—standing too close to another man's "hedge," or shouting loudly, to the detriment of other workers, or attracting the attention of the "flattie" (police constable) and suchlike unworthy practices. Street-tipping is also illegal, and the tipster is continually hopping and dodging from one pitch to another in order to have a quick sale before the "flattie" blows along.

A versatile worker will be selling the "rub," or "rub-a-dub" (a preparation which removes stains and grease from clothing by rubbing) one day and "cough slum" the next. He may be a "windbag-worker" (a seller of lucky packets) at one market and a vendor of "knob fake" (hair restorer) at another. But the best men generally settle on one line and stick to it. The king-pin of all workers is the "crocus."

The "crocus" stands at the top of his profession because he is endowed with high qualities. He must have a good speaking voice, a striking personality, and a convincing manner. His task is not an easy one, and few men are able to do it at all. First he has to gather a crowd. Having got them together, he must hold them by his voice and powers of speech until his purpose is achieved. He has to convince them that they are ill. Having succeeded in that, he has then to persuade them that he, and he alone, is in possession of the remedy, the only remedy, for their ailments. Some of them are not ill, have never had a day's illness in their lives. These, however, are provided for. A special passage in his "fanny" ("fanny dale": tale) is designed and arranged to capture the attention and the shillings of these robust ones. "Some of you men and women within the sound of my voice," he declares in ominous tones, "imagine that, because you are in apparent good health at this moment, you can afford to do without my remedy. You need no pills, no medicine, no physic; you laugh at the very idea. Poor blind fools that you are! Mark my words—and may I never move from this ground upon which I stand if I speak without knowing the terrible responsibility which rests upon me—a time will come, when you least expect it, when you will be stricken down. You will be taken with pains in the back, difficulty in breathing, tightness across the chest. You will wonder why your heart thumps at your ribs against the use of nature; why you have shooting pains all over your body; why you have specks before the eyes and spots behind the ears; why you are troubled by dizziness, blind, bleeding, or itching piles; why your head aches; your teeth ache; your stomach aches; your feet ache; you ache all over from the crown of your head to the soles of your feet. You will wonder then, I say, why you had so little sense as to ignore the warning given you by a man you saw on your common market-place, standing under the blue canopy of heaven. You called him a 'quack' maybe; you despised him because he stood on your common market-place. Be warned—for God's sake be warned—before it is too late, before you reach that stage when no medicine in the world

can do you good! Remember the words of Aristotle, the greatest philosopher the world has ever known: 'Prevention is better than cure.'"

By this time the healthiest persons in the crowd are beginning to wonder whether they are as well in health as they had always believed themselves to be. One never knows. A few more telling illustrations from the great healer, and by the time he comes to his "bat" the most healthy and the most indifferent ones are stretching out their hands for a box of his wonder-working pills.

"I am no quack!" our friend will say, in solemn and impressive tones. "My father was a well-known doctor in your city of London, who lost a huge fortune—the savings of a lifetime—in a disastrous bank failure, which is fresh in your minds today. Thirty years ago I had to forget my university education, pocket my pride, sell my house in Park Lane, give up a lucrative practice, and come into your common market-place. I have lost my surgery, my degrees, my titles, and my wealthy connections; but I have not lost my skill, my medical knowledge, my surgical training, my power to heal the sick and cure the afflicted. That skill, that knowledge, that learning, I place at your disposal here today. Here, men and women, is the pill that has made me famous, that has saved thousands of lives. Won't you trust me? Won't you place yourselves in my hands and let me cure you? I will give you a clear eye, a steady hand, a strong heart; I will bring back the rosy hue of health to those pallid cheeks; I will give you life, men and women—LIFE! I do not charge you ten guineas, I charge you the working-man's price—One Shilling!"

It was always a firmly held article of faith that to appeal to reason and commonsense was fatal to a market-worker's chance of success. To admit that there were certain diseases he could not cure, to let it be thought that any one "under the blue canopy of heaven" might know as much as he did about the anatomy of the human body or the treatment of disease, to speak highly of the medical profession, to refuse to himself the attributes of God Almighty, was to forfeit the confidence of the public and court disaster. The more incredible his claims, the more preposterous the statements to which he gave utterance, the greater his talent for barefaced and shameless lying, the more warmly would the market-going public take him to their hearts and the more swiftly would the money flow from their pockets into his.

All crowds are credulous, the educated no less than the ignorant. All crowds like to be blarneyed and bluffed into buying something they don't really wish to buy and in the merits of which they have no real faith. All crowds can be mesmerized and victimized by the authority of the spoken word. When I was a less experienced speaker than I am now, I used to address myself to the one imaginary intelligent man in the crowd. I aimed to reach him, I stood in fear of his disapproval, I set out to win his appreciation and good will. No greater error can be made by any public speaker. It is the mob that matters, not the intelligent minority, whose existence is mythical in any case. It is the ignorant, gullible, mutable many, not the intellectual and skeptical one (if such a figment has any objective existence), that count. It is to them you must appeal. They are your patrons and your paymasters. God help you if you fail to give them what they want.

Even if there should be an intellectual person among them, he is not the sort that will buy anything. Only the very young and inexperienced ever think of him at all. Intellectual persons are not noted for their generosity, and their judgments are always hollow and shallow. These individuals who stand at the back of the crowd with a superior expression on their faces are known among market-workers and stall-holders as "wide mugs." The description is apt and true. The superior person who thinks he cannot be caught is the easiest of all to deceive. It is the solemn duty of every one who is in a position to deceive him to do so. Let him have it good and hard, for it was for this purpose he was sent into the world.

Market vendors, like actors, are extremely law-abiding people. Just as actors who rifle tills, hold up bank-managers, and murder their wives are as rare as honest lawyers, so "crocuses" who forge checks, practice white-slavery, or pour poison into beer-jugs are as scarce as thinking freethinkers or cultured communists.

The chartered markets, of which there is one in practically every city and town, and the London street-markets, are an ancient and valuable feature of the national life. They are not what they were. Bad trade, changes in public taste, vexatious restrictions upon individual enterprise on the part of poor men, the increasing bureaucratic regimentation of everything and everybody, are robbing the country of everything outstanding and colorful in individual personality, and sweeping away the many virile and romantic types of whom the "crocus" was one of the most splendidly picturesque.

CHAPTER XIV

Dramatic Recitals

EARLY in my career as a socialist advocate I tried to intro-
duce a touch of art into my work. Just before the war,
while I was spending some weeks in Manchester, I suggested
a series of lectures upon literary subjects to the Independent
Labor Party and other socialist bodies throughout Lancashire
and Yorkshire. Many of the branches availed themselves of
my services. I charged a fee of ten shillings a lecture, and
they were successful enough. Yet, much as these lectures were
appreciated, I could not help feeling that the subjects were
alien to most of the audiences. They applauded warmly and
asked sympathetic questions, but I knew in my heart that
they would have preferred the old economic stodge. They
wanted to hear again the old stereotyped phrases of socialist
propaganda. They never tire of these. They do not even
desire the old ideas to be presented in a new form of words.
They want the old words and shibboleths, the old arguments
and illustrations, hoary with age, the old jokes stale with
use, the old instances and analogies, worn by constant usage
and stringy with long chewing by a thousand tongues. What
is to be done with such people? Nothing. They must be
left mouthing and rolling their dusty, mildewed old phrases
round and round their tongues until the world's sanitary
inspector, Death, comes to condemn them and their mouths
are stopped with dust.

I next struck the idea of giving dramatic recitals, a task
for which nature has fitted me rather well. I threw off one
or two little verses and pieces of my own composition at
concerts and socials and found them well received by all.

238

Then I was asked to give a whole evening at a socialist club in Manchester. I was not certain if my repertoire could be stretched to last so long, but I promised to learn something suitable for the occasion. I decided to give Oscar Wilde's famous poem *The Ballad of Reading Gaol*. I had learned some of the verses after coming out of Strangeways Prison, the theme of the ballad naturally interested me at that time. For the recital I learned the whole poem off by heart. It is fairly long, and takes thirty-five minutes to declaim in its entirety.

The recital was a great success. The *Ballad* is a difficult thing to do because of the length and the absence of dramatic action. There is no scope for the use of gesture or any kind of effect, other than that which lies in the striking and beautiful words of the poem, yet it elicited such applause as I had seldom received before. The audience, I am glad to say, was deeply affected, handkerchiefs being freely employed in the course of the recital. There is no spectacle more gratifying to an artiste than the sight of strong men and stronger women weeping copiously as a result of his efforts. It is a bracing tribute to his talents as an actor.

I responded to the terrific cheering by giving the speech of Buzfuz from the *Pickwick Papers*, which I had learned in jail. This was equally successful, the audience laughing as to the manner born. Having tasted blood, as it were, they demanded more, and I followed with Mark Antony's speech, Shylock's vindication of his race, and Hamlet's "Rogue and peasant-slave" outburst. I then burlesqued a few Labor leaders and well-known propagandists, hitting off their mannerisms and tricks of speech, and finished with an imitation of Tom Mann which swept the whole crew of them right off their feet.

I continued to give these dramatic entertainments all over the country for many years. There was little competition. I had the field to myself, no one could imitate me. Speakers ape and copy each other continually, but no one has ever been able to imitate me, either as speaker or entertainer. It would seem, therefore, that I am unique and inimitable, a distinct entity with a distinct identity.

Yet, although I was cheered to the echo whenever I spoke or recited, nothing happened. I never got anywhere. It took me a long time to realize that this was because I did not fit into any place in the British socialist movement. They don't really want art and beauty, or wit, or any of the things that men think distinguish them from the beasts that perish. They want lead, not gold. Big chunks of lead. Leaden ideas, leaden dogmas, leaden economics, and leaden politics. A leaden philosophy for leaden bodies, leaden minds, leaden souls. Many of them enjoyed the poetry and drama which I gave them, but in their hearts they were ashamed of enjoying it. The socialist oracles had instilled into them the idea that life must be taken solemnly. They could not grasp the difference between taking life seriously and taking it solemnly. They could not recognize a truth unless it came in mourning attire. They would reveal their Anglo-Saxon Puritanism in everything they said and did. The mention of beer, for instance, would set them sniggering. Those who drank it were as ashamed of doing so as was the long-faced teetotaler of seeing them "put it back." The atmosphere of the prayer-meeting and the Nonconformist conventicle hung over the workers' political parties like a thick mist.

On the question of sexual morality or personal conduct the English revolutionaries have always followed the lead of the Nonconformist bodies. On matters of ethics and religion they

take their cue, like the freethinkers, from the Protestants. On
most other matters they take their cue from the industrial
capitalists of the early nineteenth century.

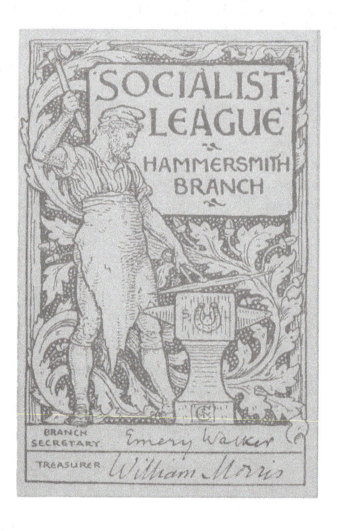

William Morris, the greatest figure the movement was ever able to capture, died worn-out and heartsick at the failure of his efforts to bring an understanding of the rich and vital art of the Middle Ages into the minds of the drab dullards of British socialism. Morris was one who loved his fellow-men in spirit and in truth. He was an artist and an artisan, a poet and a craftsman, a painter and a singer. He spent his magnificent physical powers in a vain endeavor to bring beauty into the lives of the industrial workers. A lover of all that was rich and fine and noble and beautiful in life and art, he broke himself against the rock of Puritanism. Morris was continually urging the socialists to cultivate beauty in their houses, their dress, their furniture, their books and their thoughts. He loved color, rich decoration, heraldry, pageantry, and civic ritual and ceremonial. He appealed to the socialists to turn their minds upon these things. He might as well have talked to the dead. What they wanted—and Morris came to realize it towards the end of his life—was to read Karl Marx and ask silly questions about "the economic basis of art," that is, if they ever asked questions about art at all. They wanted to fight and squabble and scratch and call one another "twisters" and "traitors" and "renegades," and air their own little egos, instead of acquiring education and developing intelligence and self-respect. They hated beauty because they had no conception of it. They dared not openly say so, but in their bleached and stringy little souls they hated and feared all that was noble and beautiful in life. Such things made them uncomfortable. Karl Marx, the world's champion bore, with his mean, selfish, peevish disposition and his constitutional inability to say a good word about any living creature, is their hero and their god. It is to the eternal glory of William Morris that he refused to have anything to do with the dreary old misery-monger. Like many others of a generous nature, he could not stomach the man.

My dramatic recitals were splendidly received in Scotland and Wales, and on the occasions of my visits to Dublin or Belfast the response of the people was overwhelming. Never, outside London, have I been insulted by some one complimenting me, after a two hours' recital of the best in the world's literature and drama, upon my wonderful memory. I am not naturally homicidal, but that remark makes me see scarlet.

CHAPTER XV

Old Victorian Nights

A FTER a long absence in the north of England and in activities with frequent bouts of socialist propaganda, lured into it, as I have said, by a charming lady who eventually left with a handsomer—and richer—man, I returned to London. By 1924 I had grown tired of market-work. It was very exhausting, and no longer as lucrative as formerly; and I hated the birth-control stuff so heartily that I could no longer endure to sell the book; so I resumed speaking in Hyde Park.

Ten years had wrought few changes in the personnel of either the speakers or the crowds. The war had taken toll of the nation's manhood, the bravest and the best, but the same old faces still haunted the meeting-ground at Marble Arch. Ranters and hot-air merchants, who had gone into hiding during the war, had crept out of their funk-holes and clambered on to the platforms once more. They had learned nothing. The same old jargon was still being mouthed. Capitalism, of course, was collapsing. It always is. There has never been a time within living memory when the capitalist system was not crumbling, tottering, rocking to its doom. It always has been and it always will.

A new factor had, I should mention, entered into the economic and political speeches and discussions: the Russian revolution. This event had given fresh hope and inspiration to every malcontent and sorehead in Europe. The sadistic aspect of the revolution made a strong appeal to the yobs and Yahoos who abound on the fringes of the revolutionary circus. Vast numbers of vicious dunderheads had been cut down on all sides in the course of the change from Czarism to Leninism. The squealing and grunting round the pig-trough was deafening. Whites, Reds, and all sorts of stiffs and saps had been put through the mill with enormous gusto. There had been a terrific fury of blood-letting, thousands having been hanged, shot, burned, disemboweled, and generally ill-treated. The prisons were crammed. Trotsky was mowing down the opposition, and Denniken and Koltchak were ripping up the Reds. Our home-bred Bolshies were in their element, howling, weeping, and caterwauling in true yobbo style. A great number of the middle-class intellectuals–what the Americans call the "radical bourgeoisie"–were squeaking and twittering in a nauseating manner. Oxford and even Cambridge were all hot and bothered over the Sickle and Hammer. It was all extremely tiresome.

Hyde Park was swarming with these new communists. It was impossible to move without treading on one of them. Free speech had gone by the board: only a communist or socialist could get a hearing. There was a stand in the Park called the "Open Socialist" platform. I was invited to speak from this. My address created a sensation. I had been away so long, and so many things had happened since 1914, that I did not quite realize how good a speaker I had become. To the Park crowds I was a second Cicero. I did not mention any specific socialist organization by name, I just orated as an independent revolutionary propagandist. This, I thought to myself, is not too bad. I must turn my popularity to account. So I let it be known that I earned my livelihood by speaking alone, and invited my listeners to see me at the receipt of custom—outside the gate.

For two years I was a regular speaker on the "Open So-cialist" platform and a great favorite with the wrong kind of people. But the opponents of the revolutionary idea liked me almost as much, though the thick-headed "comrades" did not know this. I had hardly an enemy for a long time, and attained a dazzling popularity; more important than this was the fact that I made a good thing out of it. The crowds flocked to the gate and pressed money into my hands, shillings, half-crowns, and ten-shilling and pound notes coming thick and fast. During these two years I took, on the average, six pounds a week in collections and donations outside the gate. People seldom spoke to me without giving me something. It was money for old razor-blades. I made some good friends, people who did not care a rap what side I was on as long as I spoke.

I often noticed the presence of celebrated people in my audience. Actors, actresses, members of His Majesty's Government, bishops, authors, musicians, and all sorts of public characters well known in their different spheres. I became a sort of cult. My revolutionary ideas were passed over and I was studied from the artistic point of view. A famous actor, Mr. Baliol Holloway—for whom I am glad to say I have unbounded admiration as man and artiste—wrote to say how much he had been struck by my technique as a speaker. "I am a Conservative, though not a bigoted one," he said, "but it is your technical accomplishments which astonish me, not your political views." I had many communications from men and women of prominence, but Mr. Holloway's praise gave me a thrill of genuine pleasure.

During the summer of 1925 I visited the Old Vic theater to see an actor who had impressed me greatly when I saw him at Leeds towards the end of the war. He played "Oswald" in Ibsen's *Ghosts* with such power and originality that I had never forgotten him. He had joined the Vic company to

play a round of leading parts in Shakespeare, and I made
my way there especially to watch his acting. This actor,
who is now famous, was Ernest Milton. As a consequence of
the interest which he aroused in me by his wonderful art, I
have been an enthusiastic Old Victorian since that day, and
have not missed a Shakespearean production for nine years.
The emotional and artistic stimulus which this has brought
me can hardly be overestimated. It gave me a new interest
in life, when things had become pretty bleak intellectually,
and revealed to me something of Shakespeare which I had
not known of before. Shakespeare has spoiled me for all
other writers, except Dickens, Walter Scott, and the great
Irish dramatist Sean O'Casey, who is Shakespeare's only
successor in force and power and beauty and imaginative
sweep. O'Casey's characters pulsate with urgent life, and are
so real and vital that they vibrate in the mind with greater
reality than living friends. O'Casey is a poet. He loves words.
All Irishmen love words and use them as they should be
used: lyrically, poetically, and rhetorically. Their speech is
rhythmical and full of musical cadences. When their orators
speak, they use language with accuracy and precision.

I have lived for many years in the society of persons who
use words continually without regard to their meaning and
are the victims of phrases and slogans which convey nothing
definite to them. Their way of arguing and debating is to
answer one phrase with another phrase. They never see a
thing as it is, but as an aspect or reflex of something of
which they have read. They know nothing, yet they have
theories about everything. Reality is no more than a blur of
words and phrases to them. As a consequence of this horrible
mental malady, the revolutionary knows nothing whatever a-

bout anything, and cannot give an account of anything whatever. He is a brain in chains.

The dyer's hand is so often subdued to what it works in that I should have become one of these awful types myself had I not been born with a disposition which reacts more against my environment than to it. I did not take color from my economic or social surroundings. On the contrary, I grew as unlike the people I associated with as possible. Most people, says a brilliant writer, are other people. I have never had any difficulty in remaining myself.

Though I was never a saluter or salaamer of big reputations, there are certain things and persons to which I have responded with great fervency. Eggs-and-bacon have always affected me profoundly. Sitting around in a comfortable position, talking with some one whose personality and conversation is congenial, makes a strong appeal. Great literature and good clothes, good tobacco and plenty of leisure, make me happy. There has never been any difficulty about the great literature, but the lack of good clothes and comfortable surroundings and the right kind of food and company has irked me all my life. I hope to have an abundance of material comforts and of those things which gratify the senses before I die.

I think, however, that on the whole I have enjoyed the things of the mind more than the things of the body. Indeed, I have often put mental and spiritual satisfaction before physical or material gratification. I have gone without food so that I might enjoy a play I wanted to see or a book I wanted to read. I found in Shakespeare such deep satisfaction as might be compared to the eating of a good breakfast or the embraces of a beautiful woman—but with something added. Shakespeare touches chords and rouses thoughts and emotions of which one had not suspected the existence. Above all, he harrows and shakes the soul by his superb, his incomparable mastery of words. I never read or hear a line from Shakespeare without feeling a tremendous thrill of emotional exaltation. Even the sight of his name in print moves me greatly.

The performances at the Old Vic taught me a great deal and gave me greater intellectual and emotional pleasure than almost anything I have ever experienced. For the last nine years, as I have said, I have not missed a production of Shakespeare at this house, and I must raise my headgear in token of gratitude and appreciation.

Shakespeare has never found, I am convinced, a greater exponent than Ernest Milton. This actor makes a particular appeal to me because his personality and style is exceptional and unusual. He brings upon the stage a note of strangeness which is akin to the quality one finds in certain poets and artists whose personality and achievement astonish the world. Ernest Milton is as far removed from the commonplace as it is possible for an actor to be. He is the antithesis of the ordinary. In parts calling for an interpretation of the uncanny, the eerie, the macabre, the spiritually isolated and remote from common experience, the psychologically disturbed or the profoundly tragic, there is no one who can approach him. He possesses a subtle intelligence and a far-reaching imagination. These great gifts come into play in his interpretation of such characters as Hamlet or King Lear. In the Richards Two and Three there is no actor to compare with him. His Shylock is the most striking of all Shylocks I have ever seen. His Hamlet is the greatest since Irving; his Lear is sublime.

There is also a strain of the exotic, a suggestion of tropical luxuriance, something Panlike and other-worldly in his personality, which affects people strangely. The audience are put under a spell. I found that Milton's acting gave me the same kind of thrill that I got from Irving when I saw him in *The Bells*; the same feeling of exhilaration and tremendous emotional excitement that I experienced when seeing Bernhardt, Duse, and Mrs. Patrick Campbell. Every one is not so convinced of this actor's greatness as I am, but that is their misfortune. He has been called a "genius" by the dramatic critics, and high praise has been bestowed upon him, but it generally seems to me to fall far short of a true understanding of Ernest Milton's significance as an artist. The Anglo-Saxon mind is too puzzled and baffled by unusual genius to assess it truly; the standardized judgments and perfunctory estimates of an actor's work are insufficient and misleading. The critics carp and cavil and emphasize unessentials and wander off into personal reminiscences of some one else. The habit of comparing one thing with something entirely different is a mania with most of them.

But to Hades with other critics and their opinions. It is enough that I find Ernest Milton to be the greatest acting genius of our time. If I think so, then it is so for me, and that is the thing that matters. I assigned him his place at the peak of English acting a long time ago. He creates—amid so much that is passing and perishable in the traffic of the stage—moments of unearthly beauty that shine out through the darkness of our modern world.

Another actor whose work gave me great pleasure at the Old Vic was Baliol Holloway. This lively, virile, essentially masculine actor has been called by Henry Ainley the best Shakespearean player in this country. I know only one who excels him. His manliness is predominant in his acting, as in his life. Dullness or staleness cannot live where he is.

A cheerful tornado, a laughing whirlwind, a good-natured volcano. He bears himself like an athlete and has a grayhound-cleanness and swiftness about him. His features in repose are grim and stern. A great Richard III, a splendid Henry V, a lean and hungry Cassius, and the best Othello of our time. An actor and a man.

These two personalities stand out in a waste of stereotyped miming, and both have given me so much intellectual and esthetic stimulus that this book would be an inadequate record of my career if I left them unmentioned. As it is, it must prove unsatisfactory in many ways. I am no great writer, but an orator who started late in life trying to say in print what he has not been able to say before, even on the public platform. During all those years I spoke continually, but seldom bothered to write anything, not even a letter. If the whole of my correspondence was collected it would not amount to more than a thousand words. I received a great many letters, but often left them unanswered. Two things I have always disliked doing: writing letters and visiting people at their houses. The fear of being bored has prevented me from cultivating many acquaintances that might have helped me greatly in my career.

I did make a few friends among the Old Vic audience, though at first I tried to avoid talking to them. But we formed a little group after a time, and our judgments on the actors, although not loudly voiced, were drastic in the extreme. The Old Vic audience has been praised on all hands, by both actors and critics; they certainly provide that enthusiastic response which is of immense value to the players. The scenes on first and last nights and on Shakespeare's birthday nights are without parallel in the history of the modern theater. I have never failed to do my share of clapping, shouting, and cheering on these occasions. I always applaud at curtain-fall when I go to a theater, and I loathe the unresponsive blocks of wood who sit silent at the end of a powerful and beautifully played scene. I look upon such persons with feelings of intense hatred. As for the swine who not only refuse to applaud themselves but look at those who do with an expression of disdain, I could cheerfully turn a machine-gun upon them. There is a particular type of theater-pest who, as soon as applause breaks out among the audience, starts "shishing" in an indignant manner. I always wish I had the physique of a Dempsey or a Tunney when these scoundrels start their sabotaging activities. A few smashing blows to the body and a good uppercut to finish would teach them a well-needed lesson.

At the same time, more harm than good is done by the kind of indiscriminating applause one hears so often at the Vic. To cheer a bad actor or actress is an insult to a good one. Every year the Vic company begins the season with a number of actors who cannot act at all. These novices are in the company to be trained. This would not be so bad if these small-part players improved as the season advanced. In very few cases has this been so. My seat at the Vic is, and has been for many years, at the left-hand side of the gallery, facing the stage. This corner is monopolized by myself and a few companions, who watch everything with close attention. More than once we have been on the verge of revolt at the tortures inflicted upon us by certain actors who, with each play, get worse instead of better. Only loyalty to the Vic as an institution, and sympathy with the rest of the cast, have prevented us from shouting out our disapproval of these pitiable touts. I could mention names, but I will refrain. While fine actors and actresses are out of work it is an outrage that these beginners—beginners from whom nothing is to be expected—infest the stage with their detestable activities. The Old Vic audiences are to be heartily condemned for not only suffering but encouraging them.

Another thing I object to is the presence of too many "Nancy-boys" among the small-part players. I have no prejudice about a man because he is homosexual—many geniuses have been and are so constructed physically—but I resent having to watch the languishing and listening to the squeaking and twittering of these youth while there are good men unemployed. Let these young perverts take up dressmaking or needlework, instead of plaguing theater audiences with their ninnying and neighing in the name of art. One in a company is bearable—he arouses an indulgent smile—but half a dozen is far too many, especially for an audience so virile and proletarian as the Old Vic.

It is amusing and amazing to find that the Vic audiences, who attend the plays so regularly and listen so attentively to the glorious lines of the greatest spirit ever born among men, are incapable of giving any opinion or criticism of either the plays or the acting. They have preferences and prejudices, but cannot tell any one why. They have to read what the critics say before they know what to think about a performance. In Dublin, for instance, the members of a theater audience can explain quite clearly and cogently why they like or dislike a play or a player; they may be sometimes mistaken, but they are not so mentally debilitated as to be unable to state why they hold a point of view. Londoners are the most mentally and morally weak of any section of the British people. Their minds are a blank; they know nothing about anything, not even about the work or business by which they earn their bread.

Yet, compared with a West End audience, the Old Victorians are monuments of taste and intelligence. To sit in a theater "up West" while a good play, well acted, is being performed, is to suffer the agonies of the damned. The stupidity, the emotional and intellectual insensibility, the inability to see a point or seize the meaning of a line, the cries of "ooer" every time anything intelligent is said upon the stage, the loud laughter during the poignant or tragic scenes, the icy silence when anything witty is said, the whispering and tittering, the munching and crunching of sweets and chocolates, the continual passing and repassing of patrons during the progress of the play, and the general boorishness and brutish ignorance of the bulk of the people in all parts of the house are so appalling that one stands aghast with horror and disgust.

There is nothing of this at the Old Vic, and for that, at any rate, the audiences are to be eternally blessed. An ideal way of seeing a play is from a box shut off from the sight and sound of any one, but perhaps the next best way is from the quite comfortable seat in the corner of the Old Vic gallery, left-hand side facing the stage. I say left-hand corner because the other corner is often occupied by a collection of the most objectionable hounds I have ever seen at that historic house. They chatter away like monkeys during the intervals, about the plays and the acting, but what they say is the most puerile rubbish. They have about as much knowledge of the drama between the six or seven of them as would half fill the back of a postage-stamp. How different is our corner! What high and critical intelligence; what artistic perception; what culture; what vast knowledge of the drama! An added advantage of sitting in this corner is that we hear the lines twice, once from the actors, and a second time from Miss

Pilgrim, a foundation-member who knows all the plays by heart and repeats each line as it leaves the actor's lips.

It is rather trying, to have to put up with the actors making speeches from time to time. "I thank you for your wonderful reception. It has all been too wonderful." One actress, for whom I have the greatest admiration, makes the same speech on all occasions. "I thank you for your wonderful reception. It has been awfully ripping." She has never been able either to add to or take from those beautiful and wonderful words of thanks. A few speak quite well, and Ernest Milton is nearly as good a speaker as he is an actor, but most actors should keep silent and content themselves with taking their calls.

The Old Vic is a glorious institution, and I have derived immense emotional and spiritual stimulus from the great playing and production I have been privileged to witness there.

I continued to speak on the "Open Socialist" platform until just after the General Strike in 1926. In that unfortunate attempt to pit themselves against the forces of the State the organized workers were beaten and smashed beyond hope of recovery. The strike might have strengthened the unions and wrung substantial concessions from the employers, had it not been for the usual sabotaging tactics of the communists, who hung on like obscene parasites to the saner body of workers who were working hard to check the drastic wage-reductions the masters were seeking to impose. Those Simon Tapper-titts bellowed and trumpeted about the need for an armed revolution so much that the Government made up its mind to stand no more nonsense, so they broke the trade-union movement, passed emergency legislation, and compelled the strikers to crawl back on their hands and knees.

From that time onwards the working-class political movement has been utterly powerless. It is doubtful if it will ever amount to anything again. English socialism gradually died, the rank and file melted away, and the whole thing petered out as a serious factor in the national life. The great swarm of communists who made Hyde Park hideous with their yelping and baying also began to break up. Within less than six months there was hardly a Red to be seen near the meeting-ground.

With the slump in socialist enthusiasm came a falling-off in my takings outside the gate. I found myself deserted by the vast crowd of socialist supporters who had formerly contributed to the collection.This was no surprise to me. I have never placed any reliance upon the rank and file of the workers' movements, the kind of cattle who gathered round the walls of the prisons while their leaders are confined within, and whose contribution to the class struggle is to sing the "Red Flag"—outside. One soon learns to disdain the fickle homage of the mob, the beast of muddy brain who will crown a leader today and crucify him tomorrow.

But it came home to me with greater force than before that the people who called me "Comrade" were a squalid collection of insincere and petty-minded weaklings, the ideals I had subscribed to in my youth were shabby and grimy ideals, and the movement I had been identified with so long a shoddy and grubby movement. The social aspirations of these people were not of the least moment. For a long time I had been traveling towards the dawn of nothing. The time had come to call a halt.

I left the "Open Socialist" platform and set up a platform of my own. Since that moment until the present time I have been known as an unattached speaker, a freelance, reserving the right to support or oppose any party or no party. I gradually eliminated the extremist elements from my audiences and from my personal acquaintances. Sometimes one or two would try to interrupt my meetings, but I used my old weapon of ridicule so mercilessly that they soon melted away. My answer to all who asked me why I had left off advocating socialism was, "Because it has pleased me to do so." That is my reply to all persons who inquire why I do or do not do this, that, or the other. "Do you believe in the emancipation of the working class?" a man once asked me about this period. "No," I answered. "Why not?" "Because it does not please me to do so." That, I think, is the most reasonable and honest attitude to take, though whether it is reasonable or honest is a matter of small concern to me. It pleases me, and that is sufficient.

I have always had a strong objection to explaining my actions or being responsible to any one but myself for what I say or do. I have addressed so many meetings in my time that most of them have passed out of my mind, but I recall one or two because of certain incidents which made them worth remembering. For many years now I have refused to answer any questions from members of the crowd, but I recall with great satisfaction an answer I made at the end of a lecture during the General Election of 1924. A man rose at the front of the hall—the lecture was indoors—with an expression of strong disapproval on his face, and in a grim, accusing voice put the following question: "Tonight you have attacked the Labor Party in the most uncompromising language, yet only last evening in a building only a few yards from this place you spoke on behalf of a Labor candidate and praised the Labor Party to the skies. What explanation have you to offer?" I rose at once and in a firm and decided tone answered, "None whatever." The questioner collapsed in confusion, while the audience laughed heartily and applauded loudly. I regard that answer as the most brilliant I have ever given to any questioner, and I have given some pretty sharp answers in my time.

There have been times when I have wondered how I have been able to get away with some of the things I have said. Any other speaker would have been laughed at, bowled down, or torn to pieces. I have taken the most outrageous liberties with crowds, and I have never had a rowdy meeting in my life. An attempt was once made by a handful of tiddly-wink communists to break up one of my meetings, but they paid dearly for their folly. I have never believed in giving an inch to any one who tries to upset a meeting, and employ the most ruthless and unscrupulous measures to suppress them.

Unless you let it be known that it does not pay to trifle with you, these scum will give you no peace. Other speakers are continually subjected to heckling and interruption, but interrupters have always given me the widest of berths.

For a time after I had broken with the "Open Socialist" platform my collections fell off considerably. I let them fall. My pockets were lighter, but I felt much freerer. I soon began to gather round me a better type of listener—the kind of listener who has no set views about anything, who is free from bigotry and is not a partisan.

To all who have ever listened to me I have given full measure, pressed down and running over. If the millions of people who have enjoyed my speeches paid me what they owe me, I should be living in Park Lane. Most of the crowds who stand rubber-necking in the public parks never pay a penny towards the speakers who provide them with entertainment on the cheap. They imagine that the speaker should be at their service at any hour of the day and night. "Hi, Mr. Speaker; answer my question!" This cry is always heard at the meeting-grounds. It is heard at nearly every meeting, but never at any meeting of mine. My hearers seem to know by some sound instinct that it would not pay any of them to set up such a cry. The degrading practice of answering questions should be discontinued. Unless it is stopped, free speech will cease. There is something humiliating in the sight of a speaker battling with nit-wits and half-wits for a right that is already his by law—the right to express his views without let or hindrance. But my fellow-speakers have themselves to blame for pandering to the crowds as so many of them do, begging leave to submit this, and asking to be allowed to suggest that. They unbend their noble strength and pay dearly for it.

As for the peculiar types who ask questions, they should never be encouraged. Persons of that kind should be nipped in the bud at once and told that there are Free Libraries where they can find answers to all questions. If they are too lazy to take a book from the shelves and find out the difference between one "ism" and another, they are certainly not fit to be taken seriously by hard-working platform-men, who have something better to do than provide free education for intellectual spongers and loafers.

For my part, I will not stoop to it. If it pleased me to do so, I should do so; but it does not please me. I have never hesitated to make it clear that I am no man's servant. If any one wishes to bribe or buy me, they will have to pay a pretty stiff price.

For the last eight years I have continued to speak from my own platform as a freelance, independent of all parties, relying upon my own personality and talents for a livelihood. It is not easy work. I live upon nervous force. One must expend a vast amount of this nervous energy in order to hold the crowds together. As soon as I notice the slightest sign of inattention among the listeners I know that I am not at my best, and finish as soon as possible. Unless you are in fit health, it is not possible to throw out those waves of magnetism which infect a crowd and root them to the spot. Personality is vitality. And one does not always feel in the mood. It is better at such times not to speak at all. I have often been forced, by economic stress, to speak when I was not in good form. The effect is seen at once. The crowd is flat, sluggish, unresponsive, and fidgety. It is amazing how a crowd reflects the speaker's mood. The listeners take their cue from him. If he is dull, they are dull; if he is irritable they are irritable too. As soon as he livens up, the crowd livens up. He sets the pace. At least, it is so with me.

Yet I have long ceased to get any thrill out of public-speaking. The conditions are too dire. The struggle for existence is too keen. The possession of the actor's temperament enables me to simulate an intense interest in what I am saying, and to give spontaneity to everything, but it is more of a penance than a pleasure to speak nowadays. The disparity between the apparent success of the meeting—the laughter, the cheers, the enormous mass of people under the sway of the spoken word—and the meager financial reward—is grotesque. It is as though Kreisler got no salary for playing the violin so divinely, and had to stand outside with his hat in his hand, depending upon what his audience liked to give him. Only two per cent would take the trouble to donate, and, in addition, the police would move him on for obstruction. He would do fairly well in Ireland or Scotland, or in the North of England, but he would have a very thin time in London.

The fate of the freelance speaker is in the hands of the capricious multitudes, fickle and feather-brained, who will lap up his eloquence like dogs and leave him to starve in the end. He has to compete with the half-witted and lunatic speakers who, in a place like London, naturally draw the largest crowds. To a shallow public, who try to look intelligent, and fail, he pours out the treasures of his mind. He has no status. He receives no tangible recognition for his services. He bears the stigma of a Hyde Park tub-thumper, even though he has never thumped a tub in his life. He is the outcast of the oratorical world, the Ishmael of politics and the prey of time.

The profession of a speaker who cuts himself adrift from the herd, who cannot submit his intelligence to the rule of a party, is a blind alley. He must die worn-out and unwept, soon forgotten.

I have arranged to have the following simple inscription recorded upon my tombstone:

BONAR THOMPSON
BORN 1888
DIED 19—
THE COLLECTION WAS NOT ENOUGH

CHAPTER XVI

The Black Hat

FOR a long time I used to dream of running a paper of my own, an official organ through which I could reach a larger public than was possible by means of the spoken word. It was not until 1930 that I found it possible to achieve this ambition. I happened to be discussing homosexuality in a cafe near Shaftesbury Avenue one night with a group of artists and poets of the intellectual underworld. Seated at our table was a tall, stern-looking, well-dressed man of military bearing, who said little but looked rather bored and derisive. I was introduced to him by a young man who is now a well-known pictorial artist, and we struck up a conversation which turned out to have interesting consequences. His name was Harold Kelly, a West-country man, who had been in business, but, having been hit hard through the General Strike, had migrated to London in hopes of making a career in journalism. He had already placed several short stories with magazines, and was writing a play, but was open for anything that would speed things up in the literary racket. I mentioned my idea of a weekly or monthly review of my own, which would be utterly different from anything of the kind then in existence. The upshot of our talk was a determination to launch the paper as soon as possible. Mr. Kelly had no money, neither had I. I decided to try some of the high-lights of the Labor and socialist movement and others who knew me as one who had spent many years as an ardent champion of the workers' rights. I drafted a number of letters, which were dispatched to well-known men who might be likely to support me in an individual venture of such a kind.

The reactions of some of the "comrades" provided food for my natural cynicism. That celebrated forward-looker, the Hon. Bertrand Russell, replied as follows:

> Dear Mr. Thompson,
> I am sorry I cannot persuade myself that there is any chance of success for such a journal as you suggest, and therefore do not feel that much good would be done by helping you to found it.
>
> Yours sincerely,
> Bertrand Russell.

Professor Laski's letter is, in my judgment, a masterpiece, and I shall preserve it for posterity, if it is possible to do so:

> Dear Mr. Thompson,
> If I thought that there was the slightest chance of your proposed journal being a success, I would gladly give my mite towards starting it; but I am sure you will be wasting your ability and energy in the project, and I do not feel able to lend myself to what can only be a disappointment to you.
>
> I am,
> Yours very truly
> Harold J. Laski.

I felt angry at receiving such letters. If these gentlemen did not wish to help me with the paper, they were quite entitled to withhold their support, but why pour cold water on a comrade who was trying his best to earn a living? It was not the refusal to subscribe that annoyed me, but the smug assumption that I was doomed to failure before I started. If one listened to advice of that kind, one would never achieve anything.

A different kind of response came from Laurence Housman:

Dear Mr. Thompson,
I have been in at the death of too many journals to have any high hopes of success in your case. As an experiment, however, I send you a pound and wish for the best.

Yours sincerely,
Laurence Housman.

Professor Tawney sent a guinea with his good wishes, which I appreciated as a compliment, coming as it did from a man for whom I have great respect. I am afraid both Mr. Housman and Professor Tawney were rather disappointed with the paper when it appeared, as I had led them to expect something more sympathetic to the socialist point of view. Neither has written to me since. Mr. A. W. Haycock, M.P., was the only Labor member—with the exception of Joe Toole—who helped in any way, though I had helped many of them into office and was known as a man who had done much work for the Labor cause. Mr. Haycock was a real friend, putting himself to great inconvenience in his efforts to assist.

The appeal did not yield very much. Most of the money was subscribed by poor people who admired me as a speaker. The rest was borrowed from friends and had to be repaid in installments of so much a week. I raised, in all, the sum of twenty-five pounds. With that sum the paper was launched upon the reading public.

For many years I have worn a black hat—many people who visit Hyde Park make for the platform where the speaker with the black hat is to be found. Mr. Kelly suggested the title *The Black Hat* as the most appropriate and original. The whole of the paper was to be written by Harold Kelly and myself. Both of us had something to say, and we felt that we knew how to say it. Our trouble was to prevent other writers from dumping their stuff into our paper. We pointed out very firmly that we had not gone to the trouble of starting a paper so that others could write for it, but in order that Mr. Kelly and I could write for it. In the first number we made it plain that if any one wanted to see their stuff in our paper, they must pay a high fee for the privilege.

It is amusing to realize the effect of the printed word upon most people. We were continually being told that we should soon dry up and would have to have assistance with the articles. "Why don't you try and get an article from H. G. Wells, or some one like that?" was the kind of thing we had to put up with. "What the devil do we want with articles by H. G. Wells?" I used to say. "Harold Kelly and Bonar Thompson write for the thing. Isn't that good enough for you? You can read Wells any day, or Shaw, or any of those people. Haven't you had enough of them? Why are you such a snob? Do you think nobody can write unless he has a big name?" They always looked mulish and sheepish when talked to like that.

I never realized the power of human servility and snobbery and shallow stupidity until I began to write. It is pitiable. The way the modern person crawls before the pontiffs and popes of literature and journalism is sickening. Nor did I ever imagine how truly dense, thick-headed and slow-witted the reading public is. Apparently the average leader is convinced that writing an article is a wonderful feat. He pictures, I suppose, the writer sweating and straining, with towels round his head, in order to get a few thousand words on paper. No wonder book-writers make fortunes and are looked upon as oracles. I began writing seriously for the first time in my life just a little over three years ago. At first I did not think it would be so easy, though I never believed it to be very difficult. I had no difficulty at all. I could sit down and dash off a couple of thousand words without stopping to draw breath. It has been so ever since. I have no smug conceit in my ability as a literary man. That what I write has many faults of composition and treatment and style I am the first to believe, but that any one with anything to write about

has to rack his brain for words, thump his forehead, and cry,
like Hamlet, "About, my brain," I find incredible.

The copy for the first issue was all ready within a week, a
printer was found, the job started, and in ten days or so *The
Black Hat* was born. It was, of course, a personal venture.
The sales were mainly outdoor sales—at places where I was
known as a speaker. At Tower Hill, a dinner-hour speaking-
pitch, over five hundred copies were sold by Mr. Kelly and
myself within two hours. The crowds fought for them, and
we were nearly mobbed in trying to hand them out. Four
hundred copies, approximately, were disposed of outside the
gates of Hyde Park every Sunday. At a well-known bookshop
in Charing Cross Road fourteen quires a month were sold
regularly each month while the paper was published.

The Black Hat was a success. We sold six thousand
copies of the first issue within three weeks. We did it all
ourselves. We carried parcels, addressed wrappers, licked
stamps, interviewed prospective advertisers, sold the copies
at meetings where I talked about the merits of the great
review, and wrote the thing as well.

But it is not possible to keep any paper afloat today
on sales alone. You must have advertisements, and that is
where we fell down on *The Black Hat*. We got a few, but
not sufficient. And we had to pay for everything on the nail.
We were short of working capital; we were often short of
postage-stamps. We worked like galley-slaves, but we were
beaten in the end. We stuck it for five months. Had we
only been able to get some money into the concern, it would
have lived and become a feature of modern journalism. We
had good supporters, and most people liked the paper. One
encouraging feature was that the sales did not drop after
the first number, as is so often the case with mushroom

magazines. Our readers were enthusiastic—they were always asking for the next issue long before the previous one had been out a month. Kelly and I kept them on the tiptoe of expectation. We were up to all sorts of stunts.

The Black Hat was unusual. It was different. It was unlike any other journal. Original, unexpected, exceptional, provocative, pungent, trenchant, piquant, and never twice alike. We were never able to realize our ambitions because of lack of money and other considerations. Our great ideal was to produce an issue so tingling with virility and at the same time so utterly outrageous that most of the readers would go raving mad. But we did not want to achieve this by the usual methods—not by pornography, which is already played out; nor by attacking the things which every one attacks; but by simply writing as we felt. This is seldom done, and there is a fortune for any one who can do it well and in an original way. We continually contradicted ourselves, for instance, because we felt like that. We attacked bitterly one month the ideas we had violently endorsed the month before, and so on. That is what I mean by writing as you feel. And Mr. Kelly and I feel quite a lot of things that the average intellectual does not feel, I assure you.

Mr. Kelly is, like myself, an individual. That is why we had a terrific advantage over the average writer and all who traffic in ideas. We had no inhibitions or reservations, and, even if we had, we should tell those who don't like it to go to hell. That, in fact, was our motto and our message to all and sundry.

A host of imitators have sprung up since, and they have all been forgotten. They have been forgotten because they were what they were: imitators. Imitation is the curse and plague of our time. It has become a racket, a mania, a disease. Our imitators are forgotten because there was nothing in them. Nothing at all. But *The Black Hat* is not forgotten. It was read by all sorts and conditions of men. Galsworthy, Edgar Wallace, C. B. Cochran, Martin Harvey, Rosita Forbes, Lord Dunsany, Baliol Holloway, George Relph, Marda Vanne, and Gordon Craig all read and appreciated it. I mention these well-known people because they are all distinct personalities, working in different spheres. I have not left out the names of obscure people because they are any less important, but because, being obscure, a list of their names would mean nothing to the reader. I cannot abide writers who are always slinging famous names about, but there are times when it is necessary to refer to some of them. Some of the most famous people in the country read *The Black Hat* and expressed their liking for its contents in solicited and unsolicited letters to its editors. Such men would not have committed themselves to an expression of commendation had they not been genuinely pleased with what was in it.

Our means of advertising the paper was limited. I boomed and boosted it at all my meetings, of course, thus whetting the curiosity of audiences and inducing them to speculate twopence on the purchase of it. It is emphatically true to say that "once a *Black Hat* reader, always a *Black Hat* reader" was our experience from first to last. Our method of advertising it, apart from platform boosting, was to post a copy of the first issue to every well-known or influential person in the kingdom. And we had quite a number of readers in America.

Miss Rosita Forbes wrote:

I think it is a very plucky effort to try and write all of a paper between the two of you. I wish I could help with some practical assistance, but, alas, I don't think it is possible for any one to be more broke than I am. Get hold of a plutocrat if you can, because brains are powerless without the sinews of war. Best of luck.

From Richard Aldington a message came:

Your paper is fine. I am sending a guinea to help. Why don't you try Shaw? He is said to be generous to struggling writers, and, as you know, he has plenty of money. I like the vigorous tone of your paper.

From the late John Galsworthy:

I don't suppose I agree with many of your views, but you seem to have them. Good wishes.

Mr. Galsworthy, with characteristic generosity, sent five pounds.)

We ran a column each month under the title, "This Month's Bore," which elicited the following letter from the famous Irish poet and story-writer, Lord Dunsany:

Dear Mr. Kelly,
Here is one of the twenty pounds that you need: Mr. Snowden requires the rest from me.
I have just been reading your column headed "This Month's Bore," and wondered how you saw so deeply into the character of your subject. I only know him, as probably you do, from his occasional pronouncements, and yet I feel that you have undoubtedly put your finger on as much as he has of a soul.

                                        Dunsany

A letter which gave us great honor was one from Walter de la Mare, enclosing ten shillings and wishing us good fortune and great success.

A letter from Mr. Warwick Deeping, in which he congratulated us on our enterprise, besought us "to go on being natural," and sent two guineas, caused us to revise our critical estimate of Mr. Deeping's writings in the light of that experience. I had read *Sorrell and Son*, and, while enjoying the story, would not have placed the author by any means in the front rank of modern English novelists. I felt it nothing less than my duty to turn again to a more serious examination of Mr. Deeping's work, with the result that I found my first impressions had been hasty and ill-considered. In view of my further study, and as a result of more mature thought on the matter of his work as a novelist, it is my considered opinion—advanced with the full support and approval of Mr. Harold Kelly, the critic, journalist, short-story writer and playwright—that Mr. Warwick Deeping is a writer of the first flight and worthy of a place among the best of our present-day novelists; and I challenge successful contradiction.

I cannot, I regret to say, make the same claim on behalf of Mr. Hugh Walpole, Mr. Gerald Bullett, or Mr. A. E. Coppard. I do not doubt that these authors are good husbands, faithful sons and well-conducted fathers; but I should be false to my trust if I said they were anything more than efficient craftsmen at their trades. I would praise them effusively if I dared, but my literary conscience will not permit me to do so—they all failed to send subscriptions to *The Black Hat*.

In the fourth issue (December 1930) I reviewed Gordon Craig's *Life of Henry Irving*, but did not send a copy to Mr. Craig, as he is a bird of passage and seldom to be easily found. I was agreeably surprised one morning, therefore, to receive the following letter:

Dear Mr. Thompson,

I came across a copy of *The Black Hat* today, and I shall be glad if you will send it to me for the rest of the year—beginning with the first number. Please count on me to subscribe yearly.

Thank you very much for your review of my book—I am glad you liked it. I enclose a cheque for 6/-.

Yours sincerely, with every good wish,
Gordon Craig.

The great stage-designer and genius of the theater enclosed a list of prominent people whom he thought would like the paper and become regular subscribers. I regard it as a great honor that Gordon Craig should have written to me like that, and shall keep his letter among my possessions.

From Maurice Browne and Sir John Martin Harvey we had friendly congratulations and subscriptions, which were most encouraging to us both. We were complimented by Mr. Garvin on our "spirited venture;" Edgar Wallace sent us "a pound for luck;" while Rathmell Wilson, the "Wandering Gentile," gave us practical help over and over again.

We did not go on our knees to any man, large or small; we sent our paper out with a typewritten note asking for a subscription towards an individual experiment in journalism, and left the rest to them. Not only have we nothing to complain of, but the support extended to us was in excess of our most optimistic expectations.

The paper was popular with all sorts of people, but especially with those who were tired of the squeamish, the namby-pamby, the platitudinous, and the standardized. Stupid persons, of course, could see nothing in it; and for a very good reason, there was nothing in it—for them. We had only two abusive letters—a record, I think, for any journal. We tore up the first one with a laugh, as abusive letters are nearly always funny and rarely clever. I would welcome an abusive letter as much as any man, if it was well written or clever, but I have never had one like that. I therefore invite readers who dislike my personality and way of writing not to hesitate to write and tell me so, but the letters must be clever, otherwise they will be ignored and no prize will be given. Upon the writer of the second abusive letter we played the following trick. His letter was badly phrased and venomous. We therefore revised it a little. It appeared as follows:

Dear friends,

Why did I not read your paper earlier? Please send the back numbers. I have never enjoyed anything so much. You have shaken some of my prejudices pretty severely. Go on hitting the humbugs hard. We need men like you to counteract the humbug of the age.

Yours gratefully.

The fool had given his correct name and address, and we published it in full. That will teach the ass to write abusive letters, we said. It taught him not to, I hope, for he was never heard of again. He probably left the country, or put his head in the gas-oven, at the disgrace of it all.

The Black Hat sales continued good while the weather held, but with the coming of the November cold and fogs there was, naturally, a slump. We were unable to stand up against these handicaps. Although we did everything possible to save the paper from collapse, we had to skip a month; but, after a campaign of borrowing and begging, we got it out again. We could not let the readers know how desperate our position was—that would have destroyed confidence; it would also have scared away the prospective capital we so badly needed. We were always on the look-out for a capitalist who, struck with admiration for our work and alive to the business possibilities of the paper, would come forward with a sum of money sufficient to run the thing on a business footing. We nearly landed one several times, but something always happened to frighten him at the last moment.

It was a good business proposition. Such a journal is needed in this country, and if we had only had a little money to keep it going during the initial stages *The Black Hat* would today be a power in the land. Our experiences proved that beyond doubt. But we were fighting against ingrained prejudices and a stupid conservatism, which can see nothing profitable in a thing unless it is on approved lines. We were continually met with the suggestion that we should copy some other paper. "No, no, no," we replied. "*The Black Hat* is only valuable and commercially possible because it is different from all other journals or reviews." But we could not make capitalists see that. We could not get them to see it despite the fact that every one who read the paper liked it immensely. "If the five thousand who read it now," we pointed out, "like it, as they certainly do, then surely there are at least fifty thousand more who would like it just as much, if we could get it to them." Men with money to invest admitted all this, admitted that they liked the paper themselves, but either underrated or misjudged the intelligence of the wider reading public and decided to wait and see how the paper prospered before risking their money. While they were waiting, we were crippled to death for lack of a few pounds to keep it going.

We received, as I said earlier, help of a practical kind from our friend Mr. A. W. Haycock, who was at that time the Labor Member for West Salford. I had known Haycock before the war, while he was lecturing for a peace organization. He was the only Labor Member who remembered the work I had done in those days and later, and knew how little I had got out of it. Kelly and I never appealed to him in vain for assistance with the paper. We went several times to see him at the House of Commons, and he put himself out to raise subscriptions for *The Black Hat*. His efforts brought us in many a half-crown—the yearly subscription. He tracked down his fellow-Members and put it to them that I was the kind of man it was their duty to support.

The reactions of some of these champions of democracy was very interesting. The patronizing way in which they paid their half-crowns was quite typical. One representative of the toiling masses was beginning to put me through an examination as to what I intended to do with the money, when I told him to go to hell. The air of superiority towards me, as if I were some kind of dependent who was not able to look after himself, was characteristic. The reason for this was that these persons had got on in the world and I had not. Many of them, I noticed, adopted the same attitude towards Haycock. They had worked the racket successfully; Haycock seemed not to know on which side his bread was buttered. He took socialism and the Labor movement seriously, and was always ready to discuss matters affecting the welfare of the workers. His comrades used to pull his leg over this. They looked upon him, in fact, as a damn fool for bothering about such things. One evening, while Kelly and I were sitting in the smoke-room of the House of Commons, waiting for our friend to finish a speech in the Chamber, a well-known Labor Member said to us, "Haycock is a good chap, but he is a fool to himself; he ought to be doing well here, instead of running about to address meetings in all sorts of hole-and-corner places." The Labor leader meant that any member of the socialist movement was a fool who did any work for socialism while he could do well for himself as a grafter in Parliament.

Kelly was delighted at the naïve way the man spoke. "These are the men who fight the battle of Labor on the floor of the House of Commons," he said to me. "Look at them." At a table in the middle of the room there sat a group of men whose names are familiar in our mouths as household words. They were busy drinking whisky-and-soda, beer, cognac, and coffee, and telling one another all the smutty stories they could think of.

Haycock joined us and we had a cup of tea at his expense. While we talked, a Member joined the group at the table and ordered a large brandy before starting on his favorite risqué joke. The Member was a well-known and widely respected rabble-rouser, who sobbed bitterly on the platform over the sufferings of the poor working mothers and the toil-worn fathers.

It was a ludicrous thought that these beefy, broad-shouldered, well-fed men were the chosen representatives of the poor and the down-trodden. There they sat, licking their lips, wiping their heavy mustaches and drinking expensive drinks. To think that without a working-class to suffer and go short and have their wages reduced they would still be toiling in mill and mine was an amusing reflection. The Labor Government was then in office, and these *bon viveurs* were making laws for us. It was grand.

When the House rose and the cry of "Who goes home?" rang through the rooms, our governors rose unsteadily and rocked out into the night. Kelly and I have often laughed at the recollection of one Member who was so drunk that he could not move from his position against the smoke-room wall and had to be helped across Palace Yard and into a taxi by two policemen. This sort of thing happens every night while the House is sitting. Long live Parliamentary democracy! I have no objection to these men—on the contrary: I wish them the best of luck in their great fight for socialism.

With the help of our friend Haycock, we raised thirty shillings in subscriptions from the drunken champions of the New Social Order. It was, at any rate, thirty shillings more than we should have got from the teetotal section, who are always holding up their hands in holy horror at these orgies. It would have been fun, for instance, to have tried Dr. Salter for a subscription, but we had not the time to spend on the experiment.

I had an interesting experience among the *bourgeoisie* at this time. A patron of ours, a man who invested twenty pounds in *The Black Hat*, arranged a debate for me at a Feminist Club near Victoria. It was felt that my appearance at this haunt of wealthy ladies with intellectual views would help the paper. The question to be debated was, "Are women intellectually inferior to men?" I agreed to maintain that they were. My opponent was to be a French lady well-known in the literary world, though none of us had ever heard of her.

Our backer suggested that I should dress for the occasion, as there was to be a dinner before the debate. I have never possessed a dress suit in my life, and explained how impossible it was for me to procure one. He offered to lend me his, and it fitted me fairly well, though the cut was a trifle old-fashioned. Kelly and I set out for the club with three-halfpence between us. It was quite a lengthy walk from Bayswater to Victoria, and we arrived hungry and hard up. Fortunately, we were well dressed.

The dinner was first rate, the wine of excellent vintage, and the cigarettes of the finest blend. The room was crammed with women, old and young, masculine and feminine, all highly educated, well nourished and overloaded with the riches of this world which are but as dross. Excellent speeches were made for and against the motion, all well delivered and lacking in originality. The lady who led the opposition to my contention was an efficient-looking, well-poised, and smooth-spoken Frenchwoman. She had no case, and knew it, but this did not deter her from speaking fluently in a sleek, polished manner, reeling off the well-known arguments in favor of woman's intellectual equality as though she had originated them herself.

In the course of my address I had asked how it was that little creative work of an intellectual nature had ever been achieved by women. There have been no female philosophers, no women scientists, painters, sculptors, poets, playwrights, or thinkers of any significance. Why have we not had—if women are intellectually equal to men—women the equal of Shakespeare, Molière, Euripides, Homer, Mozart, Cæsar, Napoleon, Mussolini, Dickens, Einstein, or Bernard Shaw? I gave them Emily Brontë and Jane Austen, though I pointed out that the same kind of fiction had been written better by men. I gave credit to Madame Curé for the valuable assistance she had given to her husband in handing him his instruments, taking down notes at his dictation, and answering the door. I accused Jane Welsh of having driven Carlyle to his death by worrying him to read her literary attempts (this preposterous assertion was not challenged), and charged Lady Burton with burning her husband's MSS. I explained how Christina Rossetti's poems had been licked into shape by Dante Gabriel, made fun of George Eliot, and told several things about George Sand of which the world had previously been kept in ignorance. The French lady winced slightly when I said that but for her love affairs with Chopin and De Musset, George Sand would never have been heard of. I praised Mrs. Henry Wood, Mrs. Humphry Ward, Miss Braddon, Maria Edgeworth, Marie Corelli, Florence Barclay, and Ethel M. Dell. I began and ended by assuring those present that I had no lack of admiration and respect for women, as women, but that for them to claim a faculty peculiar to man—the creative—was futile, in view of what was known to the contrary.

The French lady made no attempt to refute my contentions, but said the reason why women had not excelled in the creative arts was because they had never had a chance. They had been fettered, restricted, and suppressed. I knew this point would be made, as I knew in advance the arguments that would be used. It is a great advantage to be able to anticipate all the arguments that will be employed. I simply asked how women came to be suppressed at all, if they were the intellectual equals of men. You cannot suppress an equal. But I went on to show that women had never been suppressed in any essential sense. They are too clever not to take advantage of their sex to win the favor of their would-be suppressors. I congratulated women on their sense in avoiding warfare while men were dying like flies, on accepting favors from men although they had independence and economic equality, and on their general ruthlessness in getting what they wanted.

The vote went in my favor by a substantial majority. It was rather amusing to think of a majority of intelligent women admitting by a show of hands that they were intellectually inferior to men.

A lady who had spoken in the debate with excellent sense and humor and had taken my side was introduced to me later as Miss Berta Ruck, wife of Oliver Onions, and novelist in her own right. "Pleased to meet you," I said. "I have read many of your books." This brazen lie did not deceive Miss Ruck, who said, "No, you haven't. It is my husband who is the genius. I'm only a writer of popular romances." Miss Ruck is a Yorkshire woman, and I liked her very much indeed.

I should have enjoyed the evening more if some of the ladies had foamed at the mouth, or shown symptoms of chagrin and bitter mortification; but they took my attack with perfect composure. They retained their poise. I suppose they could afford to.

Kelly and I have always regretted that we allowed ourselves to be mentally intimidated by the pressure of a false tradition. We felt that to allow it to be thought that we were hard up would have lowered our status in the eyes of these wealthy ladies. I was so concerned about this that I never mentioned *The Black Hat* for fear I should be suspected of using the occasion to cry my own wares. We realized afterwards that the dress-suit had been a mistake. It would have been better to turn up badly dressed, mention that the dinner had been a perfect godsend, and let it be known that we were out for all the money we could get. I am certain that I could have raised several pounds for the maintenance of the paper if I had asked for it. As it was, I did not even receive a fee. I shall never make such a mistake again.

After a long-drawn-out struggle against overwhelming difficulties, *The Black Hat* went under. We had given our best and got nothing out of it except the thrill and the fun. And it was a great thrill, both for ourselves and the readers. We had trampled on toes and trodden on corns to right and left. Our readers had gasped with surprise and heaved with laughter, and we had won golden opinions from all sorts of people.

During a period of nine months we had brought out seven scorching numbers. We had the reading world to bustle in, and we kept that world alive while *The Black Hat* lasted.

The paper was a raging success in every sense except the financial, and it was not our fault that sufficient capital could not be raised to place the paper upon a sound financial basis. *The Black Hat* went down into the dust and mire of defeat, trailing clouds of glory and showing a total loss.

The Mystery of the Bernard Shaw Letter

HAROLD Kelly and I were depressed at the failure of our little enterprise. I was depressed, too, by illness, which rendered me good for nothing for some months, during which I had a hard struggle to keep base life afoot, and was so disgusted that I had not the heart to put pen to paper. Neither of us, however, had abandoned faith in *The Black Hat*. We resolved to revive it again at the first opportunity. The original readers could always be counted on to rally as soon as the paper reappeared. There were over three hundred yearly subscribers on our list, good and true men and women who had sent their half-crowns and had only had seven copies in return. Letters were frequently coming in demanding to know when *The Black Hat* was appearing again.

The months passed and nothing of a hopeful nature seemed likely to occur. Kelly found work on another paper, and was no longer available for anything involving a full-time effort. A year elapsed before anything happened. Then I made one of those sudden decisions for which I am noted. I borrowed ten pounds from a solvent friend, agreeing to pay him back at the rate of ten shillings a week, and restarted *The Black Hat* with myself as editor, sub-editor, news-editor, political and foreign correspondent, dramatic and literary critic, proof-reader, distributor, seller, and chief advertiser. I had no fear of the labor involved, as I am a fiend for work where my own interests are concerned, providing I am in charge of the proceedings. I find it irksome to be at any one else's beck and call, but delightful to have others fetching and carrying for me.

But I felt the need of Harold Kelly. He was, from my standpoint, the ideal colleague, a man after my own heart. He had no blind spots or warts on his mind. At handling a pen, manipulating ideas, thinking out schemes and stunts, he was a tower of strength to such a venture as *The Black Hat*. A man loaded, but not overbalanced, with ideas, he possessed a free, unusual, and amazingly fertile mind. His company and conversation were stimulating and refreshing—oh, how refreshing!—in the waste land of London's intellectual life. I had to go on without him, as he had been appointed to a position on a City paper which took up most of his spare hours. He pushed ahead from that time and had a play produced, *What the Doctor Thought*, at a West-End theater that winter—1932—which was well received, and is now striding rapidly forward to fame and fortune. Having found a printer, I made up the first issue of the resurrected *Black Hat*. Apart from the crowds at Hyde Park and Tower Hill, there was no public within my immediate reach. I could count on about three thousand copies a month being sold within the limited orbit of my own personal activities as a public speaker.

How to bring the paper under the notice of the wider reading public was the big problem. "Why not try and get a letter of commendation or condemnation from Bernard Shaw?" asked Kelly, who was prepared to assist to the extent of his time and opportunity. We had tried Shaw more than once without result. A word from him would certainly have a bracing effect on the sales, for his publicity value is very great. A friend of ours, Lionel Britton, had found

Shaw a tremendous help in bringing his play and novel before publisher and purchaser. He had stopped the great man in the street and held him, as it were, to ransom. Shaw had promised to read his play to get rid of him, and, having read it, was so pleased that he gave Lionel his public blessing and shoved him into fame.

But *The Black Hat* was not likely to appeal greatly to Shaw. It was too irresponsible in tone and gave forth no message for humanity. It was not socialistic. If we could have induced him to curse and condemn it in public, we should have been made. But he was deaf and disinterested. "We must have a message from some big-pot," I said, "even if we have to send the message ourselves." "Exactly," Kelly said. "You will have a message from Bernard Shaw in the morning." The following letter arrived next day:

Dear Thompson,

It is mere impertinence for you to ask for a message to the readers of your paper. If the people who are foolish enough to pay twopence a month for such twaddle want to read articles by me, which I doubt, they can get my books from the library.

I am ashamed to say that I enjoyed reading a copy of *The Black Hat* once, but if you send me any more my secretary will put them in the waste-paper basket. People like you should not be allowed to remain at large, much less propagate your ideas, in any country but your own. You seem to imagine that your being an Irishman establishes some claim on my consideration. That, of course, is nonsense. If you were a blood-relation or a Central African Pygmy, holding the same outrageous opinions, I should enjoy having you shot.

You also remind me of your connection with the socialist movement some years ago. It does not surprise me that you no longer hold the same views. If people became socialists from impecuniosity, there would be as many socialists as failures—not that that would do socialism any good.

I am an old man and a capitalist, and I have not changed my views. If you regret your defection, go to Russia. I suppose you will publish this letter and make capital out of it. You would be a fool if you did not, but will you please remember in future that I earn my living—a very good one too—by writing, and do not ask me to supply you with articles until you can afford to pay my proper fee.

Yours truly, G. Bernard Shaw.

The letter went to the printer the same day and appeared in the new issue without editorial comment. Tongues began to wag before many days had gone by. I referred to Shaw's message casually in the course of my speeches. The paper sold like hot cakes. That the Shaw letter helped is certain. People spoke to me about it frequently. "You will be offered a big price for the original," they said. "Oh yes, but I don't want to sell it," I replied—"not if it can be avoided." One or two gave me a quizzical look when the subject came up, but I preserved a grave or careless expression. The press made only one reference to it. The collectors were silent. But the letter helped the sales.

"We must keep it up," I said to Kelly. "A message each month from a world-famous figure. What about Mussolini or Einstein?" "No, that would be overdoing it," he said. "The readers will refuse to believe it when you get a real message.

They will think you have invented them all." "I don't know what you are talking about," I said. "Are you insinuating that the Shaw letter was a fake? Be careful, man, be careful; there is such a thing as the law of libel, you know." "Well," said Kelly, "you would have no objection to a big libel case if it advertised *The Black Hat*, would you? If Shaw brought an action against you, it would send the sales up to half a million; you would be a made man." "Shaw had better be careful," I said. "I am in no mood to stand any nonsense from him; he has insulted me enough already."

"What about an article from James Joyce?" asked Kelly. "He might be induced to send you one for the next issue." "I am no Joyce fan," I said, "though, like every one else in the country, I have read *Ulysses*. But if he cares to send me an article, I will print it. It will help the sales, and that is the one thing needful." "I'll drop him a note and see what he says," answered my erstwhile co-editor as we separated for the night.

Two days later an article signed James Joyce reached me through the post. I was glad to have it, and asked no questions. The name "Joyce" is not so very uncommon, and "James" is a well-known Christian name. The next issue contained an article of about five hundred words in Mr. Joyce's characteristic manner and style. It was entitled "Holidays" and began as follows:

> Unwounding scissor-blades of sunlight cut. Dust expanses scintillate on window-panes. Inch-bound universes have grain-high acclivities, spot-deep declivities. China like peasants' ankles. Corpulent fishwives have bulging curves set on splaying bases,

and ended with:

> Life is short and nothing is heavy to carry away. No reputation must be lost till death, and lose a good one then. Mounds of flesh, mounds of respectability. But all that is to-day and all that is tomorrow and tomorrow will not always come.

"Yes," I said to myself, "that's Joyce right enough. This will set the literary tongues a-babble." And it did. But the press was silent.

Number Two sold as well as Number One. The weather kept fine, and great crowds bought their copies outside the gates of Hyde Park, where I had three men posted to catch the passers-by and the vast throngs from my meetings. In my determination to advertise the paper, I carried on something shocking. I warned my hearers that an attempt was being made to suppress the paper. "But I'll beat them yet," I thundered, "and if you stand by me we shall strike a blow for a free press in England for which every man who loves liberty will thank and bless us. Buy your copies outside the gate." And they did.

In the third issue I made a ferocious attack upon W. H. Smith & Son.

> The notorious bullies of the newspaper trade [I wrote]. A ghastly octopus. The insufferable mandarins of the newspaper trade. *The Black Hat* cares not a snap of the fingers for them, or a thousand like them. The editor has fought bigger and better enemies than W. H. Smith and beaten them to a frazzle, and he is not deterred by any threat from any quarter whatever. It is just as well that this should be clearly understood, so that trouble may be avoided.

Considering that I knew next to nothing about W. H. Smith, or Son, that they had made no attempt to interfere with me in any way, and that the whole thing was sheer nonsense, it was surprising how many letters I received congratulating me on my great fight for freedom. Nor was there any attempt to suppress the paper. Why should there have been? Yet I was thought to be waging a grim fight against authority. A lone figure with his back to the wall, and the world against him.

I never realized how easy it was to review books until I started *The Black Hat*. I gave a couple of columns, for instance, to reviewing half a dozen of Upton Sinclair's novels. I praised them highly, but not too highly. I spoke well of Sinclair as a man with a highly developed sense of social justice, though I no longer agreed with his radical opinions, and I wrote at length about *The Wet Parade*. I have not read *The Wet Parade*. I compared the book with the film. I have not seen the film. The only books of Sinclair's I have read are *The Jungle*, which I have forgotten, and *Oil*, which I have almost forgotten. I do not, in fact, care much for his work. Yet an official of the publishing house which issues his books here was delighted with my notice and struck by the insight I had displayed into the author's mind and work. Book reviewing, in my opinion, is child's play, and any person who knows his or her way about in the book world can do it without bothering to read the books at all. And why should they? Very few modern books are worth reading.

I was guilty of a little sharp practice over Sinclair. About eight years ago I had a cordial letter from Upton in connection with a socialist pamphlet I had written. I had kept this by me, and I published it in *The Black Hat* with no date on it, as though it applied to the paper, although Sinclair might not have approved of the paper at all. But I did naught in hate, but all in honor. I stuck at nothing in the great cause of circulation. And as long as the readers were thrilled and tickled, I was more than justified, for an editor's first duty is to his readers, just as Selfridge's first duty is to the customer.

Alas, the third issue of the revived *Black Hat* was the last. Again it was the bad weather and lack of working capital that brought all my efforts to naught. The sales were good, over four thousand the first and second months. The fall in sales synchronized with the coming of the winter weather. With summer all the year round I could have done the trick, but bad weather killed the outdoor sales, as it kills outdoor meetings. I got a few advertisements, but not sufficient to keep things in a solvent condition. I had no time to nurse the baby into health, so it died. The shops which stocked the paper maintained their level of sales until the end, But I had not the means to extend the circulation through the newsagents. I got nothing out of it except, as before, the fun and the frenzy of trying to do the impossible. When I started *The Black Hat* I was broke; while I was running it I was broke; and after it failed I was ruined. But it was great fun, and I learned a lot about many things. I regret to say that, as there was a certain amount of mystery about the "Shaw" letter, I am unable to throw any further light upon it; yet it helped the sales.

CHAPTER XVII

Personalities and Places

A blow was struck at the livelihood of the freelance in 1926 by the appearance in Hyde Park of a large number of racing tipsters. These turf-guides attracted vast crowds. They were speaking on an important subject, of greater interest than any "ism" known to man—horse-racing. More people followed them outside the gate than had ever been known to follow any class of speaker since the Park was open for public recreation. Unfortunately the usual busybodies got to work, backed by a large body of lack of opinion. It was the contention of these prigs that the tipsters were a nuisance, that they lowered the standard of public discussion (the funniest statement ever made) and should be driven from the meeting-ground. The Calvinist communists and Nonconformist revolutionaries, together with all the Little Bethelites and professional spoil-sports, tin-horn redeemers and ardent humanitarian kill-joys, had their way as usual. An Amendment to the Hyde Park Regulations Act of 1872 was hurried through, and it was made illegal for any speaker to ask his listeners to follow him outside the gates for the payment of wages due to him for work done. This awful crime was called "Unlawfully soliciting donations," and is punishable by the imposition of a fine not exceeding five pounds.

This has made a considerable difference to the collections. I have used my brains and succeeded in devising a form of words by which I let the audience know that I could not be expected to work for nothing. This formula has served me fairly well since 1926, but I have been summoned and fined three times. The police have treated me with great consideration and allowed me considerable latitude, but no doubt they are compelled to take action occasionally. The rule forbidding the announcement of collections is vexatious and against public equity, but nobody cares about that. I do not myself. The only thing that concerns me is the loss of revenue which has resulted from the new regulation. But I do not complain; the fault is mine, for being a public speaker at all.

It must not be imagined that I thank those who cheer or contribute to the collection. They are paying for services rendered—that is all. I am entitled to whatever they give, and much more than I imagine any of them have ever thought of giving. I owe them nothing. The boot is on the other foot.

Three years ago I was approached by an official of the British Broadcasting Corporation and invited to speak to the listening millions from Savoy Hill. I was asked to avoid the subjects of sex and religion, but no other restrictions or conditions were imposed. The B.B.C. gave me a free hand to say what I liked. My talk was arranged for the third of May, 1930, and I was told by the director, as he handed me a very liberal fee, that my effort had been a great success. His opinion was confirmed by all sorts of people who wrote or spoke to me about it. It seemed that I had a good recording voice and a distinctive style of delivery, which gave general satisfaction. I was treated with extreme courtesy and liberality by the B.B.C., and enjoyed the experience very much. I should like to speak in future to none but invisible audiences, and hope that it may some day be possible for me to do so.

By 1930 I was established in Hyde Park as the leading freelance speaker. I had gathered round me an audience which knew me and understood something of my attitude. These choice and master spirits would tolerate no interference of any kind with their right to listen to their favorite speaker. It was generally understood that I could do no wrong. Every one had to accept me as an orator unique among public speakers. I had no policy, no program, and no plan, no wish to uplift anybody, no concern for any social or political problem, and no message for humanity. I spoke on any subject, or no subject. Sometimes I put forward two mutually exclusive points of view in the same speech, and won general approval. I dominated the situation and did as I liked.

The large collections of former days could not be looked for. The depression had made a vast difference to every one. I did better financially than any other speaker, but there is no big money to be made in that way nowadays. My takings, on the average, during the last five or six years have ranged around the neighborhood of fifty shillings a week in the summer and thirty in the winter. Now and then I might have a record collection, but this would invariably be followed by a wet Sunday. I got engagements from time to time, to lecture or recite, but in view of my independent non-party attitude these became fewer and fewer. Whereas at one time I was in demand continually by Labor Party branches and other bodies, I seldom heard a word from any of them now. This pleased me very well. I had grown to look upon all movements as intolerably frowsy and silly. It was worth the money to be relieved from the awful boredom of lecturing to economic and political enthusiasts who were always yearning for a social system in which I was not interested. I was glad to be away from all that, never to associate again with the malcontents and puling protesters against everything which sane people take for granted. I would not lend my voice to the advocacy of socialism or any other "ism" for any sum of money.

When I look back upon my early career as a world-builder I sometimes wonder if I was entirely sane. The blindness, the stuffiness and stiffness, the fixity and rigidity of the people I cast my lot among, were incredible. Many of them have passed into their graves without ever having been more than half alive. It is fortunate that sane, humorous, and unpretentious humanity pays little attention to these agitators. Normal people eat, sleep, laugh, make love, get drunk, get married, and get buried without bothering their head about holding "convictions," "principles," "ideals," or any of the big bow-wow humbug of the evangelist and the propagandist. That is why communism has petered out in this country. It cannot strike roots. The people remain essentially sane. Normal society rejects such fungi and normal humanity ignores them. The working-man prefers football and horse-racing. He may lose his temper at the former and his shirt at the latter, but at any rate he retains his sanity.

In the course of the nine years of continuous oratory in Hyde Park I have addressed millions of people. I have poured out treasures of wit and eloquence to an admiring and perspiring populace. My speeches must have given great pleasure to those millions. It has not been my primary intention to give pleasure to the masses, but if they have enjoyed my performances, then they stand in my debt.

One of my frequent listeners about this time was J. A. O'Rourke of the "Irish Players." O'Rourke is not so well known as Arthur Sinclair, Sara Allgood, or Maire O'Neil, but to me his stage-work is a source of unfailing joy. Within his range he is an actor of remarkable talent. As "Uncle Peter" in *The Plough and the Stars*, Sean O'Casey's great tragi-comedy of Dublin life and character, he is an unforgettable figure of frustrated self-importance and semi-senile goatishness. The lugubrious face, with its fixed expression of peevish determination, the labored rhythm of utterance, the clamping walk, the dreadful outbursts of sheepish wrath, and the gorgeous language of indignation and unctuous rectitude, which provoke derision from his companions—with what unholy accuracy and consummate skill does Mr. O'Rourke sustain this utterly delightful role.

I found Mr. O'Rourke to be a quiet, unassuming, unobtrusive soul; too modest, if anything, for he has great gifts.

I was once in Harry Hutchinson's dressing-room, having a talk about this and that with some of the wonderful players. Mr. Hutchinson, a fine actor, told a story of how, when he was once looking for a flat in London, the landlady asked him what his profession was. "I am one of the Irish Players," he said. "Oh," she exclaimed, "how nice! And what instrument do you play, may I ask?"

SEAN O'Casey also listened to me occasionally. I first met him outside the gates of Hyde Park, where I had taken up my stand in order to collect my wages from the crowd who had been listening to me inside. "Hullo, Bonar; I want to have a talk with you afterwards," he said, and stood by while I took the few shillings I had earned. While he waited a man came up and said to me, "I wish I could speak like you, Mr. Thompson. How do you do it?" I get a lot of that sort of thing, and it makes me tired. It strikes me as about the most stupid remark any one could make. Exhausted with the intense nervous strain of speaking, I waved my hand and said, "A gift. A gift."

O'Casey broke in at once. "It's no gift at all. It's a matter of hard work and years of apprenticeship. What's the use of a gift if it is not cultivated and developed by hard work?" He took the bore off my hands and explained the thing to him in forcible language. He then took me home to dinner at his house in St. John's Wood. I have seldom spent such a profitable and enthralling evening. He talked of Yeats and Lady Gregory and Synge and the drama in such terms as showed him to be a man of intense thought and genius. I could have listened to him for ever. A kindly, sensitive, friendly man, with the stamp of great genius upon him. I felt honored to have met and spoken to him on such terms, and came away with the impression that he was the finest man I had ever met.

The rumors of his having lost his inspiration since he attained fame and success are rubbish. That sort of thing happens to second rate artists. Sean O'Casey is too hard-bitten, knows and has suffered too much, to develop swelled-head or to forget how to do good work. That his achievement is of the highest kind and will endure for all time I have no doubt whatever.

The only other man for whose genius I have the same respect (I have met a number of half-geniuses and have been told that I am one of these myself—God forbid!) is my great hero among actors, Mr. Ernest Milton. When *The Black Hat* was being started, I had a long interview with him and wrote about it in the first issue. I found him a brilliant conversationalist, cultured and witty. He is a man of great charm, a thinker and an artist of rare perception and great imagination. Everything about him is full of distinction. It struck me that this actor has something of Edgar Allan Poe in his temperament. There is the same suggestion of the demoniacal in his acting that made Irving's performances so memorable. Off-stage he seems remote, aloof, a sensitive and solitary soul. I have met him many times since then and found his conversation always attractive and delightful.

As a man and an artist, I admire him this side idolatry, a rare feeling for me to have about any of our modern celebrities, who have always struck me as commonplace and dim. It is a high privilege to be the contemporary of one who has brought to the stage such unique gifts of personality and artistic authority, who has added to the world's charm, and whose achievement reminds us that there is a realm of gold above the squalor of common existence.

IN November of 1932 I was invited to address the Oxford University Liberal Debating Society at Oriel College. The meeting was a highly successful one. I laughed at Liberalism and attacked the most cherished beliefs of the students. They gave me an ovation at the close and treated me like a lord. One passage in my speech seemed to amuse them a great deal. "It must be borne in mind," I said, "that Mr. Ramsay MacDonald is not only a strong Labor man and an ardent socialist, but he is also a keen Liberal and a die-hard Conservative as well. His opposition to the late war was balanced by his active support of it, and while he takes a firm stand against one thing, he is equally firm in his support of its opposite. This is the secret of his rise to power."

This passing reflection, which struck me as so true as to be no more than a platitude, sent the audience into convulsions, and was reported in the Oxford press as a humorous remark. Every one appeared to be delighted with me, and I could not have wished for better treatment. The Society won general applause for their initiative and enterprise in bringing, for the first time in history, a real live Hyde Park orator to put his views before them. I was not, as a matter of fact, in the best of form for speaking, as I did not feel very well. Had I been at my best they would probably have appointed me as headmaster of the college, or something equally distinguished.

My health gave me a good deal of trouble about this time. I had to give up drinking any kind of intoxicants and go on a diet. I could not afford to take a rest or have a holiday, so I just carried on as usual. As I have always known how to use my voice, I did not suffer from hoarseness or any of the usual speakers' complaints; but my vitality was lowered, and this showed itself in my work. The speaker's difficulty is the heckler's opportunity, and I had one or two interrupters. I had no difficulty in dealing with them, but the fact that they had dared to open their mouths at all caused me to realize that I was losing grip a little. The crowds were, of course, secretly delighted to notice that I was in difficulties. The crowd is always the enemy of the individual, and only a fool takes notice of either popular hostility or popular applause. I brought myself back to full strength by dieting and deep-breathing, and regained once more the old ascendancy over crowds which has enabled me to avoid hard manual work for over a quarter of a century.

CHAPTER XVIII

A Tale That is Told

TIME was when Hyde Park was free to all who cared to speak, sing, dance, juggle, conjure, recite, sell pills, give racing tips, solve world problems, or build Utopias while you waited. Collections could be taken without let or hindrance. Up to 1872 the place must have been a speakers' paradise. Those days are gone. Gone, too, are the great oratorical figures who affrighted the air of Marble Arch.

When all is said about the character of the crowd, its fickleness, cowardice, shallowness, and instinctive brutality, it is undeniable that many of the old orators of Marble Arch were warmly received and well beloved by hundreds of their hearers. A wave of genuine idealism swept through the people during the later days of the nineteenth century. There was a touch of nobility about some of the old agitators to which the crowd responded cordially. Socialism was in its dream stage. It had not become the scumminist nightmare it is today. Few communists know anything of communism or socialism, though most of them are experts in hooliganism. The modern socialist does not love the poor, he only hates the rich.

One may say that socialism as a possible solution of economic or any other kind of problems is as obsolete as the antimacassar or the magic lantern. Between a soulless communism on the one side and a soulless industrialism on the other, the industrial proletariat is being slowly destroyed. They are losing their manliness and pride. Is there any hope for them in the future? I do not think so. Their day is done.

The old warriors for social change meant well. They were limited in outlook and given to easy generalizations, but they had good intentions. Like Malvolio, they thought nobly of the soul. It is good that they are gone. They have been spared the horror of the harvest.

A visit to the Hyde Park meeting-ground as it is in 1933 is a lesson in the futility of human hopes. To what a little measure are all the glories, triumphs, spoils of free speech and libertarian fighters shrunk! What havoc has been made of the dreams of visionaries and what Mr. Belloc has called "the great rosy dawn!" The pioneers of the age of plenty, the aspirers after perfection, the foundation-stone layers of the earthly paradise, here is their journeys' end, here is their butt, the very sea-mark of their utmost sail.

My own meetings are attended by a special kind of listener who is no more typical of the average listener than I am typical of the average speaker. It has taken me some years to establish my own tradition, but it is now established. My meetings, as Mr. Hannen Swaffer was good enough to say in an article in the *Daily Herald* a short time ago, are a feature of London life. This, too, is my journey's end. A strange career truly—a futile series of struggles and adventures without significance and without result. To say that I regret having acted as I did would not be true. I have lived, loved, hated, laughed and sorrowed, and taken the whole business for no more than it is worth. What ceremony else? A few more years of sensation, of emotional and spiritual excitement, of intellectual and material storm and stress, and I shall be as though I had never been. The whole business is of no more account than the passing of a breath of wind over the grass on a quiet summer's day. It is of no less account than the most stupendous cataclysm that ever disturbed the universe.

So much has seemed important at the time of its happening, yet now and again come irrefutable assertions that nothing signifies. Three years ago my Aunt Eliza died. I remember when she, of all things and persons, seemed immutable. A year later my stepfather and my mother also died. They were my last relatives. I called at the house in Manchester where they had lived, loved, and quarreled for so many years, carrying on the traffic of daily existence as though it were a matter of supreme importance, which it was to them. Yet the people who were in occupation of the house at the time did not even know that such persons as Aunt Eliza, William Williams, or Maude Williams his wife, had ever existed. They have left behind them no record and no memory, except, perhaps, those which still stir in the brains of old Rachel Thompson and the writer of this book.

From this melancholy scene I passed to one more strange and more melancholy still—I returned to Northern Ireland for a holiday. From Belfast to Antrim, a journey so great when I was a child as to be almost mythical, is a slight distance in one of the motor coaches which run between the city and the ancient town now. But there are no means of quick or easy conveyance from Antrim to Carnearney, and, although it was a hot July day, I walked the four miles each way. I am glad now that I did. It enabled me to see aspects of the experience I should otherwise have missed.

I had remembered the place in the magnified perspective of a child. Now the old roads seemed to have shrunk, the expanses dwindled and the houses grown smaller. As I neared the mountain the Master's old house came into view with my aunt's cottage standing a few yards away. In its ensemble the scene had not altered. I recognized the trees, the slopes and stretches of the land, and even the smell of the air.

The silence which prevailed everywhere seemed strange. My ears had been attuned to the roar of towns, and I had forgotten that. Far away I could hear the sound of a reaping machine. As I reached the top of a hill I saw the waters of Lough Neigh glittering in the sunshine, and away below me the great stretch of land between me and the towns of Antrim, Kells, Connor and Ballymena. It was silent, and appeared lonely. I tried to picture myself as the odd, uncouth boy that I must have been, living in this beautiful setting and thinking of it only in terms of hard farm labor or childish escapades.

I passed along to the cottage where I had lived. It was silent and deserted, as it had been for more than twenty years. The roof had fallen in, the causeway in front was overgrown with weeds and nettles. It was a heap of stones with a few pieces of rotting wood which had once been doors. My uncle's house, for generations the scene of an intense and urgent life, had fallen in. Among the debris were some of the Master's books, pulpy with the damp, overlaid with dirt and gnawed by the rats which scuttle about the ruin. The farm was derelict; old plows and pieces of harness lay rusting and rotting in the neglected fields.

The whole countryside seemed deserted. Nearly every one I had known was gone. The few who remained were old, and, with the exception of Rachel, I did not remember them and they could not remember me. They were old; they had forgotten. Even Ladyhill School is closed. The few children of the district go to the Bush School near Antrim. Ladyhill is beginning to crumble and decay.

I could not remain there. The place was full of ghosts. The sun poured down on the deserted fields as it had done thirty years before, as it had done for centuries before that. The sun and the fields remained unchanged, nothing else had done so. This is the irony of the universe and life. The things that have no feeling, no conscious life, remain. The living things change and pass away.

My friends, the companions of my youth, those I had known and loved, who seemed to bear their lives so freshly and strongly, were gone. No great cataclysm of nature had swept them away. There had been no sensation in their passing. Time had just passed indifferently on its way and brushed them out of existence.

I passed quickly across the silent fields away from the place. The waste of it all was too depressing. It was too ironic a comment on the drama of human life that the countryside could remain so placid and unperturbed. Old Rachel alone remained apparently untouched by the years. I left her by the peat fire, smoking her clay pipe and ruminating on the past.

"Drop in again when you are up this way. Goodbye, Johnny," she said. I wished her good-by and hurried away.

When I got back to London I put the finishing touches to this book and wondered whether what I had written could be expected to interest the hurrying, distracted readers of this present age. What interest could there be in the limited adventures of a Hyde Park orator, a man who lived by spouting from a platform? Who could be expected to take such a book seriously? What had I done, anyhow? I had not flown the Atlantic or made a scientific discovery of great benefit or detriment to mankind. I had not even fought in the war. I had been true to no ideal, kept no trust, set my hand to no great task. I had achieved the reputation of being a quaint sort of public entertainer, one who had no status, who was not above making himself a motley to the view.

Yet I will not dismiss myself so lightly. Shakespeare himself had no more status than I have. He belonged to a group of players who were not allowed to ply their art within the City boundaries. He was not so well respected by the London public as even a modern Hyde Park orator. He resented his lack of standing in men's eyes and fretted about it continually. Yet his name is immortal, and what does that profit him?

Have I not done something of the same kind as he did? I have raised the intellectual and artistic standard of public speaking and taught the frequenters of Hyde Park that a man can work in a low, disreputable, and despised medium and still create something from it that has an element of worth. I am no Shakespeare. My name will not ring through the ages. Yet I have made a small contribution in my own peculiar way and in peculiar circumstances to the artistic life of my time.

I may be mistaken. Does it matter if I am? Not in the slightest degree. I, at any rate, shall lose no sleep about the matter. I have lived my life so far. What more has any human being ever done than live? The setbacks, heartaches, and heartbreaks are all an essential part of life. The ugly sights, the small annoyances, the stupid and the filthy, as much as the noble, beautiful and sublime—are life. The endless follies we commit, the illusions we hug and breed, even the illusion that we have no illusions, are as much part of and important in life as the beetle we tread on. To complain, to rebel, which seems to me stupid and contemptible, is quite right and proper. Everything is right and proper, and all is as it is. What of it?

It makes no difference what happens as long as something is happening or even if nothing is happening at all. The wind passes over the place where we have been living, where we laughed and cried and were happy or unhappy, as though nothing had ever occurred to disturb the quiet earth, or no sound had ever broken the indifferent silence of eternity.

Outside the Gates

by Trevor Blake

"Well, people, you have heard this young man's story. He is up against it. I need say no more. You can see him outside the gates."

Hyde Park Orator Illustrated (p. 112).

B Y way of *The Black Hat* we know that *Hyde Park Orator* was to be followed by a second volume of autobiography. That second volume was never published and any manuscript is lost. A great deal of Thompson's life and work is gone or inaccessible, as if it had never occurred. This new edition of *Hyde Park Orator*, the first in nearly a century, has some chance of reversing that trend if the reader will make their own exertions. To the tablets, new memories...

Hyde Park Orator intermingles Thompson's memories of Shakespeare, the Old Vic and the embrace of a beautiful woman (p. 247). In 1928 Bonar Thompson met Pat Geary. "[We] met in the gallery of the Old Vic, and we got into conversation discussing *Hamlet*. It was Shakespeare who brought us together, in my view one of his finest achievements." It could be that Geary was the glorious romance who threw him over (p. 225). Upon the publication of *Hyde Park Orator*, the two were married. "We were excellent friends and discussed Shakespeare frankly until quite recently all this nonsense ripened into love." At the time of their wedding, Geary was a clerical worker for the Southwark Borough Council[1]. Their

---

[1] "Park Orator Weds a Clerical Worker / Credits Shakespeare." *Cincinnati Enquirer*, 25 June 1939.

marriage and that Pat survived him is all that is known about Pat Geary.

Thompson spoke at Hyde Park and elsewhere as long as he was physically able. During the 1950s he was taken in by Freedom Books in London, where he continued to speak as he pleased for the remaining years of his life. When his health prevented him from even indoor speaking, Freedom Books held fund-raising meetings for Thompson. A kindness I hope sales of this book can begin to repay.

Thompson did speak again to invisible audiences (p. 292), appearing a number of times on radio as well as on television.

Bonar Thompson died at the age of 74 on the 6th of January, 1963. He was cremated at Golders Green Crematorium and Mausoleum in London. His manuscripts, letters and personal possessions appear to have been consigned to the midden.

Hyde Park Orator lacked an index in its prior publication, a deficit handsomely corrected here. This index follows the names Thompson used for the characters he described, which might not always be the names these men and women used in their daily lives.

There have been three challenges in publishing this new edition of *Hyde Park Orator*, each with its own failure. First, the book is in the public domain in the United States but not necessarily elsewhere. Therefore, at this time sale of this book in the nations where Thompson lived is unfortunately restricted. Second, permission was sought to reprint some lively photographs of Thompson. The licensing company credited in the original publication of the photographs had been sold, and the licensing company that purchased it had been sold, and that licensing company had also been sold. The licensing company that bought the licensing company that bought licensing company replied to my inquiry that to begin the process of licensing would cost $1,300.00 and $100.00 per hour afterwards. For that non-refundable expense I would be told if the licensing company was, in fact, the owner of the photographs; actually licensing them would be an additional expense. Therefore, at this time these photographs have not been licensed. And third, a biography of Thompson was published by a regional historical society in the 1990s. Including even some of the research found there would have enriched this edition. That biography is out of print and is seldom seen in the second-hand market. The author of that biography is incommunicative. The publisher of that biography has declined my offers to buy up the remaining stock, or to reprint it at my own expense, or to sponsor a reprinting of the book by the historical society itself, or to license sections of it for publication here. Therefore, at this time that biography does not compliment this autobiography.

Ushering this book back into print has been challenging, and finding Thompson material at all has been challenging. Thompson spoke in public for decades, he took part in formal debates, he appeared on radio and television, and one would think that audio recordings, films and video recordings would be plentiful. But this greatest of all atmosphere printers was profoundly under-documented. In many years of searching I have found a transcript of one audio recording that might include Thompson, and I have found mere seconds of Thompson on film. Only by employing an international private researcher was I able to locate what might be the only remaining copies of *The Black Hat*–and *Bonar Thompson's Monthly*, a publication not mentioned in *Hyde Park Orator*.

There is much more I would like to print by and about Thompson. The success of *Hyde Park Orator Illustrated* will determine if its companion volume, *The Collection Was Not Enough*, will see print. The bibliography of works by and about Thompson appearing for the first time in this edition lists only some of what waits in the wings.

In closing, I will follow the Hyde Park Orator's own advice on working the markets, speaking as he might speak, in the advancement of this book and a potential companion volume. I shall roundly refrain from paying to promote *Hyde Park Orator Illustrated*, expecting instead that I should be paid for my work. I shall readily rely on a insightful individuals to elevate *Hyde Park Orator Illustrated* by the purchase of copies for friends and family. And most of all I insult that segment of the audience–not you, friend, but those others–who rudely refuse themselves the pleasure of perusing *Hyde Park Orator Illustrated*. Will I see you outside the gates?

Notices

"The crowd is always the enemy of the individual, and only a fool takes notice of either popular hostility or popular applause."

Hyde Park Orator Illustrated (p. 299).

Books

Batchelor, F. W.: *Around the Marble Arch* (London: London Printing Works, 1945).

Bernard, Oliver: "Part One [22]" in *Getting Over It* (London: Peter Owen, 1992).

Braybrooke, Neville: "Age of Discussion, The" in *London Green* (London: Gollancz, 1959).

Coleman, Stephen: "Age of Discussion, The" and "Meetings of the Imagination" and "Pre-Electronic Orators, The" in *Stilled Tongues / From Soapbox to Soundbite* (London: Porcupine Press, 1997).

Cortney, Roger: *Dissenting Voices* (Ulster: Ulster Historical Foundation, 2014)

Darlington, Ralph: "Composition and Structure" in *Syndicalism and the Transition to Communism / An International Comparative Analysis* (Abingdon: Ashgate Publishing, Limited, 2008).

Farson, Daniel: "Wit in Hyde Park, A" in *Sacred Monsters* (London: Bloomsbury 1988).

Field, Alice Withrow: "Practical Significance of Communist Theories Regarding the Protection of Women and Children" in *Protection of Women and Children in Soviet Russia* (New York: E. P. Dutton, 1932).

Foot, Michael: "Hyde Park Sceptic" in *Debt of Honour* (London: David Poyner Limited, 1981).

Fox, R. M.: *Drifting Men* (London: Leonard & Virginia Woolf at The Hogarth Press, 1930).

Foy, R. H. (compilation): *Bonar Thompson / The Old Days at Carnearney* (Antrim: Antrim & District Historical Society 1991).

Greacen, Robert: "In Search of Bonar Thompson" in *Sash My Father Wore, The* (Edinburgh: Mainstream Pub., 1997).

Harte, Liam: "Hyde Park Orator" in *Literature of the Irish in Britain, The* (London: Palgrave Macmillan 2009).

Hodges, Jack: "Liberal Education, A" in *Maker of the Omnibus, The / The Lives of English Writers Compared* (London: Sinclair-Stevenson, 1992).

Huggon, Jim (editor) and Sansom, Philip (foreword): "Bonar Thompson" in *Speakers' Corner / an Anthology* (London: Kropotkin's Lighthouse Publication / Housmans Bookshop, 1977).

Jesson, Henry: "Sunday, January 14, 1940" in *And Beacons Burn Again* (New York: D. Appleton-Century Company, 1940).

Kearton, Cherry: [advertisement in] *I Visit the Antipodes* (London: Jarrolds, 1937).

Kent, William: "Thompson, Bonar" in *London Worthies* (London: Heath Cranton Limited, 1939).

Murray, Tony: "Irish in London, The" in *London Irish Fictions / Narrative, Diaspora and Identity* (Liverpool: Liverpool University Press, 2012).

O'Casey, Sean: "Hyde Park Orator" in *Blasts and Benedictions* (London: Macmillan, 1967).

O'Casey, Sean: "Appendix: The Divine Gift" in *Letters of Sean O'Casey, The / Volume IV, 1959-1964* (Washington DC: Catholic University of America Press, 1992).

Quail, John: "World War One - And After" in *Slow Burning Fuse, The* (London: Granada 1978).

Rose, Jonathan: "Down and Out in Bloomsbury" in *Intellectual Life of the British Working Classes, The* (London: Yale University Press, 2008).

Swasey, George H.: *Large or Small Families?* London: Liberator League, circa 1918.

Vance, Louis: [publisher's notice for *Hyde Park Orator*] in *Encore the Lone Wolf* (London: Jarrods, 1934).

Wicks, Harry: "Growing Up in Battersea" in *Keeping My Head* (London: Socialist Platform Ltd., 1992).

Magazines

"Bonar Thompson speaks." [Notice with variations in] *Freedom* (London) for 4 April 1953 ("On Oscar Wilde"); 25 April 1953 ("Oscar Wilde and the Road to Reading Gaol"); 4, 11, 18, 25 January 1958; 1, 22 February 1958; 1, 8, 15, 22, 29 March 1958; 12, 19 April 1958; 10, 17 May 1958; 7, 14, 21, 28 June 1958; 12, 19, 26 July 1958; 2, 9, 16, 23, 30 August 1958; 27 September 1958; 4 October 1958 ("Until October 8"); 18, 25 April 1959 ("Benefit Meeting: Faith, Hope and Charity"); 21, 28 May 1960 ("Benefit Lecture"); 11 June 1960 ("Benefit Lecture"); 18 March 1961.

F. A. R.: "Laughing England's Democracy Away." *Bulletin, The*, 25 April 1934.

"George Albon" in *Freedom* (London: September 1988).

Hilliard, Christopher: "Literary Underground of 1920s London, The." *Social History*, May 2008.

_____ "Provincial Press and the Imperial Traffic in Fiction, 1870s-1930s, The." *Journal of British Studies*, July 2009.

"Hyde Park Orator." *Socialist Standard*, April 1934.

"I.L.P. Evangelist, An." *Socialist Standard*, December 1926.

Moyse, Arthur: "Around the Galleries" in Freedom (London, 1 October 1960)

"One Crowded Hour." *Radio Times*, 31 March 1935.

Sanner, The: "Television News / St. George's Hall – Perhaps." *Radio Times*, 25 August 1939.

"To echo Bonar Thompson... " *Freedom* (London) 23 May 1959.

"Tragedy of Coriolanus, The." *Radio Times*, 20 April 1948.

"Variety in a Taxi Cab." *Radio Times*, 2 June 1935.

"Soapbox to Soundbite." *Socialist Standard*, July 1997.

Manuscripts

Burke, Margaret: *Patricia Lynch and R.M. Fox Papers, 1919-1972*. National Library of Ireland.

Doyle, Jennifer: *Sean O'Casey Papers, 1917-1993*. National Library of Ireland.

Edwards, Harold: *Harold Edwards / A Revolutionary Youth*. libcom.org

"John Bonar Thompson" in *England and Wales Census, 1911*.

Savile, I: *Ideas, Forms and Development in the British Workers' Theatre, 1925-1935.* (London: City University, 1990)

Newspapers

"350 London Worthies." *Norwood News*, 2 June 1939.
"Around and About." *Belfast News Letter*, 4 May 1939.
A. V. T. "Hyde Park Orator," *Winnipeg Tribune*, 26 September 1934.
"Another aspect of London life... " *London News*, 21 July 1934.
Baxter, Beverley: "Audience of Two / But This Show Must Go On." *Belfast Telegraph*, 1 August 1944.
"Black Hat." *Daily Herald*, 5 April 1947.
"Bonar Thompson... " *Era, The*, 13 April 1939.
_____ *Observer*, 14 September 1941.
"Bonar Thompson's Message." *Daily Herald*, 8 July 1916.
"Books Published Today." *New York Times*, 4 September 1934.
"Books Received." *Truth*, 14 March 1934.
Bowden, Ron: "Free Speech and Rapier Rejoinders." *Plain Dealer, The*, 11 April 1993.
"Broadcasting." *Aberdeen Press and Journal*, 3 April 1935.
_____ *Aberdeen Press and Journal*, 3 June 1935.
_____ *Belfast News Letter*, 3 June 1935.
_____ *Gloucester Citizen*, 3 June 1935.
_____ *Western Morning News*, 3 June 1935.
"Broadcasting Features." *Yorkshire Post and Leeds Intelligencer*, 3 April 1935.
Buckham, Bernard: "Listen In To." *Daily Mirror*, 27 May 1940.
Burdens, Denis: "Story of Hyde Park, The." *Gippsland Times*, 3 September 1953.
_____ *Armidale Express and New England General Advertiser*, 28 September 1953.
_____ *Longreach Leader*, 22 January 1954.
"By the Way." *Portsmouth Evening News*, 3 June 1938.
Cannell, J. C.: "Microphone Whispers / Golden-Voiced Girl Still Unspoiled." *Daily Gazette*, 20 March 1939.
Chiang, Jack: "Philosophy Deserves More Credit Than It Gets." *Kingston Whig, The*, 22 October 1997.

"City Window Smashing / Charges of Conspiracy." Manchester Courier, 26 & 27 March 1908.

"Club Society and Gossip / Hyde Park Politics." *Birmingham Mail, The,* 5 January 1939.

"Commentary on Broadcasting." *Yorkshire Evening Post,* 3 June 1935.

"Crowded Hour." *Guardian,* 3 April 1935.

"Crowded Hour of Variety." *Sheffield Independent,* 3 April 1935.

"Doyen of Marble Arch Orators." *Nottingham Evening Port,* 15 October 1940.

Eibl, Ralf: "Tourists Mingle with Hecklers at Famed Speaker's Corner." *Ottawa Citizen, The,* 27 Febbruary 1993

Eliot, Peter: "Cabbages and Kings / Mystifying Cockney." *Times Colonist,* 5 April 1952.

"Flowers Embarrass British Footballers / Utopia Unlimited." *Townsville Daily Bulletin,* 4 December 1945.

"From a Window in Fleet Street." *Ottawa Journal,* 27 January 1939.

H. H.: "Mr. Bonar Thompson." *Observer,* 23 April 1939.

_____ "Bonar Thompson... " *Observer,* 24 August 1941.

Halton, M. H.: "Most Thorough-Going Cynic in World Found by Halton / Everybody is Absolutely Right." *Windsor Star,* 26 August 1933.

"Herald League, The." *Daily Herald,* 4 November 1916.

"High Speed Variety." *Hull Daily Mail,* 3 April 1935.

"Hyde Park Corner in the Spring." *Advertiser,* 24 April 1947.

"Hyde Park Orator." *Dundee Courier,* 17 April 1934.

_____ *Ottawa Citizen,* 5 June 1943.

"Hyde Park Oratory." *Herald,* 8 October 1912.

"Hyde Park soap-box or small-platform, The... " *Calgary Herald,* 3 July 1943.

"Hyde Park Speech, A / Kings and Magistrates Denounced in Wild Terms." *Gazette,* 3 September 1912.

"I have never... " *Irwin Index,* 26 June 1954.

"In the Theatre." *Guardian,* 15 September 1941.

"It is unfortunate... " *Observer,* 9 April 1939.

_____ *Cornishman,* 27 April 1939.

J. H.: "Free Speech." *Advertiser,* 27 March 1937.

"King of Outdoor Orators Confesses." *Daily Herald,* 5 April 1934.

"Lee-on-Solent." *Hampshire Telegraph,* 3 June 1938.

"Let us have laughter... " *Sydney Mail,* 12 October 1938.

"Letter from London." *Devon and Exeter Gazette*, 13 January 1939.

Listener: "Wireless Notes." *Guardian*, 6 June 1935.

"Literature of the Week / County Antrim Man's Experiences." *Northern Whig*, 17 March 1934.

London Correspondent: "Hyde Park Orator, The." *Guardian*, 19 April 1939.

_____ "One-Man Show Man's Story / Lunch-time Lessons Turned Greaser into Orator." *Manchester Evening News*, 20 April 1939.

"London Letter / Mr. Bonar Thompson." *Evening News*, 19 May 1939.

_____ *Central Queensland Herald*, 25 May 1939.

"London Topics / Park Politics." *Lake Wakatip Mail*, 21 February 1939.

"London Topics / Hyde Park Orator." *Evening Star*, 27 November 1945.

M. R.: "Literature and Life / A Booklover's Corner." *Ottawa Journal*, 14 July 1934.

"Missing." *Manchester Courier*, 21 March 1908.

"Manchester 'Martyrs' / Unemployed's Strange Threats." *Sheffield Daily Telegraph*, 27 March 1908.

"Manchester Sessions / The Window-Smashing Cases." *Guardian*, 25 March 1908.

"Manchester Unemployed / Police Object to a Speaker." *Guardian*, 1 September 1909.

"Manchester Unemployed / The Imprisoned Conspirators." *Guardian*, 30 March 1908.

"Manchester's Unemployed / Plot Leaders Sentenced." *Bolton Evening News*, 27 March 1908.

"Manchester Window Smashing / Prisoners before the Recorder." *Bolton Evening News*, 25 March 1908.

"Men and Matters." *Westralian Worker*. 24 May 1935.

"More cheekily cynical personal narrative, A... " *Birmingham Daily Gazette*, 20 March 1934.

"Mr. Bonar Thompson... " *Northern Whig*, 17 April 1934.

"Mr. Bonar Thompson and Miss Pat Geary." *Marleybone Mercury*, 1 July 1939.

Munro, George: "Sabbath in the Park." *Era, The*, 24 March 1938.

"Next War, The." *Ottawa Journal*, 7 August 1937.

"Not all window-smashing... " *Guardian*, 24 March 1908.

"Notable Sayings." *Telegraph*, 1 July 1939.

"One Crowded Hour." *Burnley Express*, 3 April 1935

_____ *Portsmouth Evening News*, 3 April 1935.

"Open Air Oratory." *Daily Standard*, 6 May 1935.

"Orator, Author, Lecturer." *Belfast Telegraph*, 7 January 1963.

"Orator's Last Word." *Belfast Telegraph*, 11 January 1963.

"Orator's Show." *Manchester Evening*, 21 April 1939.

"Our London Letter." *Western Morning News*, 27 November 1938.

Our Own Correspondent: "London News and Views / Freedom in the Park." *Age, The*, 21 December 1940.

P. A. C.: "Man on the Soap Box, The / Book for 'The Mob' by Hyde Park Orator." *Nottingham Journal*, 4 June 1934.

Palmer, Arnold: "Books." *Britannia and Eve*, 1 May 1934.

"Park Orator in Theatre." *Daily Herald*, 21 April 1939.

"Park Orator Weds a Clerical Worker / Credits Shakespeare." *Cincinnati Enquirer*, 25 June 1939.

"Preacher Fined / Hyde Park Orator Said to Have Been in Asylum." *Cairns Post*, 15 October 1912.

"'Premier of Hyde Park' Dies, The." *Daily Mirror*, 7 January 1963.

"'Prime Minister of Hyde Park' is Dead, The." *Birmingham Daily Post*, 7 January 1963.

"Recruiter for Socialism / Bonar Thompson Now Booking Dates." *Labour Leader*, 16 March 1916.

"Revival of Old Debating Society / Manchester County Forum." *Guardian*, 8 September 1951.

Russell, Frank: "Debunking the World-Builder / Park Orator Writes Reminiscences." *Herald*, 23 April 1934.

"Sayings of the Week." *Red Deer Advocate*, 17 May 1939.

_____ *Observer*, 8 January 1950.

_____ *Sun, The*, 22 January 1950.

"Scene in Hyde Park." *Observer*, 11 August 1912.

"'Scurvy Government' / Window-Smashers' Protest." *Manchester Courier*, 20 March 1908.

"Shepherd's Bush Empire." *Stage, The*, 20 July 1939.

"Some Ulster Folks We Ought to Know Better." *Belfast Telegraph*, 1 November 1940.

_____ *Larne Times*, 9 November 1940.

326

"Still Hyde Park's Best Orator." *Newcastle Morning Herald and Miners' Advocate*, 18 July 1947.

"Stoll Theatres." *The Era*, 13 July 1939.

"Struggle in the Dock / Wild Rush by Convicted Man." *Dundee Evening Telegraph*, 25 March 1908.

Swaffer, Hannen: "I Heard Yesterday / Let Them All Talk!" *Daily Herald*, 31 March 1933.

"'Tapping' Statesmen / Easy Means of Livelihood." *Auckland Star*, 18 August 1934.

_____ *Alexandra Herald*, 26 September 1934.

Tewson, W. Orton: "Attic Salt Shaker." *Star Phoenix*, 26 September 1934.

_____ *Asheville Citizen Times*, 30 September 1934.

_____ *Tampa Times*, 4 October 1937.

_____ *Tampa Times*, 10 November 1937.

"Three of the men... " *Guardian*, 27 March 1908.

"To-Day's Broadcasting." *Northern Whig*, 3 June 1935.

"To-Day's Radio Programmes." *Sunderland Daily Echo*, 3 April 1935.

_____ *Sunderland Daily Echo*, 3 June 1935.

"To-Day's Wireless." *Leeds Mercury*, 3 April 1935.

"Tub Thumper, A." *New York Times*, 23 September 1934.

"'Unemployed' Rioters Sentenced / Wild Schemes Discussed." *Morning Post*, 27 March 1908.

"Unemployed Window-Smashers / Exemplary Sentences." *Daily Mail* (see p. 104.).

"Untold Stories of the Irish in Britain." *Irish Times*, 25 April 2009

Wendt, Nikolaus: "Open-Air Parliament of the People, The." *Vancouver Sun*, 5 May 1945.

W. H. G.: "Cheek as a Living." *Birmingham Daily Gazette*, 20 March 1934.

W. J. B.: "Hyde Park Orator at the 'Bush.'" *The Era*, 20 July 1939.

W. L. A.: "Cynic's Book that Annoyed Me, A." *Leeds Mercury*, 4 April 1934.

Williams, Heathcote: "Soap-Box in Cyberspace, A." *Independent*, 7 May 1997.

"Window-Breaking Charges." *Guardian*, 28 March 1908.

"Window-Breaking / Result of the Sessions Trial." *Guardian*, 27 March 1908.

"Window Smashing / Another Man Charged." *Guardian*, 19 March 1908.

"Window Smashing / Several Men Committed for Conspiracy." *Guardian*, 20 March 1908.

"Window Smashing Case / Smith Committed to Sessions." *Guardian*, 24 March 1908.

"Window Smasher Sentenced / Other Charges Today." *Manchester Courier*, 25 March 1908.

"Window Smashers, The / Borstal Treatment for Thompson." *Manchester Courier*, 28 March 1908.

"Window Smashers, The / Charges as Sessions." *Manchester Courier*, 24 March 1908.

"Wireless." *Derry Journal*, 3 June 1935.

"Wireless Programmes." *Lancashire Evening Post*, 3 April 1935.

"Worth Reporting." *Australian Women's Weekly*, 24 May 1947.

Further Reading

The Gospel According to Malfew Seklew

"[Malfew Seklew] had read a great deal and had been profoundly influenced by writers like Nietzsche and Max Stirner. Their doctrines, however, had been passed through the witty and original mind of a man who possessed certain odd qualities of his own. [...] I became friendly with him and learned a great deal from one who was a distinct and outstanding personality of the market and the public square."

- Bonar Thompson, **Hyde Park Orator** *Illustrated* (p. 81).

Baltimore: Underworld Amusements, 2014. ISBN 978-0988553682

Confessions of a Failed Egoist

"Egoism is the claim that the individual is the measure of all things. In ethics, in epistemology, in aesthetics, in society, the Individual is the best and only arbitrator. Egoism claims social convention, laws, other people, religion, language, time and all other forces outside of the Individual are an impediment to the liberty and existence of the Individual. Such impediments may be tolerated but they have no special standing to the Individual, who may elect to ignore or subvert or destroy them as He can. In egoism the State has no monopoly to take tax or wage war."

- Trevor Blake, author of *Confessions of a Failed Egoist*
and editor of *The Gospel According to Malfew Seklew*.

"*Confessions of a Failed Egoist* is somewhere at the crossroads between *The Satanic Bible* and *Prometheus Rising*. Everything you know is wrong, but don't worry: It's just the punchline to the great epistemic joke. Blake's book is a throwback to the days of H. L. Mencken mercilessly skewering sacred cows on the left and right, while firmly rooted in our present day victimology industry conundrums. Blake's book provides inspiration for thought. Bring it up at your next boring work party and scare your colleagues."

- Nicholas Pell.

"Trevor Blake hails and assails the 'isms' closest to his heart in a Mencken-like step-right-up, soapbox style that is smart, dense and fun to read. Blake is a meticulous thinker, and this book is bound to delight and challenge individualists, egoists, and people who would dramatically object to the idea of egoism–but then do and say exactly what they want to anyway."

- Jack Donovan, author of *The Way of Men*.

"It's hard to know [who] will like this book. I'm left-wing and I really enjoyed it but I also know a bunch of people who are themselves extremely left-wing who would loathe this book because they are left-wing in a different manner than I am left-wing. If you are a liberal who is sick of victim culture, attempts at censorship on behalf of the goals of identity politics, and the denial of personal responsibility as a social good, you will like this book. Ironically, many right-wingers who are also libertarian in their mindset will hate this book because it cuts Ayn Rand little slack and refuses to pander to Christian or doctrinaire morality. So I have no idea if you will like this book. Having a deep appreciation for word play and sarcasm will help... "

- Anita Dalton, author of *Odd Things Considered*.

CONFESSIONS OF A FAILED EGOIST

AND OTHER ESSAYS BY TREVOR BLAKE

Baltimore: Underworld Amusements, 2014. ISBN 978-0988553651

334

THE COLLECTION WAS NOT ENOUGH

The Complete Works
of
Bonar Thompson

In Production

336

Index

CPSIA information can be obtained
at www.ICGtesting.com
Printed in the USA
FSHW021208100921
84630FS

9 781944 651183